T0369674

Theodor Herzl

JEWISH LITERATURE AND CULTURE
Series Editor, Alvin H. Rosenfeld

THEODOR HERZL

From Assimilation to Zionism

Jacques Kornberg

Indiana University Press

Bloomington & Indianapolis

© 1993 by Jacques Kornberg

All rights reserved

No part of this book may be reproduced or utilized in any
form or by any means, electronic or mechanical, including
photocopying and recording, or by any information storage
and retrieval system, without permission in writing from the
publisher. The Association of American University Presses'
Resolution on Permissions constitutes the only exception to
this prohibition.

The paper used in this publication meets the minimum
requirements of American National Standard for Information
Sciences—Permanence of Paper for Printed Library Materials,
ANSI Z39.48-1984.

♾™

Manufactured in the United States of America

Library of Congress Cataloging-in-Publication Data

Kornberg, Jacques, date.
Theodor Herzl : from assimilation to Zionism / Jacques Kornberg.
p.   cm. — (Jewish literature and culture)
Includes bibliographical references and index.
ISBN 0-253-33203-6
1. Herzl, Theodor, 1860–1904. 2. Zionists—Austria—Biography.
I. Title. II. Series.
DS151.H4K68 1993
320.5'4'09569409436—dc20
93-18399

1 2 3 4 5   97 96 95 94 93

This book is for
Mona Silver Kornberg

Through us the world shall be acquainted with something that has not been considered possible in 2,000 years: Jewish honor.

—Herzl, *Complete Diaries*

Contents

Contents

Acknowledgments

WRITING THIS BOOK has meant summoning up vast amounts of *Sitzfleisch* within four walls; lonely as it has been, the book has also been virtually a shared undertaking. My debts to others are many and great. I am no less accountable for the flaws in this book.

Carl Schorske's "Politics in a New Key: An Austrian Triptych," in *The Journal of Modern History* (December 1967), was the first to disentangle the influence of Theodor Herzl's Viennese milieu on his Zionism. Though our conclusions differ, his by now classic article, republished in his book *Fin-de-Siècle Vienna*, opened up a road that started me on my way.

To Robert Melson I am deeply grateful for his boundless support. And for more too: on our many seminars during five-mile runs, he listened unfalteringly, commented with penetrating insight, and helped me hone my arguments. I am indebted to Bernard Avishai for his steadfast encouragement and shrewd and illuminating observations. I owe much to Michael Marrus for his astute and generous advice both as writer and scholar. Thanks are due to Harvey Dyck for his skilled counsel on style.

I am no less grateful to others: Ronald Bryden helped me grasp the theatrical qualities of *The New Ghetto*; Ernst Loeb helped me understand its literary aspects. Ronald Bryden and I endeavored to have Herzl's play staged in Toronto. Readers of this book will understand why our efforts were rebuffed. Helga Wischnewsky shared her fascination and skill with words, and helped me translate the German.

I am especially indebted to the Indiana University Press and to the press's readers, Marsha Rozenblit and a second who remains anonymous, who offered astute criticism and suggestions.

I am grateful to Dr. Michael Heymann, former Director of the Central Zionist Archives in Jerusalem. He and the staff helped me navigate through the vast Herzl archives, whose holdings are so clearly and extensively catalogued, they are a scholar's dream. Thanks are due to the Social Sciences and Humanities Research Council of Canada. Their Research Time Stipend freed me from teaching duties for a year, enabling me to complete a first draft of the book. The Humanities and Social Sciences Committee of the University of Toronto helped pay for my research expenses.

Finally, some very personal debts: to my parents, Henry and Frieda Kornberg, for the Jewish home they provided me, shaped by the dissonance of tragedy and triumph—the Holocaust and the founding of the State of

Israel. My children, Micah, Nicole, and Joshua, each my pride and joy, endured a preoccupied father, but also taught me that there is life beyond Herzl. To my wife, Mona Silver Kornberg, to whom this book is dedicated, my boundless gratitude for exacting editorial criticism, for wise counsel, for unwavering love, for making it all worthwhile.

Theodor Herzl

Introduction

From Austro-German Assimilationist to Zionist

No one ever thought of looking for the Promised
Land where it actually is—and yet it lies so near.
This is where it is: within ourselves.[1]

THIS BOOK COVERS a distinct period in Theodor Herzl's life, one that began in 1878, when his family moved to Vienna from Budapest, and ended in 1896, when he published *The Jewish State*. In the course of this period, spanning his eighteenth to thirty-sixth year, Herzl moved from German assimilation to Zionism. My book challenges the prevailing view that attributes Herzl's conversion to Zionism to the Dreyfus trial and offers a new interpretation of his transformation. I have not sought to understand Herzlean Zionism by investigating his career as a Zionist leader. I intend to shed new light on his Zionism by investigating its origin.

In the prevailing version, December 1894 was a crucial date in Herzl's conversion to Zionism. Herzl, a prominent journalist, was in Paris, assigned to cover the French scene for his newspaper, the *Neue Freie Presse*. That month he reported on the treason trial and conviction of Captain Dreyfus, a Jewish officer serving on the French General Staff. The antisemitic press vilified Dreyfus—and through him all French Jews—as a typical Jewish turncoat and opportunist. Herzl was witnessing the fate of an assimilated Jew, who like him had risen high in the gentile world. Several months later, Herzl conceived the idea of the Jewish state. It is widely believed that his conversion to Zionism occurred under the impact of the trial.

This view of Herzl's awakening has long served as a Zionist object lesson. The lesson begins by asserting that Herzl founded political Zionism after being abruptly and dramatically jolted out of his assimilationist delusions. In the fate of the assimilated Jew Captain Dreyfus, Herzl read the future of European Jewry. Herzl's Zionism was, then, a canny and virtually clairvoyant response to telltale signs of impending Jewish catastrophe. The object lesson virtually shouts out its moral: would that all European Jews were as insightful as Herzl! This is how Alex Bein viewed Herzl's Zionism, as a prophetic response to the growing external threat of antisemitism.[2] I will argue, to the contrary, that the Dreyfus case had no impact on Herzl's conversion to Zionism.

I do not mean to imply that Herzl had no foreboding about potential threats to Jewish life and property in Europe. However, the Dreyfus trial did not prompt this foreboding. Herzl's concern with antisemitism went back much further in time, reaching a high point of intense preoccupation by late 1892, fully two years before the Dreyfus trial. But even here we are far off the mark if we see Herzl's conversion to Zionism solely or even predominantly as a response to external threats to Jewry. Perceived external threats were filtered through Herzl's feelings and consciousness, and it is to these that we must turn.

People have long accepted the view that the Dreyfus trial converted Herzl to Zionism, because no one has put forward another explanation for Herzl's profound transformation. I shall do just that, by probing Herzl's consciousness. The Israeli scholar David Vital once expressed his uneasiness over ascribing Herzl's conversion to the Dreyfus trial: "The roots of his obsession lay deeper—that much is plain—even if they cannot now be laid bare." I believe the source of Herzl's "obsession"—aptly worded to describe a long-standing intense preoccupation—can be uncovered. Mounting political antisemitism, chiefly in his Austrian homeland, intensified a long-standing inner conflict in Herzl, at the heart of which was his ambivalence over his Jewishness. *Ambivalence* has been clinically defined as "the coexistence of antithetical emotions, ideas, or wishes toward a given object or situation."[3] It is often associated with mental illness, but it is also a feature of the normal psyche. Herzl experienced intense Jewish self-disdain and feelings of inferiority, but he was also animated by feelings of Jewish pride, loyalty, and solidarity. In this sense the contempt for Jews Herzl was struggling with was, not least, his own. That he struggled with it instead of succumbing to it makes the term *ambivalence* the operative one in describing Herzl's attitude.

The young Herzl, acculturated to Germandom, had internalized the Jewish stereotypes of the European Enlightenment. He saw Jews as inferior: cowardly, unmanly, preoccupied with money, bereft of idealism. But he also identified with their history of victimization, admired Jewish steadfastness in the face of persecution, and most important, his high standards of loyalty and personal pride ruled out deserting the camp of the victimized. Throughout the 1880s, while the promise of full assimilation and acceptance into Austrian society looked realizable, Herzl could hold such conflicting feelings in uneasy though tolerable balance. The meteoric rise and success of Austrian political antisemitism in the 1890s upset this balance, intensifying both his Jewish self-disdain and his Jewish loyalties.

Eventually Herzl resolved his conflict by turning to Zionism. As a Zionist, he advanced a radically new ideal of Jewishness. His ideal of a new Jew, heroic and idealistic, stood in marked contrast, he believed, to actual Jews, who were devoid of these traits. In this sense Herzl had absorbed Europe's negative image of the Jew. His perceptive criticisms of Jewry, motivated by Jewish pride and solidarity, were also driven by Jewish self-hate. Herzl sought to transform Jewry by incorporating German nationalist models into his new ideal of Jewishness and by appealing to a myth of ancient Jewish greatness in their period of statehood. Only after doing so was he able to embrace his reconstituted Jewish origins unreservedly and commit himself to the Jewish cause.

My study deals largely with Herzl's personal conflicts, both about being Jewish and about being an Austro-German. Such conflicts affected the deepest recesses of his personality and shaped his view of himself, of other Jews, and of Gentiles as well. However, my approach to Herzl is social psychological and not simply psychological. My interest does not lie in psychoanalytical factors, such as Herzl's relationship with his mother, or his narcissism.[4] I see the causes of his conflict as historical, social, and contextual. Herzl's experience was emblematic of that of a large number of central European Jews, which is why his resolution of his ambivalence through Zionism resonated so powerfully in others of his generation. Hence, I locate the sources of his conflicts in the historical milieu and political events of the 1880s and 1890s: in the European ideology of Jewish assimilation, in Austrian views of Jewry, in Viennese Jewish assimilation, and in the late-nineteenth-century rise of Austrian antisemitism. Herzl's conflict as well as his particular brand of Zionism will be situated firmly within late-nineteenth-century central European history and the Viennese Jewish experience.

In adopting an unsparing historical approach, it may be said that I have removed Herzl from the pantheon of Jewish visionaries and prophets and reduced him to a creature of his times. Certainly my treatment is not hagiographical as was Alex Bein's in his classic biography of Herzl. But though I view Herzl as all too human, I do not gloss over his achievement. His brand of Zionism spoke to the dilemmas of many of his Jewish contemporaries and provided them with a new basis for Jewish pride and self-assertion.

My historical approach to Herzl has contemporary relevance, for its theme is the power of stereotypes. Herzl spent much of his life shaping his personality in opposition to the prevailing negative Jewish stereotype. Stereotypes are sweeping generalizations that ride roughshod over the vast differences among individuals within an identifiable group. The recent struggles for their rights of black Americans, the aboriginal peoples of North America, and women, have taught us how much racial, ethnic, and gender stereotypes are an outcome of power relations. Invidious stereotypes encourage resignation, a feeling of inferiority, and an acceptance by those victimized of prevailing relations of domination. Such stereotypes bestow legitimacy on relations of domination. In the case of Viennese Jewry, the more fully they assimilated and the more closely they resembled their Christian compatriots, the more old anti-Jewish stereotypes were revived, and the more distance

Christians put between themselves and Jews. This way Jews were kept in their place and denied the equality due them. Toward the end of this period, after struggling with the power the Jewish stereotype exerted over him, Herzl came to understand the close relationship between stereotypes and domination. He then insisted that Jewish liberation, or what was sometimes called the *second emancipation*, required that Jews first transform themselves. As he wrote in his play *The New Ghetto*: "The outer barriers [the walls of the ghetto] had to be pulled down from the outside, but the inner ones we must uproot ourselves. We ourselves! From ourselves!"[5] To break the power of the invidious Jewish stereotype, Herzl appealed to a new myth of Jewish greatness, the myth of a glorious past in the biblical period of Jewish statehood.

A brilliant speech to the First Zionist Congress by Max Nordau, the Hungarian-Jewish writer and one of Herzl's first Zionist converts, provides a historical explanation of Herzl's dilemma. In that speech Nordau described the "spiritual misery" of assimilated Jews in late-nineteenth-century Europe.[6] His perceptive analysis deserves to be quoted at length. Nordau claimed that for centuries Jews had been shielded psychologically by their common life in the ghetto: "What did it matter that those values which were prized within the ghetto were despised outside it? The opinion of the outside world did not matter, because it was the opinion of ignorant enemies. One tried to please one's brothers, and their respect gave honourable meaning to one's life."

Then, according to Nordau, a historic change occurred. With civil emancipation, gained in France in 1792 and fully realized in Austria in 1867 and in Germany in 1871, "Jews rushed to burn all their bridges immediately." They abandoned the ghetto and sought a new belonging, and acknowledgement as fellow Frenchmen/women, Germans, and Austrians. Eagerly, they rushed to pay the full price for their admission to gentile society, shedding their Jewishness and modeling themselves after their new compatriots. Tragically, after a brief honeymoon period, the Jewish longing for acceptance was balked by an abrupt antisemitic backlash. Jews were then psychologically defenseless, for they could no longer take comfort in their ghetto refuge or from the esteem and solidarity of their fellow Jews. The assimilated Jew, Nordau maintained: "has abandoned his specifically Jewish character, yet the nations do not accept him as part of their national communities. He flees from his Jewish fellow, because anti-Semitism has taught him too, to be contemptuous of them, but his gentile compatriots repulse him as he attempts to associate with them." As a result, Nordau continued, "the emancipated Jew is insecure in his relations with his fellow men, timid with strangers, and suspicious even of the secret feelings of his friends. His best powers are dissipated in suppressing and destroying, or at least in the difficult task of concealing his true character. He fears that this character might be recognized as Jewish, and he never has the satisfaction of revealing himself as he is in his real identity, in every thought and sentiment, in every physical gesture." Nordau concluded: "He has become a cripple within, and a counterfeit person without, so that like everything unreal, he is ridiculous and hateful to all men of high standards."

It would be a mistake to assume that Nordau's somber portrait fits all— or even most—European Jews, for many had established a balance and accommodation between their Jewishness and their new loyalties. Nordau's description did apply to a number of Jews, and not least to Herzl, for he modeled himself on Gentiles and was plagued by Jewish self-contempt. The rise of political antisemitism in Austria shattered his commitment to assimilation and touched off an inner crisis. His conversion to Zionism was his resolution of this crisis. That Herzl was highly assimilated, for a while a fervent German nationalist, and that he displayed traces of Jewish self-contempt has been noted by other biographers.[7] However, I will argue that these traits formed the background to his Zionism, spilled over into it, shaping its character. To employ Hegel's concept of the dialectic: Jewish self-contempt and mimicry of Gentiles were both contained in—and overcome—in the new Zionist synthesis.

Herzl's Zionism was a natural outgrowth of his Viennese-Jewish experience, for Austro-German assimilationism had promoted extreme Jewish self-denial. Many forces contributed to this Jewish self-denial. Since the eighteenth century, enlightened advocates of Jewish civil emancipation and integration into European society had assumed that it would lead to the eventual disappearance of Judaism, to Jews sharing with Gentiles in a common Christian-based European ethical and cultural heritage. In this sense, intermarriage and conversion were the natural consummation of Jewish assimilation. Rising German nationalism in Austria fostered its own version of Jewish self-denial. Until the 1880s Jews were welcomed wholeheartedly into the Austro-German nationalist movement, provided that they shared its animosity to Judaism and to the so-called Jewish spirit, characterized by love of profit, rampant opportunism, lack of idealism, the absence of physical courage. In Austrian society in general, Jews were identified with rising capitalism. In a society in which the aristocracy, a large artisan stratum, and Catholic corporate values—rather than the capitalist middle class—set the cultural, social, and moral tone, capitalism was viewed as parasitical and exploitative. A significant number of Jews shared these views and sought to escape the taint of parasitic capitalism and to achieve higher status at the same time by entering the free professions, the arts, and government service. Up to, and through, the 1880s, a number of Jews believed that such efforts were part of the unwritten compact of civic emancipation, and would lead to increasing acceptance and integration into Austrian society.

Herzl was one of these Jews. We take up the Herzl story with the family's move from Budapest to Vienna in 1878, where he enrolled in its world-famous university as a law student. Throughout the 1880s, while the prospects for Jewish acceptance as full members of Austrian society seemed high, Herzl sought assimilation, paying the price in Jewish self-denial. In chapter 1, I show how far he had internalized the anti-Jewish biases of both the Enlightenment and the German liberal program of Jewish emancipation and assimilation. Chapter 2 deals with Herzl's involvement in the German nationalist student fraternity *Albia*. Herzl joined the fraternity fully cognizant of its conditions of membership, a willingness to shed Jewish traits, viewed as negative, in favor of Germanic traits, modeled on idealized Prussian virtues.

These Jewish issues were not abstract ones for Herzl, not sheer matters of reflection; they affected the inmost recesses of his personality. Jewishness did not entail articles of faith for him, but stood for a sum of collective traits—mostly negative—that shaped individual Jews. Herzl strained to shape his personality against the Jewish stereotype, a sure sign of his fear that he fit the stereotype. Accordingly, Herzl was plagued by the fear that he was a physical coward, a Jewish coward. Whether he was one is not the point; such fears constituted his personal myth. Joining *Albia*, a dueling fraternity, Herzl sought to allay these fears; they remained nonetheless. As a Viennese aesthete and writer, the path he chose in the 1880s, he sought to shed the taint of Jewish materialism. Accordingly, in his stories and plays he idealized the aristocracy and derided the new capitalist bourgeoisie, particularly the Jewish bourgeoisie. Finally, during this decade Herzl sought to distance himself, through mockery and contempt, from less assimilated Jews, who seemed more characteristically Jewish. Identification with such Jews was a standing threat to him, provoking fears that his own assimilation was fraudulent, only skin deep.

I go on, in chapter 3, to underscore Herzl's ambivalence both toward assimilation and toward his Jewishness: his calls for a total Jewish fusion into Austro-German culture and his pride at Jewish steadfastness in the face of centuries of persecution; his efforts to distance himself from Jews, and the evidences of his Jewish loyalty and solidarity; and finally, his erratic, conflicted behavior as a member of *Albia*, the German nationalist dueling fraternity. Nevertheless, until the 1890s Herzl's ambivalent attitude generated only limited and tolerable internal conflict. Herzl might well have remained in this contradictory state, but for the meteoric rise of Austrian political antisemitism. The rise to power of the antisemitic Christian Social party, under the leadership of Karl Lueger—taken up in chapter 4— altered the political, social, and cultural climate of Vienna. When Lueger attained the mayoralty of Vienna in 1897, the Christian Socials became the first antisemitic party to gain control of a European metropolis. The party was no extremist or marginal political movement, but represented the solid, respectable Bürgertum, the very mainstream of Austrian society. The Christian Socials were strongly Catholic and nativist, averse to Jews both as non-Catholics and as newcomers, and hostile to the cosmopolitan artistic and literary culture patronized by the liberal high bourgeoisie, circles in which Jews were prominent. The final strain in Christian Social thought was an equivocal anticapitalism originating in Catholic corporatism, which concentrated its wrath on Jewish capital.

John Boyer has described Christian Social supporters as a traditional precapitalist and protocapitalist Bürgertum, reclaiming proprietorship over their city. As such, they sought to deny Jews equal status and rights as full members of Viennese society. After decades of gradual integration and raised expectations, Jews were now viewed as intruders in a city that was seeking to restore its traditional cultural and ideological homogeneity.

Even more shocking to Herzl was the response of Austrian Liberals to the rise of political antisemitism. It was during the period of Liberal ascendancy, initiated by the constitution of 1867, that Jews had gained their full civic rights. Liberals had brought into being a secular public school system. Their procapitalist, laissez-faire economic doctrine accorded with the Jewish interest, for Liberals favored economic innovation, upward mobility, and new forms of wealth. Moreover, Jews and Liberals shared an ideological common ground, the heritage of the German Enlightenment, with its individualistic, rationalist, and cosmopolitan values. For all these reasons Jews were loyal supporters of the Liberals.

During the 1890s, Liberals betrayed their Jewish allies by responding weakly and evasively to the rise of political antisemitism. Even worse, it soon became evident that the Liberal response was not merely due to pragmatic politics and electoral opportunism; instead, when tested by political adversity, a deep-seated dislike of Jews surfaced among Liberals. When pressed by Jewish demands for support, Liberals reverted to the notion—generally expressed by indirection and innuendo—that a pall of guilt and suspicion surrounded Jewish conduct. Liberals blamed Jews for antisemitism and for saddling them with the Jewish question.

Not the rise of political antisemitism alone, but the Liberal betrayal of the Jews as well, led Herzl to question his Austro-German assimilation. If Liberals had opposed antisemitism, viewing it as a threat to the Austrian constitution and to the liberal order, Herzl's allegiance to liberalism might have remained intact, and his accommodation to assimilation, even though it was strained by ambivalence, would likely have remained undisturbed. For this reason, Herzlean Zionism was not so much a prophetic and shrewd response to threatened catastrophes about to befall Jews—as the Dreyfus legend suggests—but rather the outcome of wounded pride and the experience of rejection, ostracism and political powerlessness. Herzl's preoccupation with antisemitism grew out of the Viennese Jewish experience of rejection, after the high expectations raised by several decades of remarkable progress toward Jewish integration. Rejection was a thousand times more wounding because it came after years of Herzl's close identification with Germanness and strenuous efforts to distance himself from his Jewish origins. Herzl could no longer beat a retreat to the fortress of his Jewishness, for the fortress had disintegrated before the face of his Jewish self-contempt. His sense of rejection was intensified by his view of Jews as perpetual pariahs, scorned wanderers, and his craving to find a settled and secure place in Austria. Finally, Herzl's longing was tied to his bourgeois aspirations. Herzl was no rebel against society, no celebrator of the outsider's critical distance from the status quo. Raised in an affluent home, endowed with exceptional gifts as a writer, he expected a commensurate social status and appropriate respect. In this he was no different from many Viennese Jews, who identified—perhaps unrealistically—with the more educated and prosperous upper reaches of the German liberal Bürgertum, those who saw the Habsburg Empire as their creation and their patrimony.

Herzl's political solution to the Jewish problem was informed by psychological factors. The new Jewish politics was to involve a self-transformative, self-transcending Jewish act. Jews were to free themselves of shame and contempt and gain pride, respect, and honor. Herzl saw this need because he projected his own experience onto Jewish history, assuming that Jews had always sought acceptance and integration into gentile society and that non-acceptance had brought about demoralization and self-hate. As he observed: "The Jews had thus always fallen lower, as much by their own fault as by the fault of others. Elend [misery] . . . Golus . . . Ghetto. Words in different languages for the same thing. Being despised, and finally despising yourself."[8] In this light Zionism served as a circuitous route to honor and acceptance, for the direct route was balked by the rise of political antisemitism. Zionism served as an unservile mode of Jewish assimilation, through which Jews would no longer seek to be embraced by Gentiles as compatriots. Jews, transformed, would now win—even command—gentile recognition and respect as equals in the European state-system. Zionism was at one and the same time a refusal to be ruled by Gentiles, consequently a declaration of Jewish independence, and a way of gaining status for Jews in Europe and gentile acceptance on a new basis. Herzl was more preoccupied with issues of Jewish pride and gentile recognition than with a refuge for Jews in distress; more with Jewish honor than with Jewish power.

Herzl's conversion to Zionism was not a cheaply won certitude, the outcome of an abrupt illumination, as the Dreyfus legend suggests. Such a view trivializes his courageous and highly original struggle with issues of assimilationism, Jewish self-contempt, the pariah status of Jews, and their self-liberation. His conversion was a step-by-step, hazardous passage on trackless terrain. At first, rising antisemitism simply intensified Herzl's Jewish ambivalence. His early responses, described in chapter 5, commingled the wish that Jews disappear into the gentile world with rage at Gentiles, wounded Jewish pride with heightened Jewish self-disdain, which even included blaming Jews for antisemitism.

Herzl's initial solutions to the problem of antisemitism were expressions of his ambivalence about both Jewishness and assimilation, which is why they included such schemes as the collective baptism of Jews or, alternatively, their mass enlistment in the cause of socialism, or—a third scheme—challenging antisemites to duels. One of the conveniences of subscribing to the Dreyfus legend is that it makes Herzl's Zionism seem to emerge suddenly, full-blown, like Athena from the head of Zeus. Hence—as his previous biographers do—it is easy to dismiss these early schemes, in particular mass baptism, as products of his assimilationist phase or of an impulsive Viennese theatricality, having nothing to do with his Zionism. On the contrary, these schemes were not at all anomalous to his Zionism; they were its germ cells. As I shall argue in chapter 5, Herzl was seeking to combine assimilation with new forms of Jewish assertiveness. He was casting about for a mode of assertiveness that would entail a radical transformation of the Jews, rid them of materialism and cowardliness, restore Jewish pride, and command the respect and acceptance of Gentiles.

Herzl eventually abandoned these proposals, made in 1892 and 1893, but they had opened up a new path for him. Herzl then broke through to another crucial stage in 1894, more than six months before he embraced Zionism. This breakthrough was a personal one, for it involved a resolution of his ambivalence both about his Jewishness and about assimilation. Herzl's "conversion," a highly emotional inner upheaval, dates from that time. The famous conversion experience associated with his Zionism, though no less important, was actually a second such experience.

Herzl's first conversion experience drove him to write his play *The New Ghetto*, a thinly disguised autobiography that I analyze in chapter 6. Herzl's later Zionist tract *The Jewish State* overshadowed the play, and it has never received the attention it deserves. I would go so far as to say that *The New Ghetto* is the key text—even more important than *The Jewish State*—for those seeking a historical understanding of Herzl, one that positions him solidly in his Jewish-Viennese milieu.

The play is not about anti-Jewish violence or Jewish economic distress, but about the overcoming of both gentile rejection and Jewish self-contempt among members of the assimilated Viennese Jewish upper middle class. The source of the drama is inward, psychological, centering on issues of psychic dependence and self-esteem. The story is Herzl's own. The play marks his break with Austro-German assimilation.

When the dominant culture showed itself unwilling even to grant acceptance in exchange for Jewish self-denial, Herzl's uneasy accommodation to assimilation unraveled. Other Jews, more solidly sheltered by their pride in Judaism, were less disoriented than Herzl by the rise of antisemitism. But in his case, disorientation led to a highly productive insight. Herzl came to realize that assimilation, which had fostered his Jewish self-disdain, robbed him of inner defenses against antisemitism. Having absorbed Austrian society's Jewish stereotypes, he had drained the cup of Jewish self-contempt: he considered Jewishness a taint, servilely copied gentile behavior, grappled with fears of his Jewish cowardice, distanced himself from other Jews, and had been deeply wounded by gentile rejection. Now there was nothing left in him but injured pride and feelings of Jewish inferiority.

Commencing with this insight, Herzl moved to a new view of Jewish possibilities. As a counter to his dismal view of contemporary Jews, Herzl vaulted over two thousand years of history, reverting to a myth of the ancient Jewish past, the era of Jewish statehood. As he observed: two millennia as a persecuted minority "rendered us ugly and transformed our character which had in earlier times been proud and magnificent. After all, we once were men who knew how to defend the state in time of war."[9] When he mentioned this to a colleague in the summer of 1894, the notion of Zionism was still a good nine months off, but in fastening onto this ancient era, Herzl now saw a new potential in Jews themselves. All the virtues Jews were to gain through Austro-German assimilation, manliness, physical courage, idealism, were now seen as potential Jewish virtues, which they had once possessed. In this way Herzl appropriated assimilation to a new ideal of Jewishness, one that could serve assimilated Jews like himself as a foundation for Jewish pride and self-assertion. Herzl was still seeking status and acceptance for Jews in Europe, but now on the basis of an independent, unservile mode of assimilation. Jews would command respect, instead of beseeching it.

All these insights were contained in his play, in which the protagonist, Jacob Samuel, was modeled on Herzl himself. The continuities between the play and Herzl's Zionism are striking and have up to now been insufficiently explored. In chapter 7, *The Jewish State*, I emphasize these continuities. I go on to show how new light is shed on Herzl's Zionism when seen as the resolution of his long-standing conflict both about his Jewishness and about Austro-German assimilation.

PART I

Herzl in the 1880s

1

Herzl as Assimilationist

What else could the leeches of medieval, and—admittedly!—also of modern times do?! They were *forced* to practise usury; why else were they Jews?[1]

Germanic Beginnings

HERZL WAS BORN in Budapest on 2 May 1860 and spent the first seventeen years of his life there. His family left Budapest for Vienna in February 1878, fleeing the scene of a personal tragedy, the sudden death of Herzl's sister Pauline from typhoid fever. With this abrupt departure, Herzl had to return to Budapest to sit for his final exams at the classical Evangelical Gymnasium, so he could enroll at the University of Vienna in the fall semester of 1878. Most likely, even without the death of his sister, Herzl would have ended up in Vienna. He was strongly attracted to the city. In addition, he already considered himself an aspiring "German writer." But with rising Magyar nationalism in the 1870s, German had fallen behind Magyar as the language of the Budapest reading public. The city was no longer a promising one for an ambitious German writer.[2]

The youthful Herzl's home in Budapest had fostered Germanic acculturation. His mother, whose maiden name was Jeanette Diament, had a strong love for German literature. Like her father, she was secular and highly acculturated; some of her relatives had even intermarried or converted to Christianity. Herzl's father, Jacob Herzl, was less educated and cultivated. He too retained a preference for German and preserved his German name in an era when Hungarian Jews were Magyarizing their names.[3]

Herzl had gone to a Jewish elementary school, then attended classes in Judaism at his secondary modern school and at the gymnasium to which he soon transferred. But the family maintained an attenuated tie to Judaism. A copy of a printed invitation to a "confirmation" at the Herzl home for Saturday, 3 May 1873, can be found in the Herzl archives. Evidently the family had decided against a Bar Mitzvah, which would have been held in the synagogue with Herzl reading from the Torah, and instead observed the event at home.

Confirmation was an innovation of Reform Judaism in Germany. Adapted from Christianity, the ceremony required a creedal statement delivered in question and answer form, following the teaching method of the catechism. Such statements could range from expressions of abstract universalism to Maimonides' Thirteen Articles of Faith. The ceremony might be held in German or Hebrew. In Germany and in Vienna as well, such creedal statements were usually combined with a religious ceremony in a synagogue or temple. However, confirmation was not a Hungarian Jewish practice, not even in the modern Neolog synagogue on Dohány Street attended by the Herzls. Nevertheless, the family chose to have a confirmation with a ceremony of sorts at home, perhaps with a teacher who had drilled Herzl beforehand in the question and answer format. In later accounts of his life, Herzl never spoke of this event.[4]

As an aspiring writer, the teen-age Herzl composed countless poems, drafts of essays, and plays. None are on Jewish themes.[5] A number celebrate Christian reformers and revolutionaries: the fifteenth-century Dominican friar Girolamo Savonarola who was burned at the stake, and Martin Luther, liberator of Germany from the tyranny of the Roman church. Herzl's attraction to rebels against papal authority shows how much he was a child of the 1870s, the peak decade of nineteenth-century anticlericalism in both Austria and Germany. During that period the conflict between church and state came to a head and ended with clerical power curtailed by the state in both Germany and Austria.

In 1864 Pope Pius IX had declared war on modern ideologies with an encyclical condemning liberalism and religious toleration; in 1870, a Vatican council proclaimed the dogma of papal infallibility. In response, the early 1870s saw an outpouring of anticlerical novels and plays, both in Austria and Germany. Gordon Craig has noted that the theater sensation of 1871 in Vienna was *Der Pfarrer von Kirchfeld (The Parish Priest of Kirchfeld)*, about a priest dismissed by his superiors for providing Catholic burial to a suicide. The theme of the play was the inhumanity of the Catholic hierarchy. The struggle against the Catholic church in Germany during the 1870s marked a high point of liberal influence and came to be called, in a term coined by a prominent liberal, the *Kulturkampf*, or the "great struggle for civilization in the interests of humanity."[6] In the course of the 1870s, civil marriage was legalized in Germany, church supervision of public education was eliminated, and the state took over the right of appointing and disciplining priests and setting their educational requirements. Events followed a similar course in Habsburg Austria with the advent of the Liberal ministry of Prince Carlos Auersperg in 1867. Civil marriage was legalized; schools were removed from ecclesiastical control, and religious instruction was reduced to noncompulsory sessions; the appointment and dismissal of priests and the regulation of their educational requirements were put in the hands of the state; legal encumbrances on Jews, Protestants, and freethinkers were removed.

This sudden and drastic reduction of clerical influence raised prospects for a secular and religiously tolerant society, and along with it, Jewry's successful integration in the Germanic world. Such hopes, which seemed on the way to realization, engaged the adolescent Herzl. He proclaimed in a draft essay on Savonarola: "In our days the old war between the church and the state has broken out anew. Again men armed with the weapons of the mind go out in order to settle the relations of the church, and to put an end, at long last, to the debate." Another statement by Herzl celebrated triumphant secularism, the approaching age of reason: He noted that "the false miracles of those clever swindlers from Moses and Jesus to the Count of Saint Germain" have already been exposed by the human spirit. Reason had discovered nature's laws and would soon unravel all of life's secrets.[7]

Herzl grew to manhood at a time of high hopes for the triumph of a more tolerant society. But such values as toleration and reason, in Herzl's words, "the weapons of the mind," were not part of some dream of a cosmopolitan culture where Jews and Christians could meet on equal terms. Instead, Herzl considered these values to be carried by the "German spirit," a creation of the German Reformation and the German Enlightenment. The evidence that he believed so comes from a poem Herzl wrote in January 1875, "We Shall Not Go to Canossa." The poem recalled the act of submission by the German emperor Henry IV in 1077, when he got down on his knees before Pope Gregory VII at the castle of Canossa in order to save his imperial throne. The pope had excommunicated Henry, which released his subjects from obedience. In the medieval struggle for supremacy between church and state, Henry's penitence marked the start of two centuries of papal dominion. The poem recounted this incident, then Herzl continued: "Centuries have gone by, / The noble race has recovered / From the infirmity that weighed it down. / Through Luther's mighty force / The German spirit awoke / From the long night. / Now freedom's golden light / Shines upon its wakened visage— / We shall not go to Canossa." The poem's significance lies in Herzl's equation of modern freedom with the awakening of the "German spirit."[8]

The phrase "We shall not go to Canossa," was a byword in the 1870s. Bismarck had employed it in a much-quoted speech in 1872 to show he was resolved to gain the upper hand over the Catholic church.[9] The phrase reflected Protestant pride in the newly unified Germany and the belief that the Roman church and the Catholic powers of Europe, including Habsburg Austria, had held Germany back from fulfilling its political destiny.

Herzl's poem suggests that he identified with the newly unified German Reich, an attitude shared by many Germanizing liberals in the multinational Habsburg Empire, who were intent on maintaining Austro-German political and cultural hegemony. For them German culture encompassed the Reformation, the great eighteenth-century literary flowering, the German Enlightenment, all considered part of the universalistic German heritage. Catholicism, the state religion of Austria, stood, in this view, for intellectual tyranny and political servitude. Herzl, in associating Luther's rebellion with "freedom's golden light," adopted a widespread German liberal belief that Luther's assertion of the primacy of individual conscience in religion played a part in fostering later ideals of political liberty. Furthermore, in this view, medieval Catholic reformers and Catholic mystics—Herzl's hero Savonarola among them—were considered forerunners of the German Reformation. In sum, it was Germany, not Austria, that had brought forth a progressive German cultural and political heritage. Herzl's youthful writings suggest he identified with that heritage.[10] Jewish integration, for the young Herzl, presupposed the adoption of Germanic culture by both Jews and Christians.

The young Herzl, by the time he moved to Vienna in 1878, had absorbed German culture in its liberal mode, was a nonbeliever in Judaism, and was optimistic about the prospects for Jewish assimilation in central Europe. Four years later, while a law student at the University of Vienna, Herzl gave impassioned, detailed and precise expression to his belief in Jewish assimilation. His convictions were noted down in his personal diary, in reviews of a novel sympathetic to Jews and of an antisemitic work.[11] These reviews merit detailed interpretation, for they establish the view of Jewry held by Herzl through the 1880s, while he still held high hopes for Jewish assimilation.

A close interpretation of these reviews first requires an excursion into German conceptions of Jewish emancipation and assimilation, for the images of Jewry embraced by advocates of integration shaped Herzl's thinking and stayed with him for the rest of his life. In making the German heritage his own, Herzl also absorbed its view of Jewry. The starting point of these notions was the belief that Jews were beset with vices and deficiencies that could only be eliminated through their integration into Christian society. Such theories, seeking the improvement of the Jews, offered a diagnosis of Jewish pathology and a cure. The image of the Jew and the theme of Jewish improvement developed in these theories were to resonate in all of Herzl's writings, pre- and post-Zionist. Herzl was ambivalent toward his Jewishness and sought Jewish improvement through assimilation. The basis for his ambivalence lay in the German program of Jewish emancipation and assimilation.

Jewish Improvement: An Enlightenment View

Emancipationist theory found its classic and most influential expression in Christian Wilhelm Dohm's *Concerning the Amelioration of the Civil Status of the Jews*, published in 1781. Dohm, a Prussian state official, wrote this work at the request of his friend the Jewish Enlightenment philosopher Moses

Mendelssohn, who had been asked by the Alsatian Jewish community to present the case for Jewish emancipation. Dohm blended enlightened premises with inherited stereotypes. He believed that the Jewish character had been corrupted by centuries of Christian persecution, but emancipation and integration into civil society would improve Jews. The view that Jewish vices were the result of persecution formed the basis of the argument for ending the unequal legal status of the Jews. Dohm believed that policies that freed Jews of residence restrictions and special taxes, that made it possible for them to enter the gamut of occupations, to acquire a modern education, to serve in the army, to enter state service—in short to be full citizens of the state—would eventually normalize the Jewish character and eliminate Jewish vices. The philosophic basis for the expectation of Jewish improvement lay in the Enlightenment notion that human nature was malleable, a *tabula rasa* or blank slate, on which the environment imprints a definite character. In Dohm's words: "Human nature is the same in all people"; cultural differences were only skin deep, and once faulty environments were eliminated, all peoples would display common traits.[12]

Dohm's account of Jewish vices included the usual eighteenth-century stereotypes. Jewish moral corruption took the form of "the exaggerated love . . . for every kind of profit, usury and crooked practises." As a result, Jews were "guilty of a proportionately greater number of crimes than the Christians." What is more, preoccupation with commerce had bred a certain kind of intelligence in Jews, a quick, calculating cleverness, geared to profit-making. Jewish greed for profit was understandable. Restricted to commerce, granted no other scope for their talents, living out a precarious existence under the shadow of arbitrary power, hence never secure, is it any wonder, Dohm concluded, that Jews became grasping and unscrupulous materialists, since "love of profit" had become their "sole means of survival." Such vices were, moreover, "nourished" by Judaism, which was "antisocial and clannish" and fostered "antipathy" toward non-Jews. Dohm was no less convinced that these traits were chiefly the consequence of Christian oppression: "We were always the rulers, and therefore it would have been up to us to induce the Jew to feel humanely by proving that we have such feelings ourselves. In order to heal him of his prejudices against us we first have to get rid of our own." Treated inhumanly, is it any wonder Jews developed "antipathy and hatred against the Christian"? Denied social status and "civil honors," indeed, treated with contempt, is it any wonder Jews had abandoned honorable behavior?[13]

According to Dohm, Judaism too had "deteriorated." He ascribed this religious decline to the unique history of Jewish persecution, lengthier than that endured by any other people. Denied rights and opportunities in society and the state from the 5th century A.D. on, Judaism lost all regard for the duties of citizenship. Judaism had once embraced such ideals in the biblical period, when Mosaic law served as the basis for "a permanent and thriving state" and promoted "civil virtue" and martial bravery. Moses, for Dohm, was a great legislator and state-founder. But once excluded from state and society and suffering unremitting persecution, Jews sought spiritual holiness instead, and "greater rights to heaven." The rabbis then took power by hedging the way to holiness with "narrowminded and petty regulations." The "freer and nobler Mosaic Law," suiting a people with a satisfying earthly destiny, degenerated into a "timid and petty spirit of ceremony." Continuing persecution had the effect of making Jews cling ever more defiantly to their religion. But emancipated Jewry would either purge Judaism of its rabbinic spirit, or perhaps even convert to an enlightened form of Christianity.[14]

Accordingly, Dohm ascribed Jewish deterioration to their exclusion from citizenship and concluded that only full citizenship in the modern state would normalize Jews. Dohm's argument was buttressed by the notion of a Jewish golden age in the biblical period of Jewish statehood. Jews had once been virtuous peasants and warriors in a thriving state; they could be so again. When he became a Zionist, Herzl had only to push Dohm's argument one step further. The cure for Jewish decay was full citizenship in the state, but in a state of their own.

It is not hard to account for Dohm's view of Jews and Judaism. Jews had lived in Europe for centuries, but they did so as a diaspora people among host societies. Not only was their religion distinctive, but by the fifteenth century they were the only non-Christian people in Europe. Living in a still localized and self-segregating society, Jews were able to maintain a high degree of separateness for centuries. The subsequent rise of the modern unitary centralized state entailed accepting Jews as co-citizens and compatriots. But instinctive hostility and myth-making about strangers did not disappear overnight. The image of the Jew as a nomad, an oriental migrant into Europe's heartland, rootless and parasitic, bent on employing mercantile acumen to subdue honest Christians, shaped modern European sensibilities. At the same time, belief in progress, in the rule of law, in the modern state's need for cultural homogeneity, in Europe's superiority and assimilatory power, all contributed to the emancipationist notion that once Jews were integrated into the modern state they would shed their "Jewish" character and become worthy citizens.

Dohm's view was not based merely on inherited stereotypes, but on current realities as well. For him Jewish moral corruption centered around commercial practices. Indeed, Jews in eighteenth-century Germany were for the most part desperately poor, managing in the interstices of a rural economy, engaged in *Nothandel*, or "the irregular or distressed trades": peddling, pawn-broking, moneylending, buying and selling junk and old clothes.[15] A life dedicated to exchange and hard bargaining rather than production seemed morally repugnant and harmful in a society still oriented to agriculture and a guild economy. Moreover, Judaism had been self-segregating, and the continuing desire of many Jews to be ruled by Talmudic law raised questions about their suitability as members of civil society. Understandably, emancipation and integration would have to entail drastic changes in the Jewish occupational structure and in Judaism.

Jewish Improvement: A Nineteenth-Century Liberal View

Dohm was a civil servant in eighteenth-century absolutist Prussia, but his view of Jewish emancipation, typical of the Enlightenment, was taken over by nineteenth-century German liberalism. Recent scholarly work by George Mosse has sharpened our understanding of the liberal ideology of emancipation. An influential statement of the case for emancipation, combining liberal premises and negative Jewish stereotypes, can be found in the novel *Debit and Credit*, published in 1855 by the German liberal publicist Gustav Freytag. Emancipationist views were not limited to programmatic treatises, but pervaded the image of the Jew in literature. The Freytag novel demonstrates the psychological power of images and stereotypes far more sharply than Dohm's tract.

Freytag's message was that Jewish traits, moral, intellectual, physical, behavioral, were to be shed; Germanic traits were to be embraced. In his novelistic portrait of the "good Jew," the young Jewish scholar Bernhard Ehrenthal, Freytag demonstrated the realized promise of Jewish civic emancipation. Bernhard is noble, lofty, unmaterialistic, entirely worthy of the friendship of the Christian Anton Wohlfahrt. Contact with Christian Europe and the prospect of a scholar's vocation has transformed him. Freytag's novel was a plea for integration, the result of which would be Jewish improvement.[16]

The setting for *Soll und Haben* was Breslau in Silesia, an area inhabited by Germans, Poles, and Jews, a Prussian borderland, where the government was engaged in Germanizing what it considered a primitive "semi-Asiatic" Polish population. Jews in Silesia, many of whom were recent arrivals from the Polish heartland, were traditionalist and self-segregating and considered part of the "Asiatic" influx. Freytag judged them differently from their Germanized coreligionists such as Bernhard: "The second generation goes to Berlin, the third to Frankfurt. Since it is here in Breslau that the distillation begins, it follows that most of the filth remains with us."[17]

In the novel, Bernhard, the good Jew, is set off against both his merchant father Hirsch Ehrenthal and Veitel Itzig, a self-made success who rose from lowly beginnings. Bernhard is virtuous in that he has shed his "Jewish

traits." Indeed he would rather have been born a Christian. The characters
in the novel are not shaded in light and gray, but are abstract embodiments
of virtue and vice. Bernhard's goodness and Itzig's calculating amorality are
played off against each other. Bernhard is the exceptional Jew, highlighting
the moral stigma of Jewish existence. Itzig is immoral, untouched by a sense
of honor, unmoved by beauty, and himself physically pale and puny. His
physical appearance is an outward sign of his inner ugliness. Thus, Jewishness
even carried a physical stigma. But such traits, according to Freytag, were no
longer, in an age of emancipation, an unalterable destiny. As Bernhard tells
his father: "You have thought of nothing but making money. Nobody taught
you anything else, your faith kept you away from intercourse with those who
understood better what gives value to life." As Christian Bensen commented
in the introduction to the English translation of the novel: Bernhard "had
departed in his inmost soul, from Judaism, that he might turn to the Chris-
tianized spirit and to the poetry of the Gentiles."[18]

Freytag, like Dohm, ascribed Jewish corruption to the Jews' persecution
and isolation. He condemned unequivocally the German treatment of Jews
in the Middle Ages, branding it "a shame of the nation." Freytag ascribed
the lack of gentility and sense of honor among Jewish merchants to their
insecure, inferior position in gentile society. An essay of 1869 evinced warm
admiration for German-Jewish achievements in art and science, testifying to
the Jewish potential once they were assimilated. In the 1890s, Freytag was to
strongly condemn the antisemitic movement in Germany. The reason for his
opposition was that antisemitism hindered the process of Jewish disappearance.[19]

Images of the Jew in emancipationist ideology were embraced by Jews
as well as Gentiles. *Debit and Credit* was immensely popular and widely read,
not least of all by Jews. Such images exerted a powerful influence upon Jews
of Herzl's generation.[20]

Jewish Improvement: Herzl's View

Herzl shared these emancipationist images of the Jew. Ironically, Herzl's
furious response to a German antisemitic tract provides our first piece of
evidence for his negative image of Jewry. In 1882 he read Eugen Dühring's
*The Jewish Problem as a Problem of Racial Character and Its Danger to the
Existence of Peoples, Morals and Culture*. Dühring was a professor, and his
learned arguments gave antisemitism intellectual respectability; the book was
read and talked about by antisemitic students at the University of Vienna.
Dühring's "teeth should be smashed in," Herzl exploded in rage.[21] The
source of this rage was Dühring's racism, for he was one of the first antisemites to define the Jewish question in terms of race. For Dühring, contrary

to Dohm or Freytag, race was destiny, hence Jewish vices were ineradicable. Occupational constraints had not forced Jews into moneylending; rather their materialistic inclinations had drawn Jews to usury. The Jewish leopard could not change its spots, and even Jewish conversion to Christianity was unwelcome to Dühring, for he considered it a ruse by Jews to better insinuate themselves into European society. Germany had to be protected from "Judaization" by repealing civic emancipation, restoring Jews to subject status, and barring them from key professions. Dühring had angered Herzl by demanding that Jews be prevented from assimilating and thereby disappearing into gentile Europe. Years later Herzl was to say that reading Dühring had raised his Jewish consciousness.[22] His memory of the incident was shaped by his later Zionist convictions. At the time, it was Dühring's repudiation of assimilationist hopes that disturbed him the most.

Herzl confessed that Dühring caught many Jewish traits with "much subtlety and rigor." "The crookedness of Jewish morality and the lack of ethical seriousness in many (Dühring says in all) Jewish actions is exposed and marked out unsparingly. There is much to learn from this." Jews were the financial "leeches of the Middle Ages—and admittedly, also of modern times," Herzl acknowledged. He also agreed with Dühring that the German-Jewish poet Heine had betrayed a Jewish tendency to seek the glitter of "external and ephemeral success."

While agreeing with Dühring that the Jewish character was "deformed," Herzl disagreed about the cause. For Herzl, drawing on liberal emancipationist notions, these Jewish vices were the result of history, hence potentially eradicable. Forced into degrading occupations, squeezed for gold relentlessly by the powerful, Jews became "avaricious and eager for plunder" in order to survive. Environment, not racial determinism, had shaped the Jewish character. "Religious-legal arrangements" in the Middle Ages had pushed Jews into "tainted occupations," and made them easy marks for plunder. Herzl blamed Christian oppression for Jewish vices: he sarcastically equated "Christian morality" with "greed for plunder." Darwinian imperatives had compelled Jews to become plunderers in turn. Now that this oppression had been lifted, the Jewish character would be transformed.

Dühring's tract did not drive Herzl back to an affirmation of his Jewishness, nor did it dim his optimism about the prospects for assimilation. He considered Dühring's racism, in spite of its modern scientific dress, a fading echo of medieval anti-Jewish attitudes, rooted in atavistic religious fanaticism and in the desire to plunder Jews. Dühring's claim that Jews appropriated Christian wealth was simply a modern version of the medieval ritual murder charge, no longer credible in the nineteenth century. Herzl maintained: "The Christian child has been transformed into Christian capital." Both charges were "old-wives tales"; one was simply, "more refined." Racial theory, he went on, was "the modern petrol poured over the medieval wood-pile now become somewhat damp, no longer able to burn properly." Dühring's book and the concurrent pogroms in Czarist Russia were inspired by the same primitive motives. Herzl looked forward to the day when "every cultivated person" would judge anti-Jewish hostility as dimly as they now did medieval fanaticism and superstition. In viewing Dühring's antisemitism as a remnant of the Middle Ages, Herzl had not yet grasped late-nineteenth-century anti-semitism as a postemancipation phenomenon, a backlash response to the entrance of Jews into European civil society, part of a rising tide of opposition to changes brought about by liberalism and capitalism in European politics and society. This view of antisemitism would come to him only a decade later.

Ghetto Isolation: Herzl's View of Jewry and Judaism

Herzl shared not only the German Enlightenment and German liberalism's view of Jewish vices, but their view of Judaism as in decay. At the classical gymnasium he had attended in Budapest, the curriculum had included Latin and Greek. In his diary there is a reference to "the power that Greek life exerts over us." "In Greece," Herzl exclaimed, "we are . . . at the world's cradle."[23] Culture began at Mount Olympus, not at Sinai. We have seen that in his youthful essays Jewish themes were absent. Instead, he wrote on Savonarola, Magyar heroes, the Cataline Conspiracy, Napoleon, who embodied "the virtues of our century," and of course, the poem celebrating Germany's national resurgence, "We Shall Not Go to Canossa." Herzl's view of Europe's dynamism and progress forms a striking contrast to the utter paralysis he saw in Jewish history and in Judaism.[24]

Herzl's views on Judaism are to be found in comments on a novel, entered into his diary on 8 February 1882, just one day before his discussion of Dühring. *The Jews of Cologne*, published by the German writer Wilhelm Jensen in 1869, was based on a fourteenth-century episode, in which Jews were charged with spreading pestilence among Christians by poisoning wells. Herzl called Jensen's work a "preliminary" protest against the "Jew-baiting" currently taking place in Czarist Russia and in Germany, for in 1881 pogroms had broken out in Czarist Russia and a massive anti-Jewish petition campaign had been organized in Germany. What Herzl singled out in the novel was its depiction of the Jews as "an aristocratic race, brought down by history," subjected to the "gloomy constraint and cage of the ghetto"; "enclosed by the ghetto like a coffin."[25] Reading the novel had spurred him to formulate his view of Jewish history.

Herzl believed that centuries-long imprisonment in the ghetto had isolated Jews from the mainstream of history, rendered them superstitious and fanatic, and made them physically weak, cowardly, and incapable of "honest, manual labor." "The ghetto-walls of intolerance," he declared, "had restricted them [Jews] both in mind and body." Herzl was castigating Christian Europe for its mistreatment of Jews, but he also considered the malformations caused by this mistreatment as no less real. Ghetto walls were impenetrable to the winds of change, creating a fossilized Judaism. This view of the Jewish past as one of unrelieved incarceration reflected both Herzl's understanding of Judaism and his case for Jewish equality. If Jewish history was a litany of victimization, then its rabbinic and Talmudic culture could be dismissed and explained away as the product of an unnatural, imposed isolation from the mainstream of humanity, as the pathetic consolation of distressed spirits, rather than as the bold creativity of free spirits. The emphasis on Jewish victimization reinforced the Jewish claim on European society to fulfill the promise of emancipation. Viewing Jewish isolation, so-called, as externally imposed rather than internally willed, one could argue that Jews had always preferred integration into the larger society and that their tendency toward self-segregation was merely a response to persecution. All this constituted an argument for Jewish equality and opened up the prospect of Jews shedding a Judaism produced under conditions of quarantine, once they were free.[26]

Images of the ghetto had come down to Herzl from the great literary figures of the German Enlightenment. These images ran deep in eighteenth-century Germany where ghettos still existed, where a mass of poor Jews pursued the "distressed trades," and where the large Jewish population in the Polish provinces recently annexed by Prussia were considered just like Poles, as semibarbaric. Typically, Goethe, the greatest of German poets, considered Jewry untutored in anything comparable to Europe's high culture. To him, Judaism was the embodiment of fanaticism and religious zealotry. In *Wilhelm Meister*, a rabbi is etched in repulsive features, all "fanatic zeal, repulsive enthusiasm, wild gesticulations, confused murmuring, piercing outcries, effeminate movements." Visiting the Frankfurt Ghetto, Goethe saw only "filth," heard only "the accents of an unpleasing language." For Herzl, Goethe's writings were an integral part of his literary heritage; in his diaries and letters he would often turn to a line from Goethe to better express his own thoughts or feelings.[27] The difference between their views was that Goethe considered these Jewish traits as fixed, while Herzl saw them as the result of unrelenting persecution, hence changeable.

By contrast, other Jews, desiring to maintain Judaism's status in the modern world while seeking equality, argued, as did Herzl's Viennese contemporary the orthodox Rabbi Moritz Güdemann, that medieval Judaism was marked by cosmopolitan learning and lively cultural interchange with the outside world. As such, Judaism was influenced by European culture and was not the product of distress and isolation. Such a view was far from Herzl's.

While Güdemann stressed Judaism's Europeanism, in the Jensen review Herzl emphasized Judaism's Oriental character. Jews in the medieval ghetto in Germany were an "Oriental tribe," like the Moors in Spain. They wore "Oriental costume"; their speech was Oriental. Herzl emphasized Judaism's foreignness to Europe, its incompatibility with European culture. Again by contrast, in 1869 Adolf Jellinek, the chief rabbi in Vienna, had described the Jewish people as an ethnic mix of both non-European and European origins, "mediators" between east and west, reconciling the two in a "higher unity."[28] Jellinek, like Güdemann, was claiming status for Judaism in modern Europe by endowing it with a special mission. In emphasizing Judaism's Oriental character and foreignness to Europe, Herzl was closer to anti-Jewish polemicists who claimed Jews were too alien to European culture to make integration possible. But while they argued that Jews would always constitute a self-segregating Oriental nation, Herzl argued that Jews would gladly shed Judaism as the price for equality.

Herzl attributed all that made Jews distinctive to Christian persecution. In a suggestive metaphor in the Jensen review, he compared ghetto existence to a tight ring on a finger, painful and constricting, digging into the flesh, creating an "unnatural . . . furrow." Jewry had become the "disfigured ring finger on the hand of humanity." Jews had for a long time "prided themselves inordinately on being this chosen ring finger," but "gradually the ring grew into the flesh," and they were relieved, indeed overjoyed, to have it removed. Herzl continued, applying the metaphor even further: now the furrow would "even out," the finger would gain its natural shape. Jews would become "indistinguishable" from others. The fingers on the hand of humanity would all be the same. The metaphor of the torturous ring is revealing: for Herzl, Jewish distinctiveness and disfigurement were one and the same.

For Herzl, Jewish disfigurement extended to the physical features of Jews. In Freytag's novel, Veitel Itzig's pale and puny physique was the physical embodiment of an inner ugliness. Jewishness, for Freytag, carried a physical stigma. Similarly, Herzl observed in the Jensen review that Jews "had a different bodily and mental physiognomy, a strange, even, alas, a despised physiognomy." This was because of constraints against intermarriage. For the sake of the "improvement" of the Jewish "Folk-profile," these constraints would have to disappear. He concluded: "Crossbreeding of the western races with the so-called oriental one [the Jews] on the basis of a common state religion—that is the desirable great solution." Herzl sought not so much the improvement of the Jews as the disappearance of Jewry. Intermarriage on the basis of a revamped Christianity subordinate to the state, a religion emphasizing ethics more than theology, would solve the Jewish question.

Intermarriage, in late-nineteenth-century central Europe, meant, practically speaking, that the family would be non-Jewish. In Austria in the 1880s intermarriage between Jews and Christians was disallowed by law. Either conversion by one partner or a willingness by one of the partners to accept the social and career impediments of *konfessionslos* (without religious affiliation) status was a prerequisite. Intermarriage involved either religious disaffiliation or integrating Jews into formal membership in a state-established Christianity.

Herzl's proposal of intermarriage and conversion was not made in a vacuum. The subject was much talked about in the 1870s and 1880s, favored by many Christians and some Jews as well. The case for intermarriage was articulated by liberals, advocates of Jewish emancipation and assimilation, in both Germany and Austria. Against those who preached racial exclusivism, the German liberal Rudolf von Gneist insisted in 1872 that "mixed blood" was the key to a nation's "growth and vitality." In Austria in 1882 a prominent advocate of assimilation, the Jewish industrialist Baron Ludwig von Oppenheimer, saw in English history a model for Austria's absorption of the Jews. Race mixing among Anglo-Saxons, Normans, and Celts had created a dynamic new breed. Intermarriage between Jews and Christians was the bridge to a comparable fusion in Austria.[29]

The call for intermarriage was based not only on the presumed merits of race mixing, but on the liberal belief in a unitary culture. Liberals considered Judaism a source of divisiveness, a stimulus for mutual fanaticism among Jews and Christians. Christianity in its enlightened form was, however, thought to be at the core of Europe's ethical and humanistic heritage. Accordingly, Austro-Liberals wished to subordinate the church to the state, maintaining Christianity as a "teacher of social ethics and civic morality."[30] They were not anti-Christian or even anticlerical in the French revolutionary mode. Christianity would be transformed into a moral and cultural force, linking together a unitary, universalistic European civilization. The liberal advocacy of emancipation was meant to provide Jews with the opportunity to share in this common culture. Theodor Gomperz, offspring of an eminent Viennese Jewish family and in 1873 professor of classical philology at the University of Vienna, understood this to be the condition for emancipation. As he observed: "Whatever differentiates human beings, also divides them." Jews had to strive for "union and brotherhood, not isolation and separatism." This entailed becoming partners in "the great Christian-European society," or "complete fusion with . . . the majority." Religion he regarded as an ethical force, not a body of theological doctrine. Consequently, he considered baptizing his three sons. For these reasons some liberal German Jews as well advocated conversion. By the same token Herzl, sharing liberal hopes, saw intermarriage and conversion as a way of levering Jews into a new unitary liberal culture where they would shed their distinctiveness and, as he put it in the Jensen review: "exert themselves diligently for the sincere well-being of humanity."[31]

Before closing this discussion of Herzl's view of Jewry, a contrary side to him must be mentioned, which was to surface repeatedly as he pursued assimilation during the 1880s. If Herzl had been single-minded and without conflict in his assimilationist views, he never would have ended up a Zionist. As early as the Dühring review his assimilationist bent was mitigated by fury at Christian persecution and by outbursts of Jewish pride. Feeling compelled to acknowledge the truth of much of what Dühring had said, "so many good, original and judicious thoughts," Herzl nevertheless exclaimed: How could the Jews "survive so long, through a century and a half of inhuman oppression, if there was nothing good about them at all." Their one great virtue was "their heroic fidelity . . . to their God." This too is a theme found in Dohm's tract, the notion that unrelieved persecution engendered a "steadfast adherence" to Judaism.[32] Dohm concluded that only the cessation of persecution would eliminate Jewish steadfastness. Herzl drew a measure of Jewish pride from this trait. His comment also reflects another deeply held attitude that was to shape his complex reaction to burgeoning antisemitism in Vienna in the 1890s, a strong identification with Jewish suffering, with a history, as he believed, of constant and unmitigated persecution.

Jewish Civic Emancipation in Habsburg Austria

In the early 1880s Herzl was prepared to conform to the terms of emancipation and assimilation at the price of his Jewishness. Though shaken by his reading of Dühring, he was optimistic about Jewish prospects in Austria. He had every reason to be so. Over the previous thirty years Jews had attained civic equality, had risen to become a solid and respectable bourgeoisie, and had achieved a measure of social integration with fellow Austrians. Antisemitism existed, but it lacked respectability and was a marginal political force. For the rest of this chapter, I shall review Jewish progress in these realms, the legal, occupational, and social, and assess the impact of Austrian antisemitism in the early 1880s.

Barriers to Jewish emancipation had been gradually lifted by the Habsburg authorities as part of an overall policy of modernization, prompted by a series of political and military reverses: the shock of the revolution of 1848, then two stinging military defeats inflicted by the Kingdom of Sardinia in 1859 and by Prussia in 1866. After the Prussian victory at Sadowa, the monarchy moved rapidly to modern constitutionalism. The fundamental laws of 1867, in effect a constitution, granted broad powers to Parliament and established equal rights under the law for all, regardless of religious creed. As

John Jay, the American minister to Vienna, reported to Washington: "From the defeat of Sadowa, Austria has arisen to the astonishment of Europe and of herself, with modern ideas, free principles, and a new life."[33]

Progress toward Jewish legal equality had begun even earlier, in the 1850s; 1867 merely marked a pinnacle. Though the government soon abrogated the constitution it had granted in the wake of the 1848 revolution, which guaranteed full equality under the law to all regardless of religious origins, pre-1848 Jewish legal disabilities were never fully restored. During the 1850s, Jews gained the right to buy state land, keep Christian servants, and be witnesses in a trial when the defendant was a Christian. In 1852 a royal statute granted Jews the right to establish a religious community in Vienna, with the power to tax and to regulate its mode of worship. The industrial code of 1859 abolished guild restrictions in the trades and in commerce. Virtually all occupations were now open; guild membership was no longer a prerequisite. In 1862 Jews were granted residence rights in all municipalities and attained both passive and active electoral rights. In 1864 all restrictions on Jewish land ownership were dropped. In 1867 Jews became citizens of a modern constitutional state.[34]

A further stage in civil equality came in 1871 when the Liberal Auersperg government abrogated the 1855 Concordat with the Vatican, thus asserting state control over the Catholic clergy. Auersperg had called the concordat "a printed Canossa in which nineteenth-century Austria was forced to wear sackcloth and ashes to do penance for eighteenth-century Josephinism."[35] Liberals saw themselves as returning to the Josephist Enlightenment tradition of state supervision over the Church. Along these same lines, the school law of 1869 had provided for compulsory and free education until the age of fourteen, while the school system itself was taken out of the hands of the clergy and put in the hands of the state. Liberals were far from seeking to disestablish the Church, but they wished to curtail its influence in the public realm, to give greater rein to secularist currents, and to promote civil equality for Protestants and Jews.

The Rise of a Jewish Bourgeoisie

The Jewish advance into the Viennese middle class began even before 1867, when civil emancipation was attained. Social mobility was rapid because of the nature of the earliest Jewish influx into Vienna. Marsha Rozenblit has marked off three overlapping waves of Jewish immigration: the earliest, in the 1850s and 1860s, was mainly from the Czech lands; the second wave, from about the 1860s through the 1880s, came chiefly from western Hungary, including Budapest; the third wave, from approximately the 1890s to World War I, was mainly from Galicia. Bohemian and Moravian Jewish immigrants, the first wave, tended to be prosperous and highly acculturated; Hungarian Jews, dominating the second wave, were a mix of the prosperous and acculturated with a fair number of poor; Galician or Polish Jews, the third wave, tended to be poor and least acculturated. Accordingly, earlier immigrants were more adaptable to Vienna than later ones.[36]

The earliest wave, Germanized Jews from the Czech lands, were far more able to achieve rapid social mobility. Sigmund Freud's family had come from Moravia in 1860, as had the Jewish publishers of the *Neue Freie Presse*, Moriz Benedikt and Eduard Bacher, Herzl's later employers. The socialist leader Viktor Adler was the son of a well-to-do Jewish merchant who had come from Prague in the 1860s. The family of the eminent historian of Greek philosophy, Theodor Gomperz, had come from Brünn, in Moravia.

As a result, Jewish upward mobility did not develop slowly, over several generations, but was relatively sudden. To cite an example, four Jewish deputies sat in the Reichsrat of 1867–1873. In the next session, 1873–1879, there were thirteen Jewish deputies. This last figure remained fairly constant over the next three sessions, extending to 1897. By the same token, as early as 1863, four years before full civil emancipation, three Jews sat on the Vienna City Council. In 1868, there were four. This proportion did not increase in later decades; indeed, it diminished in the 1880s.[37]

Sigmund Mayer, the Viennese-Jewish merchant and Liberal notable, dated the formation of a Jewish middle class from the mid-1860s. By then, Jews in Vienna were no longer a thin, unrepresentative, privileged stratum of wealthy private bankers. Jewish enrollment in medical school made up 30 percent of the total number by 1869 and was to rise to 48 percent by 1889, while the proportion in law school was 19.8 percent by 1869, rising only to 22 percent by 1889. These students were often the sons of an already established Jewish middle class, seeking the higher status of professional careers. Others came from humble origins. The young Arthur Schnitzler, a medical student in the late 70s and early 80s, described Jewish medical students from Hungary as talented, hard-working, hungry, and poor. Whatever their income level, Jews stood out by their drive for success and status and, as an already urbanized, bourgeois, and Germanized population, by their ability to use the Austrian educational system to achieve mobility. By contrast, most Christian students at the gymnasium or the university were there to maintain an ascribed status already won by their families, not to seek upward mobility.[38]

Jews came to Vienna seeking economic and social mobility, and they found it as respectable shopkeepers, solid merchants and manufacturers, clerks and managers, doctors, lawyers, teachers, and journalists. Summing up the Jewish position in Austria in 1883, Wilhelm Goldbaum acknowledged that the Galician Jewish usurer (*Wucherjude*) and the Hungarian Jewish tavern keeper (*Schankjude*) were continuing presences in the empire's benighted rural areas, no less than the Hasidic wonder-rabbi of Sadagora in backward Bukovina, before whom "a fanatic Jewish rabble" sank to their knees with cash offerings in search of miracle cures for their physical ailments. These old patterns represented "acquisitiveness in its degenerate form," while the new Jewish occupational patterns in Vienna represented the striving for gain "within proper bounds." Jews now pursued a range of middle-class occupations. In Austria's economic rivalry with the great industrialized states of Europe, Jews as productive citizens played a key role in enabling Austria to hold its own. Herzl had labeled as slanderous Dühring's denial that Jews would "rather have pursued respectable occupations with their heads raised high and free" if they had not been "shoved" for centuries into the "tainted trades."[39] The sheer unrelenting energy with which Viennese Jews pursued middle-class respectability demonstrated this. Reality seemed to be proving Dühring wrong.

Jewish Integration into Viennese Society

The degree of social acceptance Jews enjoyed, the extent to which they were considered fellow Austrians, is a more complex question, though here, too, what stood out at the time were the signs of progress.

In the retrospective testimony of Jewish contemporaries, the 1860s and 1870s seemed a honeymoon period in Jewish-Gentile relations. Later on, Freud was to recall the atmosphere of the 1860s, an era of Liberal rule when "every industrious Jewish schoolboy carried a minister's portfolio in his knapsack." Such prospects led the young Freud to consider studying law in preparation for a political career. In Schnitzler's novel *The Road to the Open*, a friend notes that in the 1870s Heinrich Bermann's father, a Liberal parliamentary deputy, "had come within an ace of being Minister of Justice." Sigmund Mayer pointed out that the votes garnered by Jewish candidates for public office were a sign that differences between Christians and Jews seem to have been "forgotten."[40]

Such retrospective assessments were too glowing, perhaps colored by the antisemitic crisis that began in the 1890s. Though their economic rise had been precipitous, the Jewish entrance into civil society was after all quite recent, and they were still regarded as outsiders. Attaining positions of public authority was difficult. From the early 1880s on, Jews began to be recruited into the public service—by Mayer's account selectively and "in very modest proportions"—in the judiciary, the Board of Trade, the Railway Service and the Patent Office. Several were even appointed heads of departments in state hospitals. A number became university *Dozenten* [instructors], not only in the faculty of medicine, but in law and philosophy as well. Particularly in the medical faculty, a few rose to become associate and full professors; these too were public appointments approved by the state. Still, by Mayer's account, the number of such appointments was "very modest."[41] For the most part, Jews were brought into the lower echelons of government and the academy, and it was understood that baptism was a condition of advancement. Certainly no unbaptized Jew would have been granted a cabinet position. For Jews to hold positions associated with the authority of the state was still considered inappropriate. Though several Jews sat in Parliament, gentile acceptance was begrudging and strained. There were at that time two Jewish Liberal members in the Reichsrat who apparently were referred to as "the two Jews."[42]

Jews remained a distinctive group, by no means fully integrated into Austrian society. In her study of the Jews of Vienna, Marsha Rozenblit has pointed to the important distinction between acculturation and structural assimilation. Viennese Jews were acculturated; they were educated in the German language and culture, they held values in common with other Austro-Germans. But Austrian society was no social melting pot. Group distinctiveness and identity were sustained by residential, occupational, and social separation. The kind of Jewish structural assimilation characteristic of late-twentieth-century North America, with high rates of intermarriage and mixed primary social relationships—close friendships and family relationships among Jews and Gentiles—was unknown in Austria. Jews tended to cluster in certain districts of Vienna, and in specific occupations. Rates of intermarriage and of conversion were low.[43] Even Jews who had abandoned religious observance, indeed, who regarded Judaism as backward and superstitious, moved in exclusively Jewish middle-class circles. Stephan Zweig's literary colleagues in Vienna were all Jewish. Martin Freud, Sigmund Freud's son, described his Viennese family as having abandoned Judaism while remaining identifiably Jewish and moving only in Jewish social circles.[44]

There seems to have been considerable mixing between Jews and Gentiles in upper bourgeois circles, but it was of a formal kind, often stemming from common membership in organizations. Sigmund Mayer recounts that in the 1870s prominent Jews vied for political posts on school boards, the city council, and Liberal party executive boards. Common political work led to "lively, mutual contact." Jews joined Austro-German music and gymnastic organizations and political associations; they were active in Liberal associations and in organizations promoting Germanization. In liberal circles, Mayer contended, Jews were in fashion; politicians, officials, businessmen "documented their liberalism by visiting a Jewish salon." The "better bourgeois stratum," according to him, mingled with Jews on public occasions, at theaters, concert, lectures, and in restaurants.[45]

This was the situation Herzl encountered in the early 1880s. Progress in integration had occurred. A modest number of Jews had been appointed to government posts. Maintaining progress depended upon Jewish willingness to consider intermarriage or conversion. Formal mixing was on the increase, but against a background of continuing group segregation. Schnitzler recalled that during his year as an officer in the Army Medical Corps in the early 1880s, socializing between Gentiles and Jews "was very narrowly circumscribed."[46] Jewish emancipation was too recent to allow for spontaneous, unconstrained relationships between Christians and Jews.

Antisemitism in the Early 1880s

As for antisemitism, Herzl's optimistic assessment in 1882, that antisemitism was a lingering survival of medievalism that would eventually disappear, was not a case of self-deception. Austrian antisemitism in that period was judged by many a German import. Anti-Jewish attitudes in the 1880s were far more prominent in Germany, where its adherents included prestigious figures such as the historian Heinrich von Treitschke and the court chaplain Adolf Stöcker. Eugen Dühring was a German academic whose audience in Vienna was limited to pan-German university students. In Germany, Bismarck's break with the Liberals and alliance with the Junkers, coupled with the rise of integral nationalism, had created a climate of respectability for anti-Jewish sentiments. Theodor Gomperz considered Austria "an El Dorado" in its relative lack of Jew hatred, compared to Czarist Russia, Rumania, and Germany.[47] In the Jensen review Herzl singled out imperial Germany and Czarist Russia as centers of anti-Jewish agitation, but excluded Austria.

To be sure, the Vienna stock-market crash of 1873 had unleashed anti-Jewish hostility. In the *Gründerzeit*, the era of stock promotion of the 1860s and early 1870s, numerous joint-stock companies were formed on shaky economic foundations. Profits were astronomical, and thousands of Austrians were caught up in the investment fever. The bubble burst in May 1873, and hundreds of firms collapsed. In the economic depression that followed, thousands of artisan businesses and peasant holdings suffered foreclosure. Public anger concentrated on Jewish financiers and capitalists. However, by 1880 stock-market promotion had been curtailed by legislation, and the stratum of Jews in banking and the stock exchange was much less representative than it had been. A solid and more diverse Jewish bourgeoisie now far outstripped them in numbers, influence, and significance.[48]

In the early 1880s antisemitism lacked respectability; its advocates belonged to politically marginal circles. Schnitzler observed that "anti-Semitism existed . . . as an emotion in the numerous hearts so inclined," though the sentiment was without significance socially and politically. The term *antisemitism* had not yet been coined, and those hostile to Jews were instead called

"Judenfresser" (someone whose antipathy to Jews makes him/her lose his/her appetite), a pejorative label. Schnitzler remembered one such *Judenfresser* at school, who was considered "ridiculous" by other Gentiles.[49]

Austrian antisemitism in the early 1880s found its main political advocates among three circles: artisans, a minority wing of the Clerical-Conservatives, and Georg von Schönerer's pan-Germans. Radical artisans, the chief cradle of popular antisemitism, were not only excluded from political power, but subjected to government repression. The antisemitic *Oesterreichische Reformverein* was established in February 1882 by a group of affluent artisans, small factory owners, lawyers, and schoolteachers. Formed to protect artisans from the effects of laissez-faire capitalism, the association sought to restore compulsory guilds. The *Verein* linked capitalism to Jewish economic hegemony, calling for restrictions on both Jewish landownership and occupational freedom and their exclusion from all public posts. The *Verein* claimed a membership of one thousand, and it was for some years the stronghold of antisemitism in Vienna. However, its record was one of abject failure. Torn by internal divisions, the *Verein* remained a coterie of political outsiders unable to muster electoral support.[50]

In 1883, a Jewish commentator termed Austrian antisemitism "the formula of the reaction."[51] Antisemitism's strength seemed to lie in precapitalist social strata that many believed were fated to disappear. This applied to artisans and Clerical-Conservatives, who had been the chief source of anti-Jewish agitation after the stockmarket crash of 1873. Karl von Vogelsang's *Vaterland* and the *Wiener Kirchenzeitung*, both Clerical-Conservative papers, ranted against modern liberal individualism and Jewish "Manchesterism." During the Liberal high tide of the late 1860s and 1870s this clerical anti-Jewish agitation had seemed an impotent cry in the face of Liberal gains. When the Clerical-Conservative party entered the Taaffe government in 1879, the constraints of power led it to mute its radical anti-Jewish wing.[52]

The final source of antisemitic agitation in the early 1880s were radical pan-Germans led by Georg von Schönerer, who had been influenced in his racist views by Dühring. Schönerer's following was mainly among university students. As a pan-German extremist, he advocated the annexation of Austria by Germany. Coupled with this Prussophile militancy, his racist views seemed a foreign aberration. In 1883 Parliament lifted Schönerer's immunity as a deputy, so the courts could proceed against him for a treasonous statement about Austria's promising future under the German kaiser.[53] At the height of his popularity, in 1885, his newspaper, *Unverfälschte Deutsche Worte* (Unadulterated German Words), had a circulation of less than seventeen hundred. Schönerer's tone was too violent and inflammatory for most Austro-Germans, who prized law and order. The government regularly confiscated the antisemitic tracts printed by the *Deutschnationale Verein*, the party founded by Schönerer. His student following, the pan-German student societies, were repeatedly dissolved by the authorities, student meetings forbidden, pan-German and antisemitic literature confiscated.[54]

Antisemitism in the early 1880s was a movement on the defensive. Antisemitic speeches in the Reichsrat were considered unparliamentary and were met with indignant counterattacks.[55] Sigmund Mayer observed that "the better people" considered anti-Jewish agitation uncivilized and were ashamed to be associated with it. Moreover, the government had made its position clear. It was well known that the emperor—different in this from the German kaiser—despised antisemitism.[56]

What Herzl could not have predicted in the early 1800s was the subsequent decline of imperial power and the rise of mass parties in the Habsburg state, a precondition for the later stunning rise of political antisemitism. In reality there was an incipient conflict between the Habsburg state and Austrian society on the Jewish question. Up to the Reichsrat elections of 1885, Habsburg governments were based upon an extremely narrow franchise, constituting six percent of the adult male population. Hence while anti-Jewish sentiment had a broad foothold in the petty bourgeoisie, until 1885, with the widening of the suffrage, this stratum lacked political expression and influence. The Josephist state bureaucracy was secure in its hegemony. Jews felt they could count on the goodwill of a powerful state authority, whose policy of integrating Jews into civil society was a matter of long-standing commitment and considered beneficial to Austria.

It was the interventionist bureaucratic state that had advanced the integration of the Jews, often in the teeth of public opinion. In the Josephist tradition, the state in all its majesty loomed above civil society; its mission was to mold civil society in the common interest and educate the subjects of the crown. Up to the time of the 1867 constitution, the rights Jews had gained had all stemmed from imperial decrees, often at odds with popular opinion. The Patent of Toleration of 1782, granted by Joseph II, was an act of raison d'état, meant to enhance the economic usefulness of Jews and transform them into dutiful subjects of the crown. The stipulation that Jews could enter schools and universities was opposed by the Catholic episcopacy. The guilds opposed the provision allowing Jews to enter trades. Even during the period of reaction from 1815 to 1848, the thin stratum of privileged Jews residing in Vienna, bankers and army contractors, enjoyed the special favor of the Metternichean state. Many of the crucial legal advances in Jewish integration occurred during the period of neoabsolutism from 1849 to 1860, in the face of opposition by the church hierarchy and by public opinion in the provinces. Provision for Jewish ownership of land and residential freedom came through cabinet decree. The industrial code of 1859, which abolished guild regulations and threw open all trades and commerce, was an act of economic rationalization by the state. Subsequent progress during the 1860s, culminating in the constitution of 1867, had been initiated by Liberal ministries allied to a modernizing bureaucracy, who saw the need to modify its absolutist ethos and share power and control with the middle bourgeoisie.[57] That full emancipation had, to a large extent, stemmed "from above" was seen at the time as enhancing its solidity, not as a sign of its fragility, for the full majesty and authority of the state stood behind it. In 1882 it would have been difficult to foresee the political changes that were to occur in Austria over the next decade, when electoral reform would lead to the rise of mass parties, creating new power blocs that escaped government control.

2

Herzl as German Nationalist

I worked on it [*The Jewish State*] every day to the point of utter exhaustion.
My only recreation was listening to Wagner's music in the evening,
particularly to Tannhäuser, an opera which I attended as often as it was
produced, only on the evenings when there was no opera did I have any
doubts as to the truth of my ideas.[1]

The Issues

HERZL BELIEVED JEWRY was plagued with faults and vices, the outcome
of persecution, and that Judaism was retrograde, the result of centuries-long isolation imposed by Christians. The remedy was the absorption of
the Jews into European states and societies. Herzl's starting point was a negative view of Jewry; his solution was radical assimilation. In this chapter and
the next, I will show how these beliefs shaped Herzl's life and actions.

Herzl had enrolled in the Faculty of Law at the University of Vienna in
the winter semester of 1878–1879. Both as a Jew and as a newcomer to Vienna
from Budapest, Herzl sought all the more eagerly to establish his Germanic
credentials. While at the university, he became a member of the *Akademische
Lesehalle* (Academic Reading Hall) and subsequently of the fraternity *Albia*,
both German nationalist student organizations. Both expected their Jewish
members to expunge Jewish traits and take on Germanic traits. In addition,
Albia was fervently anti-Magyar. Acceptance meant Herzl had overcome the
twin blight of his Jewish and Hungarian origins.

My assertion that Herzl was a German nationalist requires demonstration. Moreover, the assertion, once demonstrated, raises other questions.
What version of German nationalism did Herzl accept? Finally, did his German nationalism influence his Zionism?

For years the accepted view on the young Herzl's politics was the one
advanced in Alex Bein's definitive biography, first published in German in
1934. Bein considered Herzl an Austro-liberal, hostile to German nationalism.
At a time when the Nazis had just come to power, it seemed utterly offensive
to suggest that Herzl was attracted to German nationalism, now identified
with chauvinism and racist antisemitism. That Herzl joined a German nationalist fraternity, Bein considered politically insignificant. He claimed that *Albia*
"had not yet determined its political direction." Bein concluded that in any

case: "Herzl was certainly attracted more by the human side than by the ideological." Bein reinterpreted intractable evidence to fit his thesis. That Herzl's fraternity name was *Tancred*, Christian conqueror of Jerusalem and hero of the First Crusade, suggested to him that Herzl was already attracted to Palestine in 1881.[2] For Bein, who viewed Herzl's Zionism teleologically as a seed already present in the early years, unfolding with increasing ripeness, no other interpretation was possible.

The first historian to come to grips with Herzl's German nationalist phase was William McGrath. McGrath rightly contended that by the time Herzl joined *Albia* it was firmly committed to radical German nationalism. However, McGrath insisted this did not mean that *Albia* was in the grips of racist antisemitism. German nationalism glorified the "primal unity of the *Volk*," but appeals to archaic tribal memories and symbols were not meant to conjure up racism, but to counter excessive rationalism, individualism, and class inequalities, in the name of communitarianism. Though they emphasized the role of feeling and emotional solidarity in politics, radical German nationalists incorporated key liberal values—such as parliamentarianism and universal civic rights. Their radicalism was expressed in calls for a progressive income tax, nationalization of the railroads, protection for the working class. Thus, their nationalism was a brand of progressive populism on a Germanic foundation. McGrath further argues that Herzl carried this mode of nationalism into his Zionism. As such Herzl remained within the liberal political tradition, even though he was intent on mobilizing the Jewish masses by appeals to archaic symbols and ancient historical memories, linking nationalism with populism and democracy.[3] I shall argue that Herzl went through a German nationalist phase and that it exercised a powerful and continuing influence on his thought, though in a manner different from that suggested by McGrath. My first task will be to define the nature of Herzl's German nationalism.

The Evidence

To shed light on Herzl's German nationalist stance, the background of nationalist crisis among Austro-Germans in the early 1880s must first be sketched. The crisis gave rise to a variety of nationalist ideologies; Herzl's nationalism must be located on this spectrum.

During the 1870s and 1880s, the German position in the empire became increasingly weakened as the Habsburg state endeavored to balance the claims of its different nationalities. Harbingers of this trend appeared as early as the 1860s when, in concessions to the Poles, the educational system in Galicia was placed in the hands of the local authorities and Polish was made the language of internal administration. The constitutional settlement (*Ausgleich*)

Herzl with members of the German nationalist student fraternity *Albia*, to which he belonged from 1880 to 1883. Leon Kellner, *Theodor Herzls Lehrjahre, 1860–1895* (Vienna, 1920).

with Hungary in 1867 strengthened the forces of Magyar nationalism, which cut short Germanizing trends in Hungary. A far more decisive blow came with German unification in 1871, when many Austro-Germans suddenly felt cut adrift in the multinational Habsburg Empire. German unification under Prussian hegemony had laid to rest the dream of a greater German (*Grossdeutsch*) political union that would include the Habsburg domains and the other German states, ensuring German predominance in the new state. The period of Liberal governments during the 1870s had temporarily assured German predominance, but by the early 1880s the new Clerical-Conservative Taaffe ministry embarked on a policy of concessions to the empire's national minorities. The former self-confidence among Germans about their dominant position in the Austrian part of the empire ended and gave rise to a siege mentality.[4]

Reverses occurred in mixed areas such as Bohemia where the long-established German minority made up over one-third of the population. With the Stremayr language ordinances of 1880, the division of the University of Prague into German and Czech faculties in 1881, and electoral reforms in 1882, Germans felt they were losing ground they had held for centuries. The language decrees granted the Czech language official status in Bohemia, to be used in certain areas of administration and justice. This policy favored Czechs in the bureaucracy since they—and not Germans—had facility in both languages. A decree in 1881 made Czech schools available in any district with forty pupils. German taxpayers would now have to subsidize Czech education. The electoral reforms of 1882 increased Czech representation in the Bohemian Diet, an important step in altering the balance of power between Czechs and Germans.[5]

In response to threats to their dominance, Austro-German nationalists developed several political options. Pan-German extremists pushed for drastic solutions, the dissolution of the Habsburg Empire and the annexation of the German provinces, including Bohemia and Moravia, to Germany. Left-Liberals, considered radical nationalists, were less drastic, calling for the administrative separation of the non-German provinces of Galicia, Bukovina and Dalmatia. The rest of the empire, now sheltered by a German majority, would establish close ties with Germany, including a customs union, and thus preserve its German character and German destiny. Mainline Liberals, heirs of the Josephist tradition of centralization and Germanization, wished to preserve German dominance within an intact Habsburg dynastic state. They sought to establish German as the state language of the empire, the partition of Bohemia into German and Czech administrative districts, and close political, economic, and cultural ties with Germany.[6]

Universities were hotbeds of nationalist strife, and Herzl became caught up in these issues. Almost immediately upon entering the university, he joined the *Akademische Lesehalle* (Academic Reading Hall). The *Lesehalle* was an academic association, open to students of all nationalities. It provided its members with a library of almost 10,000 volumes and subscriptions to 224 newspapers and journals. Students could join its special clubs in law, science and medicine, philosophy, French, and even chess. In the academic year 1879–1880, the *Lesehalle* had a student membership of 724, which included 519 Germans, 41 Slovenes, 36 Magyars, 34 Poles, 27 Croats, and 26 Czechs. The figures corresponded to the proportion of Germans (about seventy-five percent) and non-Germans attending the university.[7]

Though the *Lesehalle* was by its statutes politically neutral, it soon became entangled in highly charged nationalist controversies. In late 1878, the executive suspended a Czech student for having organized a pro-Czech demonstration. In retaliation the student assaulted the chairman. The chairman and the executive then resigned and called for a vote of confidence by the membership. Coincidentally, in December 1878 the *Leseverein der Deutschen Studenten* (Reading Society of German Students) had been dissolved by the authorities. The society was exclusively German in its membership and included many pan-German extremists. Former members, led by its last chairman, Alfred Aschner, a Jewish law student, saw the *Lesehalle* crisis as an opportunity. Enrolling three hundred of their former members in the *Lesehalle* en masse, Aschner and his colleagues hoped to replace the executive with radical German nationalists. In response the *Deutschösterreichische Leseverein* (German-Austrian Reading Society), which stood for Austrian patriotism and dynastic loyalty, packed the *Lesehalle* membership with two hundred of its own followers. At a plenary assembly on 18 January 1879, a student, Adolf Bachrach, made a motion calling for a vote of confidence in the executive, while Aschner presented a motion calling for acceptance of their resignation and new elections. The former motion carried.[8]

Herzl was involved in these events. We have the written draft of a declaration he made on the day before the crucial vote. The draft was first published in 1932 by the Herzl scholar Tulo Nussenblatt, in an effort to prove that Herzl never was a German nationalist. In it Herzl refers to his own candidacy for the election, announced by him in a speech on 15 January and exclaims that to his "great regret" his remarks were interpreted "diametrically opposite to what I intended." He then insists "most clearly and emphatically" that he is opposed to Aschner's camp and stands with Adolf Bachrach. He asks that the resignation of the executive not be accepted and announces that he will be "forever and always the friend and companion of those who cherish patriotic Austrian sentiments."[9] Herzl ranged himself with those who reconciled their Habsburg loyalties with their Germanism.

But there is more here than meets the eye. Why was it necessary for him to correct a widespread misinterpretation of his views? How could Herzl's earlier speech have put in question his Austrian loyalties? One explanation is that he had made a statement favorable to German nationalism, though his speech was interpreted in a far more extreme sense than Herzl intended, as a pan-German rejection of Austrian loyalties. Herzl then backtracked and clarified his position. Though this explanation is a supposition, the testimony of contemporaries, as we shall see, supports it.

Nationalist quarrels continued to beset the *Lesehalle*. In the winter semester of 1879–1880, a radical German nationalist was elected to the executive. In the spring of 1880, Czech students at the University of Prague demonstrated against the rector, Professor Dr. Mach, who at a banquet publicly supported German interests. The university was in the throes of a bitter nationalist dispute, which led in 1881 to its division into separate Czech and German faculties. Reacting to the Czech student demonstration, the *Lesehalle* executive sent a telegram of support to the rector. Most of the Slavic members of the *Lesehalle* saw this as a gesture of support for the German nationalist position and called for a vote of nonconfidence in the executive. On 24 June 1880 at a plenary session the executive received a vote of confidence. Many of the Slavic students then withdrew from the society.[10]

Increasingly, events pushed the *Lesehalle* into the German nationalist camp. In the fall of 1880 several radical nationalist fraternities became affiliated with the *Lesehalle*. Among them was *Albia*, the fraternity Herzl was to join. At a banquet on 4 November 1880, Georg von Schönerer, the pan-German extremist, addressed a *Lesehalle* audience. All the affiliated nationalist fraternities took part. This was Schönerer's first invitation from a student organization. By then he had emerged as an outspoken anti-Jewish agitator, though he had not yet embraced racist ideology. In 1879 he had attacked the "semitic rule of money and the phrase" [a reference to the largely Jewish-owned liberal press] for undermining "the powers and rights of honest labor." In a vote held on 22 November 1880, a full German nationalist slate was elected to the *Lesehalle* executive. The German nationalist triumph was now complete. On 15 February 1881 the *Lesehalle* organized a Lessing banquet on the hundredth anniversary of the writer's death and invited Schönerer to speak a second time. He began in his usual confrontational fashion with a German nationalist song outlawed by the Habsburg authorities: "I hear German words again" ("Deutsche Worte höre ich wieder"). The song was greeted with thunderous applause; all joined in. On 4 March 1881, the *Lesehalle* was dissolved by the authorities for political agitation in violation of its statutes.[11]

What evidence do we have that Herzl was in sympathy with the *Lesehalle*'s political course? Leon Kellner was a Viennese contemporary and author of an early biography of Herzl. From him we learn that in December 1880, Herzl was chairman of the *Lesehalle*'s social club. The club organized beer-drinking evenings featuring German nationalist songs and comic poems by student authors. Kellner noted: "At that time the waves of the German nationalist movement were rising high in this student association; Herzl was one of its most enthusiastic champions." Confirmation comes from another contemporary, the writer Arthur Schnitzler, a fellow student and friend during Herzl's university years. Later, Schnitzler was to remind Herzl of a speech he heard him deliver in the *Lesehalle* and acknowledge his jealousy of Herzl's masterful poise and "cleverness." A witness to Herzl's activities, Schnitzler described him as a "German-national student and spokesman in the *Academic Debating Hall*." (Academic Debating Hall is the translator's rendition of the *Akademische Lesehalle*.)[12]

It is not surprising then that Herzl was an initiate (*Fuchs*, literally "fox") in the radical, nationalist fraternity *Albia* in the winter semester of 1880–1881. (The semester began in October. Herzl joined sometime in the fall.) Almost immediately, he began preparations for the fencing bout that would make him a senior member (*Bursch*), attending fencing classes daily from one to three in the afternoon and from five to seven in the evening, and in addition taking a special course with a fencing master. In view of his later idealization of dueling as a manly recourse for Jews, it is noteworthy that his duel, fought on 11 May 1881, was a disappointment by *Albia* standards. Karl Becke, *Albia*'s historian, called it "tame child's play." The duel lasted fifteen minutes and ended in a draw, with both adversaries drawing blood once. As a result of Herzl's weak performance, some were opposed to his acceptance. The insistence of his mentor and second at the duel, the influential Franz Staerck, carried the day, and he was admitted. Herzl seems to have been appreciated for his talented and witty contributions to the *Albia* newspaper and for his stylish personality. Hermann Bahr, a fraternity brother, later remembered "his gallant nature, his ironic, superior spirit, his easy masterfulness."[13]

Herzl threw himself into fraternity activities. *Albia* had rooms reserved at a restaurant where members would meet regularly to discuss politics, celebrate patriotic holidays, honor a guest, or drink beer, play cards, and sing nationalist songs. Members published a fraternity newspaper featuring comic poems and literary pieces. One of Herzl's many contributions to the newspaper was a heroic epic "die Hakenquart," (a fencing position) dedicated to his mentor Franz Staerk. Arthur Schnitzler recalled Herzl during this period. "I can remember seeing him with his blue student's cap and black walking-stick with the ivory handle and F.V.C. (Floriat, Vivat, Crescat: To Flourish, To Live, To Grow) engraved in it, parading in step with his fraternity brothers." We possess a photograph of Herzl taken shortly after his duel, arrayed with his fraternity brothers: Franz Staerk, Karl Becke, later to write a history of the fraternity, and a student by the name of Pischek. All are wearing the fraternity regalia: the ivory-tipped walking stick and the pill-box cap. Staerk is wearing the fraternity sash of black, red, and gold, diagonally across his chest. At Staerk's side is a fierce-looking dog held tightly on a short leash. All look jaunty and arrogant, though there is a touch of awkwardness in Herzl's stance. Their placement in the photo suggests that the novice Herzl had to defer to the other three. They are standing almost frontally, each taking up a wide space, while Herzl has to stand sideways so that all of him

will be in the photograph. A strip of adhesive is on Herzl's left cheek where
he sustained the customary cut during his duel. Visible in all their button-
holes, including Herzl's, is the blue cornflower, Kaiser Wilhelm's favorite
flower, identifying the wearer as a radical German nationalist.[14]

Albia's political attitude was well known, and Herzl must have been
sympathetic to it, or he would neither have sought nor gained membership.
Albia had become a German nationalist student fraternity well before 1880.
Founded in 1870 as the student corporation *Lipensia*, for German students
from the Leipa district in Bohemia, it soon included students from the Elbe
district, covering the whole of northern Bohemia. The name *Albia* was then
adopted, after the river Elbe, which flowed through northern Bohemia. As
a gathering point for Bohemian Germans from a mixed ethnic area where
national animosities were intense, *Albia* quickly adopted a militant stance.
Till 1874, *Albia* was designated a German *Couleur*; after that the term *national* was added and *Albia* became, officially, a German-national *Couleur*
(Student Color Society. Each fraternity had its distinctive colors.) In 1878,
Albia adopted the dueling practices of the German student fraternities, introduced into Austria in the 1860s. This included an obligatory code of hon-
or, according to which conflicts and insults were to be settled or vindicated
through duels.[15]

Albia was politically active in the nationalist cause. In the winter semester
of 1877–1878 it was accepted into the Assembly of Delegates of German National Fraternities (*Delegiertenkonvent der deutsch-nationalen Verbindungen*), a
rallying point for German nationalist students. The *Delegiertenkonvent* engineered the takeover of the *Akademische Lesehalle* in 1880. In June 1880, *Albia*
had helped organize protest demonstrations by Bohemian Germans against
the Stremayr Language Decrees. On 7 March 1881, at a ceremonial beer-
drinking party marking the tenth year of *Albia's* founding, Schönerer, the
pan-German extremist, was invited to speak. At this stage in his political
career, indeed until 1885, Schönerer, who railed incessantly at the Jewish financial conspiracy that was bleeding good Austro-Germans, still welcomed
German nationalist Jews into his movement, though only as "foot soldiers."[16]

If Herzl had wished to range himself with those loyal to Habsburg mul-
tinationalism and unequivocally opposed to German nationalism, he could
have joined one of the dueling *Korps*. These were resolutely antinationalist,
took in Slavs and Magyars, and included a greater proportion of Jews than
the nationalist fraternities. Two *Korps* in particular, *Amelungia* and *Danubia*,
had a large number of Jewish members from upper-middle-class families in
finance and industry, similar in background to Herzl. *Korps* members were
accomplished swordsmen, excellent horseback riders, socially ambitious. The
majority of Jewish students were to be found in the Austrian loyalist camp.
Herzl instead chose *Albia*.[17]

By the same token, it is inconceivable that *Albia* would have accepted Herzl into its small tight-knit band of brothers, never exceeding about fifteen active members, without having satisfied itself about his German nationalist credentials. Loyalty was at a premium in the fraternity. Each of the newly initiated was attached to a mentor (*Leibbursch*) who instructed him in *Albia*'s ways and oversaw his mastery of swordsmanship. The initiate owed his mentor obedience and had to be appropriately modest and unassuming toward him. In addition, *Albia* had its special rituals, colors, and uniform. Members adopted names drawn from the ancient German sagas; all were privy to a secret handshake. Every Saturday morning, members promenaded together—strutted would describe it better—in full regalia across the university grounds. This ritualized corporate self-assertion often led to confrontations with other students, sometimes ending in a challenge to a duel. Shoving matches and fights sometimes broke out with Slavic students. Membership did not end with graduation but was the start of a lifelong association. Members became "old boys" when they graduated; they met annually and claimed favors and special loyalty from each other. *Albia* presupposed and required ideological conformity.[18]

German Nationalism and Liberalism

Ideological conformity to what? What did it mean to be a German nationalist in the camp of *Albia*? Herzl never deviated from Austro-German liberalism, both before and after he became a Zionist. But he could feel a strong affinity for *Albia*'s radical brand of German nationalism, while remaining a committed liberal. In the early 1880s the doctrinal lines between liberal and radical German nationalism were still blurred. Liberals were still the dominant force in the German camp, and much of radical nationalist agitation went on within liberal organizations, aimed at pushing them in a more militant direction. All could agree on the need to maintain German dominance in the Habsburg realms as well as on the need to assimilate minority nationalities to Germandom. Andrew Whiteside has observed that Austro-Germans considered the Habsburg Empire as a German creation, an instrument of the German civilizing mission in central and eastern Europe. Germans, over one-third of the total population, were the largest nationality in the empire, the most urbanized, most educated and prosperous, dominant in government and in the army. The empire's high culture—theater, music, the arts, literature—and its academic and scientific culture, were all German. There was reason for Germans to view themselves as the "essential integrating ethnic-cultural element in the Empire."[19]

In the early 1880s, when the Taaffe government embarked on a policy of concessions to the Czechs, German liberals opposed these measures just as fervently as radical nationalists. One of the greatest achievements of the Liberal governments of the late 1860s and early 1870s had been the founding of a secular and interconfessional public school system. But now clericals in Count Taaffe's governing coalition mounted an assault on the public school system, viewed as an instrument of dechristianization. Slavic demands for provincial autonomy accorded with the clerical aim of restoring the educational system to local authorities, taking it out of the hands of a largely liberal German officialdom. Thus the defense of German dominance and of the liberal achievements of the 1860s and 1870s, hence of progress and enlightenment, were intertwined. Herzl's own student society, the *Akademische Lesehalle*, while still dominated by Austro-liberals, spoke out against government policies. Justifying its telegram of support to the rector of Prague University for opposing the establishment of a separate Czech faculty, the *Lesehalle*'s annual report for 1879–1880 considered its actions no violation of its internationalism or neutrality on political questions. The report insisted the *Lesehalle* was dedicated to "academic principles" and these "were founded and rested on German traditions, German learning and German culture." The *Lesehalle* went on to castigate the Czech clerical press for its campaign against Germandom and enlightenment. Attacked for its actions by *Vaterland*, a clerical antiliberal, antisemitic journal, the *Lesehalle* scoffed at the journal's "medieval urbanity," to be rejected by "all right thinking legitimate sons of the nineteenth century."[20]

Thus even strongly Austrophile societies turned to a more militant assertion of *Deutschtum* in response to Count Taaffe's policies. The German-Austrian Reading Society (*Deutschösterreichischer Leseverein*), founded as a counterweight to the pan-German student societies, was closely linked to the Liberal establishment. Its patrons included such former cabinet members as Eduard Herbst, the chief Liberal spokesman during the 70s and one-time minister of justice, and Anton von Schmerling and Baron von Chlumecky. Austro-liberals viewed the German element both as the foundation stone of the Austrian state and as its defense "against the encroaching barbarism of the East," as the chairman of the German-Austrian Reading Society stated in 1878. These Austrophiles opposed the division of Prague University into separate German and Czech branches and joined pan-Germans in organizing the German School Association (*Deutscher Schulverein*), set up to strengthen German schools in the ethnically mixed provinces of Bohemia, Moravia, and Styria. In so doing, the reading society lost the favor of the government, was harassed, and was threatened with dissolution.[21]

The founders of the *Deutscher Schulverein* were mainline German liberals, but its board of directors included Georg von Schönerer, the pan-German leader, and Viktor Adler, the future leader of the Social Democratic party. Engelbert Pernersdorfer, later a prominent socialist, was secretary of the association. *Albia* too was active in the organization. By 1883 the association was even granting subsidies to twelve Jewish schools. Another issue uniting liberals and radicals was the proposal in 1883 to erect a Czech school in Vienna. This was opposed by Liberal deputies, most of the university faculty, and all the nationalist fraternities, including *Albia*. All agreed that "the German character of the leading educational center of the Empire" had to be maintained.[22] The line dividing liberal and radical German nationalists was exceedingly blurred.

What helped reconcile almost all Germanophile Austrians to the status quo and moderate the radical nationalists was the Austro-German military and diplomatic alliance of 1879. The alliance carried the political assurance that concessions to the Slavic nationalities would be limited and would not endanger Austro-German predominance. As Germany now had a stake in the stability and security of the Habsburg Empire, this dampened the appeal of those pan-German extremists who wanted to dismantle the Habsburg state. In the end few pan-German students advocated the outright annexation of Austria to Prussia, a drastic course which was, in addition, treasonous. The question of annexation or political union became academic, something put off into the distant future. What was left was advocacy of close political and economic ties to Germany and a militant assertion of Germandom in the Habsburg Empire. Andrew Whiteside has noted: "A gradual revival of Austrian patriotism, fused now with loyalty to 'the whole [German] nation.' "[23] Differences between radicals and liberals centered more on appropriate degrees of militancy and on questions of timing. Liberals were blamed for not having done enough during their hegemony to assure German dominion, and subsequently for lukewarm opposition to the Taaffe government.

Liberal and radical nationalists would later go their separate ways, but when Herzl was a member of *Albia*, nationalist stances overlapped, and Germans joined together in a common cause. When Herzl later recalled his own generation's devotion to *Deutschtum*, he linked German nationalism to "the idea of civil liberty."[24] *Deutschtum* engaged Herzl's Austrian and liberal loyalties; it stood for a centralized empire under German political and cultural dominion, restraining the centrifugal forces of clericalism, aristocratic conservatism, and ethnic federalism. *Deutschtum* to him meant parliamentary institutions and constitutional liberties.

There were nevertheless some differences between radicals and liberals, and there are indications that on these issues Herzl was firmly situated in the liberal camp. Whiteside has summed up the nationalist common ground and the differences between liberals and radicals: Both "found a common cause in attempting to enact legal guarantees for the special position of the German language in government and education, safeguard 'imperial necessities' and 'German freedoms' in provinces with Slav minorities, [and] oppose clerical attacks on secular schooling, but they were bitter enemies when it came to the questions of political democracy, social legislation, and the pace at which reforms should proceed."[25] Herzl shared *Albia*'s nationalist militancy, though not its commitment to wider democracy. Even here the differences were not always wide, since many radicals sought only moderate social reform and accepted capitalism.

Indications of the young Herzl's political views are scanty. However, the few documents we have all point to the same conclusion. A statement in February 1882 suggests that Herzl had little sympathy for socioeconomic radicalism. In his review of Dühring's tract Herzl referred to "the miasma of social democratic hostility to capitalism, which most probably will lead, in not too long a time, to a great international epidemic." Herzl seems to have been unsympathetic to radical nationalist demands for an extension of the suffrage. In a poem he wrote for the *Akademische Lesehalle*, Herzl expressed supreme distrust of the masses as the enemies of freedom: "The people will continue to bow down their stooped backs to their old rulers. / Ruling over fools, we'll soon subdue the visionaries / They'll call back the old tyrants without delay." Herzl was to carry this elitist liberalism over into his Zionism.[26]

German Nationalism and Jewish Assimilation

Radical German nationalism for Herzl was compatible with his liberalism, and also compatible with his goal of total assimilation. In the early 1880s, most radical nationalists were still outgoing and assimilatory in their attitude toward Jews. William McGrath has identified an impressive array of Jewish students in the 1870s and early 1880s belonging to radical nationalist student societies. Among them were Viktor Adler, the future leader of the Austrian Social-Democrats; Heinrich Friedjung, who became Austria's foremost German nationalist historian; Gustav Mahler, the composer; Sigmund Freud; Arthur Schnitzler; Heinrich Braun, a close friend of Freud's and later a prominent Social-Democrat in Germany; and of course, Herzl. McGrath has also established that Herzl's close friend, Oswald Boxer, who was to die of yellow fever in Brazil in 1892, was a member in 1880–1881 of the radical nationalist *Deutscher Klub*, a student literary society with close ties to Schönerer.[27]

The radical nationalist combination of republicanism and anticlericalism, indeed anti-Catholicism, was appealing to many young Jews, for Austrian Catholicism was a major barrier to fuller Jewish integration into civil society. Radical nationalism offered the prospect of a more secular, egalitarian society that would remove the last barriers to Jewish integration.

Radical German nationalism may have been assimilatory, but it was also exacting in what it required of Jews. Participation in the Germanic heritage required shedding all so-called Jewish traits. Jews were welcome to absorb the German spirit, but only by adopting a brand of cultural anti-Jewishness. Schönerer's Jewish friends had no difficulty with his attacks on the Jewish domination of finance and the press or his identification of capitalism with the "Jewish spirit." Jewish radicals shared the view that Judaism was "reactionary."[28]

The nationalist circle that gathered around Engelbert Pernersdorfer and became the force behind the left-liberal Linz Program in 1882 included Jews. Yet the circle condemned "semitic traits": rootlessness, alienation from nature, love of profit. Pernersdorfer, a close friend of Jews such as Viktor Adler and Heinrich Friedjung, could write in 1882 that "the Jews with their ancient, dominating racial characteristics still confront the Indo-Germanic peoples ... as alien and unchanging." Pernersdorfer viewed Jews as a nomadic people, preying on sedentary nations; similar to gypsies, Jews were, however, more clever and resourceful. At the same time Pernersdorfer believed that a strong identification with the German nation could remake Jews, for were not Germanic traits—courage, loyalty, rootedness, the feeling for community—the exact opposite of Jewish traits? Germanic assimilation involved a total overcoming of Jewishness, viewed as utterly negative. Pernersdorfer insisted: "Jews who really want to be assimilated to the German nation must be serious about shedding their Judaism." That some Jews shared in this rejection of the "Jewish spirit" was well known and became the butt of Viennese ridicule. In his memoirs, Arthur Schnitzler recalled a popular quip of those days: "Anti-Semitism did not succeed until the Jews began to sponsor it."[29]

While Jews were to shed their Jewishness, Gentiles saw themselves as generously bestowing acceptance. Accordingly, Jews were to take the lead from so-called Aryans and keep to their place. Pernersdorfer expected Jews to remain foot-soldiers in the movement—never leaders—till they had shed all their ties to Judaism and Jewry. He acknowledged that this required "an altruistic kind of humility." This requirement was taken for granted by German nationalist Jews, who, as recent outsiders, idealized the Germanic world to which they craved to belong as intensely as they reviled Jewishness. In Viktor Adler's words: "The present of German culture is not easily repaid." Heinrich Friedjung, of Jewish origin, insisted: "Surely, Christians and Jews have the task of completing the requisite Germanization of a tenacious and alien part of the population. Above all Jews have to strive hard for this by relentless and severe mental efforts. They must not become instantly sensitive when this duty is called to their attention in a serious, even rough manner." Friedjung went on to condemn racial antisemitism for blocking such assimilation.[30]

Though the terms were steep, there is no question that German nationalists welcomed Jews into the fold. Accordingly, Pernersdorfer was to break with Schönerer when he began promoting the racist view that Jewish traits were in the blood, an unalterable inheritance. In June 1883 Pernersdorfer resigned from Schönerer's *Deutschnationaler Verein* (German National Association), explaining: "I don't believe in . . . the brutal position of *Juden hinaus* [*out with the Jews*] no, I am . . . of the opinion that there are decent Jews." Schönerer's fight, he lamented, was "more against Jews than against Jewry."[31]

Karl Becke describes *Albia*'s position on Jewish assimilation as being close to Pernersdorfer's. *Albia* did not join the Schönerer camp when Pernersdorfer split with him in 1883, nor did it support Schönerer in the parliamentary elections of 1885. While some had repudiated the liberal heritage of the revolution of 1848, it remained a force in *Albia*, one of the few fraternities still laying wreaths for the revolutionary martyrs as late as 1884.[32] Both the Christian and Jewish martyrs of the March days were buried in the same cemetery. *Albia* was paying homage to the Jewish fallen and to a revolution that had pioneered in Jewish emancipation.

Many of *Albia*'s members looked forward to the absorption of Jewry by the German nation. Both Karl Becke and Dietrich Herzog, another former member, were to speak glowingly about those Jewish brothers who "felt German" and were genuinely devoted to *Albia*. One was Paul von Portheim, a contemporary of Herzl, an ardent fencer and writer who was editor of the fraternity newspaper. Dietrich Herzog later recalled that an *Albia* brother, Karl Hermann Wolf, a leading antisemitic pan-German politician, still waxed enthusiastic about Portheim a full four decades after Wolf's student years. Another Jewish brother recalled by Becke was Jacob Julius David, who became a noted Moravian poet. David warmly embraced Germandom. Indeed, in order to absorb the German spirit even more fully, he had himself baptized.[33]

Herzl knowingly entered *Albia* on these terms, that he would shed Jewishness and embrace Germandom. The evidence that he accepted these terms, indeed that he saw this arrangement as the road to Jewish improvement, is not only his membership in *Albia*, but comes from the reviews of the Dühring and Jensen books, penned by him in February 1882. Much of what he says there would have had the full endorsement of *Albia*: that Jewish morality was deformed by trade, that the Jews were an oriental people and hence alien to Europe, that Judaism was narrow-minded and superstitious, and that the Jewish physiognomy was disfigured. Equally, his solution was the disappearance of Jewry, or in his formula, cross-breeding on the basis of a common state-religion.

Indeed, membership in *Albia* was a way of overcoming a double stigma for Herzl, since he was both a Jew and from Hungary. The influx into Vienna of relatively poor, ambitious Hungarian and Galician Jewish university students in the 1870s, particularly in the medical faculty, had led to an upsurge of anti-Jewish feeling, specifically directed against them. This feeling was articulated by a distinguished professor of medicine, Theodor Billroth. He singled out these students as lacking a vocation for medicine, and as ill-prepared for their studies. He charged that they were lowering academic standards and draining funds for student financial support. Arthur Schnitzler remembered the resentment directed against Hungarian Jews during his student years, including the complaint that they were monopolizing the scholarship funds for medical students. Schnitzler considered them uncouth and slovenly. Those on reserve duty with him in the Medical Corps lacked a military bearing. He noted that other Jews were among the chief instigators of the agitation against Hungarian Jews. Evidence confirming this comes from the *Leseverein deutscher Studenten* (Reading Association of German Students) which declared itself in support of Billroth. The society's membership and its executive included a number of Jews.[34] The more prosperous and acculturated Jews, either born in Vienna or earlier immigrants from Bohemia and Moravia, distanced themselves from the scorned recent arrivals from Hungary.

Herzl's own efforts to distance himself from his Jewish Hungarian origins are evident in a letter of December 1881 written from Budapest, where he had gone to pay his respects at his sister's grave. Since the time he had left Budapest (in 1878), he reported: Hungary "has become even more Hungarian. Too bad!" Many of his former friends and acquaintances had become "unrivaled Hungarian dolts." Jews now spoke Hungarian and had taken Hungarian names. While in Budapest, Herzl made it a point not to speak "one syllable" of Hungarian.[35]

Membership in *Albia* meant that Herzl was being recognized as German, not Hungarian. Magyars were excluded from *Albia*. The fraternity was hostile to Magyar nationalism, regarding the German minority in Hungary as unjustly separated from the German motherland and subjected to "foreign caprice and oppression."[36]

Herzl's time in *Albia* was, however, anything but untroubled. Eventually he was to resign from the fraternity on the issue of antisemitism. I have argued that Herzl joined *Albia* in full knowledge of its opposition to the "Jewish spirit." Clearly, Herzl saw such opposition as different from antisemitism. Trends to Jewish exclusion were beginning to emerge, though, by those opposed to Jewish assimilation into Germandom. It was this that Herzl resisted. Disagreement first emerged between Herzl and others over the *Turnverein der Wiener Hochschulen* (Gymnastic Club of the Viennese Universities), with which *Albia* was affiliated. Gymnastic clubs had originated in Germany during the student nationalist upsurge after 1815. The clubs emphasized manly strength and moral and physical discipline as ingredients of nationalism. Gymnasts wore a special uniform; gymnastic displays featured ancient Germanic symbolism and ritual and were accompanied by songs, speeches, holy flames. The Austrian gymnastic clubs were known for their radical nationalism and during this period included those who were culturally "antijudaic" in the manner of Pernersdorfer and out and out racist antisemites who wished to exclude all Jews from membership. The latter won out eventually; in 1885 the Vienna *Turnverein* voted to exclude Jews. *Albia* reports for 1881 state that Herzl proposed *Albia* push for a liberalization of the regulations on membership in the *Turnverein*. Probably Herzl was responding to informal Jewish exclusion and wanted the *Turnverein* to be forthcoming in admitting Jews. This may be why Becke, in reporting on this proposal, referred disdainfully to "the Semite Herzl."[37]

Albia too had become divided over the issue of admitting Jews, between advocates of Jewish exclusion and those willing to accommodate Jews who "felt German." Indeed, Herzl had been among the last three Jews admitted to *Albia*. The balance of opinion in the fraternity was such that while no Jews were admitted after the academic year 1880–1881, those already in *Albia* were allowed to remain.[38] If Herzl was calling on *Albia* to urge the *Turnverein* to welcome more Jewish members, he may well have been up in arms over the tendency to Jewish exclusionism, a sign of growing racial antisemitism. After the better part of an academic year in the fraternity, Herzl applied for inactive status, which freed him from attending meetings and contributing to *Albia* activities.[39] In full knowledge that no more Jews were being admitted to *Albia*, he did not, however, resign.

Almost two years later, on 7 March 1883, Herzl did resign from *Albia*, accusing it of having joined the antisemitic camp. *Albia* was then one of the founding groups of the Association of German Students in Vienna (*Verein der deutschen Studenten Wiens*), an umbrella organization uniting German nationalist student associations for common action.

The issue that sparked Herzl's resignation was a Wagner memorial on 5 March 1883, to mark his recent death. The event was organized by the *Verein*, with *Albia* playing a key role. The Wagner memorial was a well-orchestrated German nationalist demonstration with fully four thousand in attendance. The assembly hall was decorated with a gigantic German flag and the coat of arms of the Reich. Faculty members, Reichsrat deputies, lay organizations, had all been invited to celebrate the great composer's memory. Delegates from nationalist fraternities in Prague and Graz were in attendance. The German field marshall von Moltke had been invited but had sent his regrets. With the onset of ceremonies the orchestra played Wagner's music, then the audience was summoned to sing "Deutschland über alles." Speaker after speaker extolled German nationality and the Reich, some in near-treasonous terms. One speaker declared that "there can only be one German Reich." The *Neue Freie Presse* reported that several speakers gave vent to "coarse antisemitic utterances." Finally, it was Hermann Bahr's turn to speak. Bahr was an *Albia Fuchs*, a last-minute substitute for Ernst Hörner, a friend of Herzl's and a leading political activist in *Albia*, who had been taken ill. Bahr praised Wagner's Germanic ideology. He then called Austro-Germans a penitent *Kundry* awaiting salvation from the German Reich (the enchantress *Kundry* appears in Wagner's opera *Parsifal*. She sought forgiveness by serving the Grail knights and was freed from a curse by Parsifal). Reacting to these treasonous utterances, the police stepped forward and forbade any more speeches. At that Schönerer rushed to the platform and called for resistance, shouting: "Long Live Our Bismarck!" The police then cleared the hall. The next day reports of the event appeared in all the newspapers, and Herzl read about it. In his letter of resignation, Herzl charged that "to all appearances" *Albia* had approved of the evening's proceedings, since it had not "audibly protested" against them.[40]

Previous Herzl biographers have concluded that Bahr's speech signaled *Albia*'s turn to antisemitism and that Herzl resigned in response to this.[41] Such an explanation transforms an ambiguous story into a simplistic tale, as if antisemitism suddenly took over in the fraternity. Clearly, participation in the Wagner memorial was no turning point for *Albia*. What this explanation glosses over is Herzl's long-standing acceptance of *Albia*'s animus toward the "Jewish spirit." Moreover, none of the newspaper reports at the time singled out Bahr's speech for its antisemitism. Instead, his speech stood out for its treasonous call for one German Reich. Only *Albia*'s historian, Becke, mentions a favorable comment by Bahr about Wagner's rejection of Jewry, but this would surely have been nothing new for Herzl. Both in the *Lesehalle* and in *Albia* Herzl had been exposed to countless anti-Jewish attacks by pan-German speakers. By comparison, Bahr's speech was unexceptional.[42]

A more likely explanation is that the Wagner memorial spurred Herzl's protest against the new trend of racial antisemitism recently making inroads in the fraternities and gaining ground in *Albia*. Herzl declared in his letter of resignation that at the time of his admission to *Albia*, the term *Semitism* was still unknown.[43] For two years Herzl had been a member of a fraternity that viewed the "Jewish spirit" as wholly negative and that advocated the disappearance of Jewry into Germandom. If *Albia* had persisted in these views, Herzl would have had no reason to resign. Herzl was not protesting against anti-Jewishness, which was compatible with full assimilation, but against racial antisemitism, which sought to drive Jews back into the ghetto.

German Nationalism and Herzlean Zionism

I have argued that Herzl was a German nationalist during his student years. Herzl valued *Deutschtum* as a carrier of enlightenment values, assimilatory in its attitude to non-Germans. In joining a nationalist fraternity he sought full Germanic assimilation for Jews, to the point of Jewish self-effacement. The task remaining is to assess the impact of Herzl's student years on his Zionism.

Herzl's turn to Zionism in May 1895 unleashed memories of his *Albia* experience. In preparatory notes for his appeal to the Jewish philanthropist Baron Hirsch to underwrite the Jewish state, he concluded an exhortation with the words "Honor, Freedom, Fatherland." This was *Albia*'s old motto. In a speech to Jewish nationalist student fraternities at a Maccabee celebration in 1896, he recalled an old fighting song of the German nationalist fraternities in Vienna: "Someday there will be light again in all our brother's hearts," which concludes with, "they will return to the wellspring in contrition and love." For Herzl, this would now become "the song of the Jewish nation." After reading the early Zionist thinker Moses Hess's *Rome and Jerusalem*, Herzl enthusiastically proclaimed the Latin *Fiducit.* The term, proclaiming trust and confidence, was the customary response to a toast to fraternal comradeship during beer-drinking sessions at German *Studentenkneipen*, or student pubs. Herzl remembered it from his *Albia* days. While writing *The Jewish State*, Herzl attended every Wagnerian concert at the Paris Opera; *Tannhäuser* in particular was played. Listening to Richard Wagner, the cult hero of German nationalist students, strengthened his political resolve. "Only on the evenings when there was no opera did I have any doubts as to the truth of my ideas." If *Albia*'s impact on him was undeniable, its specific influence on his Zionism remains to be defined.[44]

William McGrath has argued that Herzl's experience as a German nationalist led him to value the irrational in politics. Nationalists were disciples of Wagner and Nietzsche, both of whom rejected liberal culture as abstract, rationalistic, and sterile. In line with this, nationalists developed an "aesthetic politics," centering on symbols and rituals, invoking primal communal memories. But Austro-German nationalists appealed both to the head and the heart, for they came out of a liberal matrix and cherished civil liberties and parliamentary institutions. According to McGrath, Herzl carried this appeal to "aesthetic politics," moderated by his liberalism, into Zionism.[45]

Carl Schorske has also pointed to German nationalist influences on Herzlean Zionism. For Schorske, nationalism was part of the broader movement of antiliberal mass politics in the late nineteenth century, which Herzl experienced in both Paris and Vienna and which shaped his Zionism. Mass politics, according to Schorske, taught Herzl to value subjective forces in history, such as charismatic leadership, sheer will, and "archaic religious aspiration." But Schorske, like McGrath, sees Herzl as appealing to both the head and the heart. Symbols and rituals, the appeal to the archaic, were considered by Herzl more as instruments, part of the "psychological dynamics of politics."

The goal of his politics was solidly in the rational heritage, a liberal, social-reformist Jewish state.[46]

McGrath and Schorske do well to single out Herzl's rationalist side, though they do not go far enough. Herzl never deviated from liberalism, neither as a German nationalist nor as a Zionist. As a Zionist leader, Herzl played down the irrational side—the "aesthetic politics"—of nationalism. It is easy to be led astray by his early diary entries with their calls for national festivals, for recreating archaic Jewish dress, for a flag, for a Jewish *völkisch* theater.[47] These were the speculations of a budding nationalist leader, and they did not carry over into his political practice. Herzl wished to create a Jewish state that he envisaged as a multilingual Switzerland; he was far less interested in resurrecting the Jewish nation as a collective or supra-individual entity. Even the Jewish flag, with its seven stars for the seven-hour working day, was to appeal to the social and economic—not the nationalist—aspirations of the masses.[48] Herzlean Zionism was more statist than nationalist and unrelentingly liberal and rationalistic, combining nationalism with cosmopolitanism.

Accordingly, there is no evidence that Herzl embraced radical German nationalist doctrines, certainly not its "aesthetic politics." What attracted Herzl to *Albia* was more its self-assertive, militant, and aggressive nationalist style than its political doctrines. Herzl's exposure to German nationalism during his university years made him an idealizer of Prussian traits, the mirror opposite of Jewish insufficiencies. He had joined *Albia* to shed Jewish traits; by the same token, Jewish nationalism for Herzl was a collective undertaking in casting off Jewish traits. What Herzl drew from the political experiences of the early 1880s was not a Jewish version of German *völkisch* nationalism, nor did he draw from the Prussophilia of the early 1880s a harsh Darwinism, a cult of force and scorn for humanitarianism. What he did derive from radical German nationalism was an image of politics as an arena of heroic deeds, courage, manly discipline, self-sacrifice, decisive leadership, and self-effacing obedience. Thus Zionist politics was to transform Jews from wary, calculating survivors lacking physical courage, into "real men."[49] Political Zionism was in some ways a re-creation of *Albia*, writ large. Herzl was simply building on the notion of Jewish emancipation absorbed during his student years, that Germanic assimilation would transform and perfect Jews.

Herzl admired the heroic self-assertiveness of student nationalists in Vienna. In late 1880 he had drafted a tongue-in-cheek epic poem, *Lesehallias*, which described the elections to the *Lesehalle* executive won by the nationalist slate as a heroic battle of Homeric proportions. Herzl reserved his most scornful epithets for the unaligned: "Many kept out of the battle, shuffling about, dully indifferent. / I'd compare them to Homer's choice oxen. Though this slanders the latter. / More like a herd of cattle, though far less digestible."

Among his nationalist colleagues Herzl found the antithesis to the unprincipled political opportunists he derided in his play fragment *The Knights of the Platitude*, those whose antennas were out for whatever phrases were in fashion with the voters.[50]

To indicate in greater detail what Herzl's Zionism borrowed from radical German nationalism, from its style rather than from its content, we shall have to describe that style more closely. Student nationalists prided themselves on their commitment to their ideals. In an October 1882 call by *Albia* for a new German nationalist student alliance, students were roused to "struggle in concert against fence-sitting and neutrality, fancy phrases and a servile outlook."[51] Schönerer's base of support in Vienna was among students; he attracted them because of his dogged indifference to consequences, his confrontational style, and his maximalist program. Students did not necessarily accept Schönerer's anti-Catholic extremism. He had advocated a new calendar, dating from the coming of the Germanic tribes, not from Christ's birth. The names of the months were to be Germanic; Christmas was to give way to a pagan Yule. All things un-German, in clothes, sports, language were to be outlawed. One historian has observed that students "toyed" with Schönerer's Germanic religion, their views a contradictory mix of liberalism, democracy, and ultranationalism.[52] It was rather Schönerer's uncompromising style, his contempt for half-heartedness, his scorn for "realism" that was an inspiration to them. This style accorded with the German fraternities' own heroic traditions, from resistance to Metternichean repression to the revolutionary élan of 1848. Roused by the state of siege mentality of the early 1880s, German nationalists called for heroic resistance and fought the enemy without and the enemy within, the compromisers, the tepid, the cowards in their own ranks. As one of them declared: at a time "when we Germans must beg cap in hand for our schools, when our art is persecuted, our language hated, our duty as German students must be to maintain the German character of the seedbed of German scholarship [the University of Vienna] and not pander to the Byzantinism of bootlicking and of the chase after honors."[53]

Student rebels faced intimidation by the Habsburg authorities. Newspapers were confiscated, organizations were dissolved. The police were present at student meetings ready to break them up if the kaiser was toasted, Bismarck was cheered, or a pan-German song was sung. From the perspective of the twentieth century with its gulags and concentration camps, Habsburg state repression may seem child's play; indeed the regime seems to have intermittently tolerated treasonous speeches and writings. Nevertheless, Hermann Bahr was expelled from the University of Vienna for his part in the Wagner memorial. Pan-German students lost their army reserve commissions. In this atmosphere, students walked a thin line. They shrank from illegal activity, but they indulged in inflammatory rhetoric, using purported cultural ceremonies and banquets for pan-German propaganda and bold treasonous gestures: wearing the blue cornflower—Kaiser Wilhelm's flower—and toasting the kaiser and Bismarck while refusing to accord the same honors to Franz Joseph. Students singled out for harassment by the regime became heroes to their peers. Bahr was lionized by radical nationalists after he was expelled from the university.[54]

To all indications, all the energy, dynamism, and sense of direction was in the radical nationalist camp. For many students radical nationalism was a stage of youthful revolt before they were coopted into positions and titles in the far-flung Habsburg Empire. For youth in that state of exaltation, the Austrophile student associations lacked the glamour and virility, ideological clarity and self-confidence of the radical nationalists.

Hermann Bahr best described the contrasting moods in the German nationalist and pro-Habsburg Austrophile camp. His account is worth quoting in full:

> The [Austrophile] patriots had no self-confidence, little courage and obviously a bad conscience. They took up their cause in a weak-kneed manner, saying that it was a pity about Austria, that once upon a time had abounded in glory and triumphs. They insisted that if the new Taaffe Ministry were to continue with its oppression of Germans and its toleration of growing Czech freedoms, if German rule over the small culture-less nations ever really seemed seriously threatened, if Austria ever ceased to be the German guard on the Danube, then they too would opt for the greater German fatherland. This business of two fatherlands, one small and provisional, with a larger one in the wings, pleased me not at all, and a tentative patriotism, qualified by whens and buts, only in force as long as it paid, appeared somewhat shabby. In that case better none at all. Moreover, it was not in my nature to be half-hearted in anything. If one could no longer believe in Austria at all cost, why not just make an end to it and go right over to the other side? If you put it that way, the patriots sighed: certainly, that would be best. They just didn't seem to believe in themselves. The traitors were more robust lads, they were honest traitors taking on the risks of censure, punishment, and injury to their livelihoods.[55]

Austrophile student vacillators echoed the sense of drift in Habsburg government policies, in stark contrast to the self-assured Second Reich. Despair over the weakened German position in Austria led German nationalist students to envy and admire everything German, another characteristic we shall see reflected in Herzl's Zionism. Bahr lamented: "Whose words rang out over the wide world with the earth-shaking clang of metal, resounding as when Wagner has Siegfried hammer out his sword? Over there they had Sedan, Bismarck, Richard Wagner. And what did we have?" It was across the

Rhine that a German empire and German power had been restored. By contrast, the Taaffe government's policy of tactical evenhandedness toward the demands of the different nationalities seemed cynical, passive, responding to events rather than shaping them. Taaffe was an adroit compromiser, " 'muddling through' by means of well-timed concessions," no imperious Bismarck altering the map of Europe.[56] Taaffe's conciliatory policy toward the Slavs was in stark contrast to Bismarck's draconian policy of Germanization in Prussia's Polish provinces. A Bismarck in Austria would surely have manipulated the party system in the interests of German dominion. Neither was the emperor Franz Joseph a Joseph II or Maria Theresa, ruling in the grand manner. The emperor's political style was consensual, responding to, rather than shaping the balance of opinions and forces in his realm.

Radical Austro-German nationalists lived vicariously on the glory of the Second Reich's triumphalism, at a time when Austro-German self-confidence was low. Germany had risen to new-found heights of military and political power and enjoyed unparalleled intellectual prestige, particularly in the sciences and in scholarship. Austro-Germans took pride in these German achievements, which raised their own morale and self-confidence in their struggle with the recalcitrant nationalities in the Habsburg realms. At the University of Vienna, students absorbed German political thought through the writings of Adolf Wagner and Heinrich von Treitschke, German philosophy through Schopenhauer and Nietzsche, and German nationalist writings through Richard Wagner. There were those who complained about the excessive German content of the university curriculum. In the law faculty the German historical school of law was taught, for Austria lacked a native school of law. A high proportion of university professors were Germans.[57]

Wandruszka has described the Austro-German attitude to Germany as one of ambivalent love-hate. The North German character, disciplined, industrious, single-minded, domineering, possessed all the traits Austrians by turns derided themselves and prided themselves for lacking, for their national character was easy-going, sensuous, and skeptical. Bahr himself expressed a mix of Viennese self-derision and pride: "In no other city has laziness so much grace, so much charm . . . work here is virtually felt as a threat to public safety, but after all the Viennese style of idleness makes no less demands on the soul."[58]

Bahr considered Austro-Germans epigones, feeding off past glories, "against the background of a great [Austrian] culture . . . of such depth that it's finally become conscious of its own inadequacies and indeed can no longer summon up the audacious self-confidence for a novel deed." The English journalist Henry Wickham Steed, a shrewd student of Habsburg Austria, summed up these traits in a sardonic comment on the Viennese love of theater: "The Viennese are still able to bear reality as a representation. . . . A real man in real life, the Viennese have never tolerated." He ascribed this to centuries of absolutist governments, compounded by "south German slackness and Slav sensuousness."

Admiration and affinity for Germany were tinged with the painful acknowledgment that a great German political destiny was being fulfilled by the more vigorous, younger brother to the north, not by Austro-Germans. For German nationalists—and this would find echoes in Herzlean Zionism— Prussian virtues, such as discipline, obedience, aggressiveness, maximalist thinking came to be identified with genuine German virtues, in contrast to the lassitude and accommodationism of what Schönerer termed the "flabby" and "washed out" Austro-Germans.[59]

These themes converged in Herzlean Zionism. Its style, daring, candid, and maximalist in proclaiming its political aims, was an echo of *Albia*'s Prussophile conception of honorable conduct, which demanded "courage, candour, and truthfulness."[60] Herzl was to oppose the Zionist policy of incremental settlement in Palestine. Instead, Jews were to aim for Jewish sovereignty immediately. Jews were to think big, to practice bold and risky self-assertion, to seek sweeping solutions that would alter their situation in one fell swoop. They were to be direct, to openly state their aims, proclaim them to the world no matter what the risk to the fragile Jewish infrastructure in Ottoman Palestine. As well, they were to develop physical strength and beauty, ridding themselves of their blighted physiognomy. The Jewish state would nurture physical courage by rewarding its outstanding adepts with medals and prizes.

In a discussion with Count Philipp von Eulenberg, the German ambassador to Vienna, on German sponsorship of a Jewish state, Herzl was to note that von Eulenberg believed German support should not be surreptitious or couched in guarded language. Von Eulenberg "thought it best to come right out with it, immediately and demonstratively. The world then has to come to terms with it." Herzl concluded: "Here I recognized the Prussian. This is the forthright grand old style. Open and above-board! This way they have accomplished everything." The politics of *fait accompli* was not the Austrian style of "muddling through," of well-timed concessions, of a calculated disjuncture between rhetoric and policy. Neither was it the Jewish style of minority survival through surreptitious temporizing. In his plans for the Jewish state, Herzl flattered himself that the kaiser or Bismarck would understand his political daring, whereas Jews would not. For Jews, the new politics would involve a supreme effort of self-overcoming. Jews as a collective would then realize Herzl's personal fantasy: "if there is one thing I should like to be, it is a member of the old Prussian nobility."[61]

For Herzl, Jews were to acquire power not merely for self-defense, not merely because it was prudent in view of antisemitic threats, but in order to transform themselves. Herzl looked to Germany, not Austria, as a model for the new Jew. It was as a political style, as deed not as nationalist doctrine, that the German model fascinated him. Politicizing Jews would transform them, but it would have to be politics on a grand scale, the pursuit of maximalist goals, not gradualist or minimalist solutions. Only such politics could elicit courage, self-sacrifice, and manly discipline and thereby effect the radical transformation of a people.[62]

3

Herzl, an Ambivalent Jew

> For their [the aristocracy's] natural refinement and great manner of living and
> dying, we may forgive them many things, especially their good fortune.[1]

Introduction

HERZL GAINED HIS law degree in May 1884 and proceeded into state service as a law intern, first in the courts in Vienna, then in Salzburg. Within a year he left state service, determined on a career as a writer. Herzl craved success and enduring recognition as a German playwright. His great dream, the "summit of his career," was to have his plays produced in Vienna's prestigious *Burgtheater*. The decade was spent making his way. By the mid-1880s, Herzl had established himself as a journalist, appearing regularly in the Vienna and Berlin press. But he was plagued by a sense of failure, for he regarded journalistic success as ephemeral.[2] In the late 1880s he enjoyed a brief period of success as a playwright, with several plays produced in the *Burgtheater*. By 1890, with several failures, his reputation as a playwright sank.

Herzl's avid desire for success and recognition as a German writer suggests that his irate departure from *Albia* led to no doubts or misgivings over assimilation. After all, student radical nationalists were youthful rebels, a small minority even among their peers. Their receptivity to racial antisemitism did not represent mainline Austro-German attitudes.

What lay behind Herzl's aspirations was his identification with Vienna's artistic culture, in part his flight from Jewish traits to a pseudoaristocratic ideal of aesthetic cultivation. Such tendencies were also expressed in his writings, which derided the bourgeoisie and idealized the aristocracy. Herzl's identification with pseudoaristocratic ideals extended to his espousal of the code of honor of the duel. All these represented modes of assimilation and Herzl's effort to distance himself from Jewish traits. Assimilationism also spilled over into Jewish self-contempt, displayed by his disdain for wealthy Viennese Jews and for East European Jews. At the same time, Herzl's assimilationism and Jewish self-effacement clashed with his residual Jewish pride and loyalty. During the 1880s and early 1890s, such tensions were kept in a tolerable balance, while Herzl pursued Austro-German assimilation with all the enthusiasm and devotion of a lover as yet unspurned.

Herzl as Devotee of Viennese Aesthetic Culture

In a diary entry on 18 July 1883, Herzl described himself as a "tender organism," a poet unable to share in the daily pleasures of the philistine, "the goblet, the favors of women, successes that come one's way," for the poet can live only in the ethereal world of memory and anticipation. By contrast the practical man takes the present "by the hand, kisses it on the mouth, has it, possesses it." The statement shows Herzl to be a devotee of Vienna's aesthetic culture. Carl Schorske has described this culture's preoccupation with "passive receptivity toward outer reality, and . . . sensitivity to psychic states," its cultivation of the poetic imagination, its search for a deeper reality behind appearances. To his friend Heinrich Kana, Herzl declared: "The lyrical poem will forever be the crown of creation." What art form was better suited to express the deepest, most mysterious moods of the psyche? Diary entries of his travels in Switzerland in 1883 were filled with lyrical descriptions of nature, time, inner states.[3]

Perhaps compensating for envy of the German Reich's new-found political destiny or its dazzling military successes, artistic culture filled Austro-Germans with pride in their excellence. Aesthetic cultivation was no marginal bohemian pursuit, but reflected the high status of art in Vienna. Art had long been associated with aristocratic patronage, and aesthetic sensibility with aristocratic refinement. Many aristocrats were themselves gifted amateurs, adept at art, music, or drama. Aristocratic status conferred high social worth; the middle class, to make up for an undistinguished pedigree, emulated aristocratic cultural pursuits. As a result, Schorske concludes: Vienna produced "a high bourgeoisie unique in Europe for aesthetic cultivation, personal refinement and psychological sensitivity."[4]

Vienna's celebrities were its playwrights, singers, and actors. Stefan Zweig observed that the Viennese turned first to the theater section on opening the morning newspaper. To have a play produced at Vienna's royal *Burgtheater* conferred "a sort of lifelong nobility on its author." High culture was centralized in Vienna, the imperial city. The *Hofburgtheater* was a national institution, subsidized by the Court and overseen by a royal administrator.[5]

Seeking to establish himself as a writer, Herzl was following a typical Jewish middle-class route to upward social mobility. Herzl's father had gone to a secondary modern school (*Normalschule*) as a route to a business career, while the son attended a humanistic gymnasium, the preparatory path to university. Herzl's father was a stock broker in Vienna. For his son to acquire a university degree was a step up in status. Even aspiring writers sought the title of *Doktor*, not only as something to fall back on, but as Zweig observed: "to assure the family honor."[6] For Jews, in addition, a university degree and professional career entailed escaping the taint of commerce. Pursuing such a career was not considered an expression of Jewish reverence for the life of the intellect, but an escape from Jewish materialism. So ingrained was this view that a Liberal deputy in Parliament felt called upon to point out that Viennese-Jewish achievements in scholarship involved "ideal activities," where "greed" played no role. Herzl later noted that young Viennese Jews sought to gain a "bit of honor outside the higgling and haggling Jewish trades."[7] But he himself sought more than professional standing; he also aspired to status through aesthetic cultivation.

In an important insight, Schorske noted that Herzl sought surrogate aristocratic status by becoming a putative heir and champion of Vienna's aesthetic culture. As a student Herzl had strolled with Arthur Schnitzler in front of the new *Burgtheater* while it was being built in the early 1880s and had turned to him to declare: "Someday I'll be in there." Association with the majesty of the imperial state in government posts was still largely closed to Jews. Herzl was well aware that no promising future in the judiciary awaited him. For Jews, aesthetic cultivation and the pursuit of art was one of the few ways of achieving a sense of full membership and high status in Viennese society. Stefen Zweig recounted in his memoirs that his fellow seventeen-year-olds in his gymnasium class, mostly the sons of Jewish businessmen, were seized by an "epidemic" of aesthetic creativity. He observed that his father would have never presumed to sit next to a member of the peerage, which would have violated his own sense of social propriety. However, art carried the cachet of aristocratic culture, and access to this realm was open to all. Accordingly, Jews filled the halls at theaters and concerts and came to play a predominant role as initiators and creators of Austria's literature, drama, and music.[8]

In addition, Vienna's artistic and literary culture provided Jews with an ideal neutral ground, for it was not steeped in Austria's Catholic memories and traditions. Aesthetic culture was grounded in a universalist ideal of the cultivated personality, overriding religious and ethnic differences. As heirs of German high culture, upholders of the arts, Jews could achieve recognition as collaborators in Vienna's glory.

Herzl's letters and diaries of the 1880s and early 1890s show him alternating in torment between fantasies of literary glory and fantasies of despair and self-doubt about his talents. Even after he established himself as a leading journalist, he remained dissatisfied, nagged by his yearning for literary fame. One can think of no greater self-delusion: the plays of his produced by the *Burgtheater* were light comedies selected to alternate with the serious plays that were the pride of the theater's repertory. On the other hand, Herzl undervalued his journalistic achievement as a master of the *feuilleton*.[9] These were literary essays on travel, the arts, politics. Schorske calls the *feuilleton* an example of the "aestheticizing tendency of Viennese journalism," for these pieces expressed a personal and subjective sensibility in a polished literary style. Tributes to Herzl's formidable literary art as a composer of *feuilletons* abounded from fellow writers. He continued to dream of writing a literary masterpiece.[10]

The desire for enduring literary achievement is common to writers, but in Herzl's case one of the factors behind his ambition was the craving for full acceptance in Austrian society, something he could not achieve as a journalist. Jews were prominent in Vienna's important liberal newspapers. Papers like the *Neue Freie Presse* or the *Neues Wiener Tagblatt* attained substantial readerships and were influential opinion moulders. Their intellectual and cultural level was high, but they had a reputation—not entirely undeserved—for serving the government, which alternated between bestowing favors and punitive confiscations. In addition, the trade of journalism was a harsh competitive scramble. Many of Herzl's colleagues resorted to shady practices. Herzl himself later alluded to Jewish involvement in journalistic corruption. In reaction to this, he was overscrupulous about his honor as a journalist; as literary editor, he refused to accept *feuilletons* for the *Neue Freie Presse* by any writer who had ever publicly praised his own work.[11]

In German-speaking Europe the terms "journalism" and "Jews" went together in peoples' minds. Wandruszka has even insisted that in nineteenth-century Austria, "antisemitism and antijournalism always went hand in hand." The common view of journalists as liars, superficially clever, pandering to an audience, referred to Jewish traits. Even polished literary journalists like Herzl did not escape this taint. He even used on himself the word *Schmock*, a pejorative for Jewish journalists.[12] Henry Wickham Steed commented on Viennese-Jewish journalists: "Their easy knack of turning out readable 'copy' on any subject seems a positive obstacle to the attainment of excellence." It was a view Herzl shared, for he implied that Jews were clever and facile, suited for journalism, but lacking the capacity for enduring creativity. The career of journalism was no way to shed so-called Jewish traits. A life devoted to art was. Hannah Arendt has remarked that "in regard to a *famous* Jew, society would forget its unwritten laws." In Vienna, such fame, sought by Herzl, was gained through artistic achievement. The high status of the arts, as no other pursuit, could redeem its Jewish practitioners.[13]

Herzl's Idealization of Aristocrats

Sir Isaiah Berlin has observed about European Jewish outsiders: "It is a well-known psychological phenomenon that outsiders tend to idealize the land beyond the frontier on which their gaze is fixed. Those who are born in the solid security of a settled society, and remain full members of it, and

Herzl as a law intern between August 1884 and August 1885. Alex Bein, *Theodor Herzl: Biographie* (Vienna, 1934).

look upon it as their natural home, tend to have a strong sense of social reality; to see public life in reasonably just perspective, without the need to escape into political fantasy or romantic invention."[14] This observation applies to Herzl, for he romanticized aristocrats.

Acculturated Jews, though secure in their civic rights and economic well-being, were still not fully accepted into the Austro-German Bürgertum. Considering such marginality a disgrace, Herzl identified with an ideal world of aristocrats who enjoyed secure status and as a result easy self-confidence. The hero of a Herzl novelette, Count von Hagenau, is a model of "quiet, undemonstrative pride" and "simple and natural certainty of bearing." Social status, Herzl seemed to be saying, accounted for the difference between insecure personalities who shaped themselves reactively against the grain of negative stereotypes, and those who were inwardly free, not having to measure their worth by the approval or acceptance of others. Herzl's aristocrats were models of quiet integrity. Some Jews reacted to their marginality by becoming free-wheeling critics of society. Marginality gave them an independent perspective, which those with secure status lacked. Herzl considered marginality a source of insecurity, and as he was later to insist, of self-contempt. His longing for status and legitimacy within the Austrian social order resulted in his identification with aristocratic heroes.[15]

In his early literary pieces, Herzl constructed an aristocratic *beau idéal*. The hero of *Hagenau*, a novelette completed in the summer of 1882, is Count Robert Schenk von Hagenau. Scion of an ancient line now in economic straits, the count has had to sell his ancestral estate, *Hagenau*, to a wealthy Bürger. In reduced circumstances, the count maintains the exacting standards of his station in life. Herzl characterized his natural grace as "tempered in his light-hearted jokes and reserved in his solemn moods!" He values the intangibles—honor, courage, physical grace and prowess, modesty, benevolence, and beauty. The obligatory dueling scar adorns his cheek. When a fire breaks out in the village, his composure and presence of mind saves the day. He then disappears, not wishing accolades. He finds solace in painting, seeking to capture "the serene and melancholy beauty of a landscape." Von Hagenau is in love with the daughter of the man who has purchased his estate, but his sense of honor prevents him from declaring his feelings, for he wishes to spare her the nagging concern that his love was influenced by the desire to reacquire his property.[16]

Von Hagenau's close friend Hans Brunner is a middle class doctor of law (as was Herzl), who idolizes the count. Hans scolds a doctor, a veteran of the revolution of 1848 and a fiery democrat, for branding all aristocrats parasites. Though the bourgeoisie have triumphed, Brunner believes they are no improvement over the aristocracy. The bourgeoisie have taken over their castles but have nothing finer to offer in their place. "This old stock," says

Brunner, "will take the secret of good taste along with it to its grave." The democratic doctor considers the count an opportunistic dowry-chaser. To Hans, the doctor simply harbors "the ancestral hatred of the subordinate."

The aristocrats of Herzl's imagination were the antithesis of the middle class he depicted, who were insecure, opportunistic, and given to vulgar ostentation. The difference is evident once more in Herzl's drafts for the play *The Knights of the Platitude.* The hero is Baron Raoul von Wangenheim, who is "noble, high-minded, ardently and enthusiastically devoted to all that is beautiful and good." By contrast the bourgeois politicians in the play are opportunists, fitting their oratory to the catchwords of the day, turning "the most sacred feelings into the sport of mindless, hypocritical and deceitful slogans." The baron, modestly concealing his virtue, is a "living, silent protest against the loathsome manner of the times, which prostitutes our tender inborn feelings and sentiments for everything noble by parading them ostentatiously."[17] Assured, self-confident in his status, freed from the consuming bourgeois need to succeed at any price and to display the outward signs of success, the baron can dedicate himself to the intrinsic values of life.

Herzl's description of the bourgeoisie was based on a partial truth, highly exaggerated by him. The stock-market crash of 1873 had tarnished the reputation of bourgeois capitalists. The crash brought an economic depression. Scores of bubble companies folded, as did solid, well-established firms. Chronic unemployment followed; wages fell. Investigation revealed the shady practices behind the stock-market rise: declarations of fictitious dividends, glowing accounts of quick profits planted in the Viennese press, dubious companies gaining charters through bribes. Liberal parliamentarians were implicated and some indicted for being involved in fraudulent stock promotion, and Liberal cabinet ministers were compromised by their participation in shady stock transactions. As a result, the Liberal party came to be known as the "board of director's party."[18]

Still, one could never gather from Herzl's disparagement of the bourgeoisie that the stock-market crash had implicated the aristocracy as well. Many had played the market and suffered heavy losses in the crash. Characteristic of capitalist development in Austria was the bourgeois-aristocratic business partnership, with the latter providing a distinguished name and important contacts with the military and high bureaucracy. A Clerical-Conservative deputy was to complain about aristocratic members of his party who served on the directorships of banks and the stock exchange.[19] Aristocrats had lent their names to questionable business ventures in the expectation of quick profits.

Herzl's romanticized image of the aristocracy can be contrasted to the novels of the Austrian writer Marie von Ebner-Eschenbach, herself a noblewoman, who castigated the nobility for their caste arrogance, obsession with issues of social precedence, frivolity, intellectual indolence, and lack of social responsibility. Such criticism was widely voiced, even by the heir to the Habsburg throne, Crown Prince Rudolph.[20]

Herzl's idealization of aristocrats ran counter to Jewish sensitivities as well. Politically, the aristocracy was allied to those clerical forces so detested by Jews and liberals. Adolf Jellinek, the Chief Rabbi in Vienna, called the aristocracy the "natural political enemies" of the Jews. Later on Herzl was to recall that Jewish liberal circles felt nothing but "hatred, fear and derision" for the Austrian landed gentry.[21]

Herzl's view of the aristocracy was not only driven by a Jewish outsider's idealization of secure status, as affording the freedom for devotion to higher values. Admiration for the aristocracy was also a way of distancing himself from Jewishness. The traits Herzl derided in the bourgeoisie—greed, opportunism, lack of idealism, vulgar ostentation—were characteristics imputed to Jews above all. Capitalism was a new phenomenon in Austria, viewed, especially after 1873, as morally shady and as a Jewish creation, arising out of Jews' proclivity for commerce. Old wealth in the form of landed property, real estate, government bonds was viewed as productive and stabilizing; new wealth in the form of mobile capital was seen as corrupting, exploitative, and socially destructive. Old wealth was softened by its connection to patrician status and social and political responsibility; new wealth was tainted by self-interest, ruthlessly pursued. Jews, considered agents of mobile capital, embodied for many its unprincipled, opportunistic, calculating nature. While the speculative fever of an aristocrat would be seen as a dashing, impulsive penchant for gambling, the Jewish, "matadors of the stock-exchange" were considered keen manipulators of the market.[22]

Absent in Herzl's literary pieces was an affirmation of bourgeois values cherished by Jews: hard work, ambition, austere self-control, familial devotion. Instead Herzl idealized the aristocracy as the Jewish antithesis.

Herzl's Admiration for the Duel

When the Viennese playwright Johann Nestroy wrote *Judith and Holofernes*, a parody of the biblical story, he incorporated a stock comic character, the Jewish coward. The Israelites in the play are avaricious and argumentative stock speculators and inept warriors. In a dialogue between two Israelite soldiers, the following conversation ensues:

ASSAD: Everyone must be armed . . . I'll buy myself a sabre.
AMMON: Assad, you will sacrifice your life, quit this fighting!
ASSAD: Who says I'll fight? The sabre is for practice only.
HOSEA: Practice and neglect the stock market? Such awful times I have to
         live through.[23]

The theme of Jewish cowardice was not just a comic device in farces. George Mosse has pointed out that even in nineteenth-century German novels favoring Jewish emancipation, Jews were depicted as physical and moral cowards, calculating and cunning, intent on survival at any cost, incapable of valuing intangibles like glory and courage. Jews died sordid—not glorious or heroic—deaths. In Freytag's *Debit and Credit*, Veitel Itzig drowns in a dirty river. Mosse has analyzed Felix Dahn's *Fight for Rome*, published in 1867 and one of the most popular German novels of the nineteenth century. The Jewess Miriam and her father Isaac have been transformed, ennobled by their close association with the Goths. Jochem, the Jew not so graced, is of puny build, cowardly, with a face bearing "all the calculating cunning of his race." Jochem betrays the Goths to their enemies and is killed for this by Isaac. Isaac and his daughter Miriam—honorary Gentiles—die glorious deaths in common cause with the Goths.[24]

Herzl's attitude was reactive in that he sought to model himself against such Jewish stereotypes, distancing himself from the taint of Jewishness. Under the spell of these stereotypes, he was beset by the fear that he was a physical coward. In an 1886 diary entry he described how as a little boy he was "always fearful of the shoemakers apprentices. I looked forward to growing up. Adults didn't brawl." However, he became "a brawler"—which is how he saw his time in *Albia*. But he lacked the inclination for it, for he had a "tragic need for peace" and "a dreadful anxiety about disaster coming from behind." Herzl's fear of being a physical coward was not merely a personal quirk of character, but was tied to his sense of Jewish inferiority. His play, *The New Ghetto*, culminates in a duel. The protagonist, Jacob Samuel, modeled after Herzl, believes he is a coward and sees this as connected to his Jewishness. The Jewish and the heroic were, after all, contradictions in terms. Herzl had expressed this view once before, in a satirical epic *Lesehallias*, written while a member of the *Lesehalle*. He compared the struggle between radical German nationalists and Austrophiles in the *Lesehalle* elections of November 1880 to a Homeric battle, until, that is, he got to some Jewish members of the society, objects of his mockery:

> Those three—the well-informed know their sonorous names
> Especially with those Greek endings—Schmelkes and Abeles
> Don't they have a well-nigh Homeric ring?[25]

To overcome self-accusations of cowardliness, Herzl idealized the duel. Even after leaving *Albia*, Herzl continued to admire the duel as a test of honor. He was involved in three challenges in the mid-1880s and was ready to launch another after he became a Zionist statesman. In his diary he considered prescribing dueling for the army officers of the Jewish state.[26]

The duel was hardly a universally accepted practice in Austria. Herzl's

Viennese-Jewish contemporary Stefan Zweig expressed his utter contempt for what he considered the barbaric cult of strength centering on the duel, the drive to constantly provoke and challenge others, the pride in a Prussian-style scarred cheek and broken nose. Zweig was categorical: For those "who cherished the freedom of the individual this passion for the aggressive, which was likewise servility to mob rule, too plainly manifested the worst and the most dangerous elements of the German spirit." In his story, *Lieutenant Gustl*, Arthur Schnitzler viewed dueling as a primitive assertion of social status, having nothing to do with genuine honor, which involved personal integrity. However, Schnitzler realized that Jewish university students, influenced by stereotypes of Jews, could not avoid dueling without suffering excruciating self-reproach. Herzl it seems, fit into this category. By contrast, the Christian Social leader Karl Leuger felt free to scorn challenges to the duel. For him the practice was a "mark of petty self-indulgence and self-gratification."[27]

Herzl's romanticizing of dueling may seem odd for someone who fought only one mediocre duel in *Albia*, while others were raising the prestige of the fraternity with scores of duels. But it is precisely the gap between aspiration and reality that is so telling. There is some evidence that Herzl was in no physical condition to duel. In December 1881 he wrote to his friend Heinrich Kana that he had been again found physically unfit for service in the army reserve. By then he had taken the physical examination several times, the first time in January 1880. His physical condition may well be the reason *Albia* made allowances and admitted him on the basis of only one duel. There was every reason for Herzl to scorn an activity he was not adept at, but for his need to exorcize Jewish cowardliness.[28]

Those who took dueling seriously did not see it as a mere cult of strength but as furthering the principle, in Kiernan's words, that "there is something higher than personal survival and advantage." While ordinary mortals thought only of self-preservation, those who adhered to the code of honor rose above such banal concerns. Herzl had confessed in a youthful fragment: "I am exceedingly captivated by knightliness and manliness." He fantasized about Guy de Montsoreau, a medieval Norman knight. Montsoreau was a "magnanimous fighter," who spoke with a "manly timber." In his daydreams Herzl spoke to Guy: "Your strong arm snatches up anything that resists it, and spurns whatever is granted it."[29] Nothing could have been more at variance with the stereotype of Jewish opportunism, apprehension, and timidity. Jewish cowardliness meant more than just ineptitude in combat; it also meant an incapacity to be stirred by ideals, to sacrifice self, or to risk all when honor or principle was at stake.

Accordingly, between the fall of 1884 and the spring of 1885 Herzl was involved in three dueling challenges. That they came so closely together can be explained by his mood of deep depression. In early 1885 his father was afflicted with an illness of the ear, which caused Herzl much anxiety. For most of that period, Herzl was working in the courts as a law intern, weighing in his mind whether he should continue or risk all on establishing himself as a writer. He was worn out by exhausting efforts to write and wracked by doubt as to whether he would ever make his name as an author.[30]

His first duel challenge was to a von Scheidlein, another law intern. Herzl learned that Scheidlein had decried his "stupid arrogance" and promptly sent two friends to obtain satisfaction, either by an apology or by arranging for a duel. Either Scheidlein was not in the habit of dueling or considered the issue not worthy of engaging his honor, for when Herzl's seconds approached him he replied brusquely that "he had no business with Herr Dr. Herzl," extended an abrupt handshake, and slammed the door. In their written account to Herzl, his seconds concluded that Scheidlein had violated the code of honor and was unworthy of further challenge.[31]

The second challenge was initiated by Herzl in March 1885. This time one Ludwig Videcky, the secretary of the Vienna stock exchange, allegedly defamed Herzl. The Zionist Archives has an exchange of letters dated 2 March 1885 between Herzl and Videcky, with mutual apologies, arranged by their seconds. Videcky wrote that he took back what he had said, and Herzl in turn excused his role in their confrontation by saying that he had been agitated by a sorrowful event in his family. Probably Herzl was referring to his father's illness.[32]

We know of the third challenge in 1885 from a letter Herzl wrote some seventeen years later, when he was literary editor of the *Neue Freie Presse*, to someone who had submitted a piece to the newspaper. The addressee is referred to only as Highly Honored Sir. Sometime in the 1930s the recipient gave the letter to Josef Fränkel, who deposited it in the Herzl archives, then in Vienna. He noted only that the recipient was a Gentile; apparently Fränkel had pledged not to divulge his name.

In the letter Herzl declared that he liked the submitted article but wished his publisher to see it before making a decision. He then observed that since the writer had ventured to submit the article directly to him, he had probably forgotten an incident that had passed between them seventeen years earlier. Herzl had not forgotten. He related that in 1885 they had quarreled over the possession of an armchair in the journalists' club *Concordia*, and as a result resolved on a duel. No duel followed because Herzl's father was severely ill at the time, and Herzl was too upset to engage in combat. Indeed, he had gone to the club at his mother's urging, seeking some relief from his vigil in the sickroom. Herzl confessed that he was still plagued by uncertainty as to whether weakness or strength had prompted him to withdraw from the duel. He recalled that he had patched up the quarrel the next day with an apology. However, he later brooded over the affair; it gnawed at him. "You have no idea," he wrote, "how dreadfully it rankled in me for years." As a result he had for years overreacted to the slightest insinuation about his courage. Finally at forty-two he felt he had mellowed, become more self-accepting.[33]

That the affair filled him with shame, that he feared he was a coward, Herzl acknowledged himself. That Herzl saw his cowardice as a Jewish trait and that this fed his Jewish self-contempt, can be concluded from his play *The New Ghetto*. Herzl made this story, reproduced in full detail, the centerpiece of his play. By that time, Herzl had gained insight into the double standards applied to Jews and Gentiles. As the protagonist Jacob Samuel exclaims to his gentile friend, Franz Wurzlechner:

> I haven't been able to forget it [his withdrawal from a duel]. Not I—you see, I'm a Jew! You and your kind can take that kind of thing in stride. When you Franz Wurzlechner, settle such a run-in peaceably, that makes you a solid, clear-headed chap. Me—me, Jacob Samuel—it makes me a coward![34]

Just as some Jews felt they had to be doubly honest to escape the reproach of shady business dealings, so Jacob felt he had to possess superhuman courage to escape the reproach of cowardice. Similarly, in the case of his own aborted duel, instead of taking pride in his filial devotion, Herzl apparently saw his action as a surrender to what Adolf Dessauer, in a novel of Viennese Jewry, called "Jewish excitability." It is noteworthy that in Dessauer's novel a Jewish character, overcome with worry over his father's illness, berates himself for giving in to "panicky Jewish anxiety."[35] To overcome such traits Herzl idealized *Albia*'s knightly ideal of stony sang-froid and dismissed his Jewish family feeling and devotion as a weakness.

Herzl's flight from the taint of Jewish cowardliness, his daydreams about bold Norman knights, enables us to deepen our understanding of the attraction *Albia* held for him. The *Albia* ideal stressed physical strength and an "Aryan" appearance: slim, blond good looks, a dashing mustache, the requisite dueling scar, an erect soldierly bearing, and physical suppleness and power. To this were added the knightly virtues of courage, loyalty, forthrightness and directness, and sang-froid in the face of danger, along with a touch of arrogance and wit. Hermann Bahr believed that *Albia*'s ideal was an antidote to the endemic "slackness" of the Austro-German Bürgertum, who lacked Prussian discipline. Swordsmanship taught a "composed bearing," and "courage to the timid." *Albia*'s ideal offered Herzl a model of behavior that was the antithesis of Jewish traits.[36]

Jews were considered highly emotional and excitable, lacking firm control over their feelings. In depicting the acculturated Jewish bourgeoisie in turn-of-the-century Vienna, Adolf Dessauer has a mother say proudly of her son that he "loathed the vociferous Jewish excitability." Jews reverted to type in such moments of excitability, talking in sing-song while gesticulating feverishly with their hands. By contrast, another Jewish character prided himself on his "Aryan austerity" and felt highly flattered when Jewish acquaintances accused him of "hardness and lack of feeling." It was believed that centuries of insecurity had made Jews extremely susceptible to anxiety, whereby they magnified their misfortunes a hundredfold. Herzl was to reproach himself mercilessly for giving in to his anxiety at the time of his father's illness, thereby canceling a duel. Jewish self-contempt had turned an act of filial devotion into a coward's flight. What Herzl admired in *Albia*'s ideal were all those traits that drew him away from the "Jewish surfeit of feeling."[37]

A final reason for Herzl's attachment to dueling was that it affirmed status honor, membership in a "socially privileged circle." Student dueling was an outgrowth of the special legal status of universities in the Middle Ages, when these institutions regulated their own affairs and were not subject to regular courts of law. The code of honor involved an assertion of superiority over those without a university education, who were judged not of sufficient rank to grant "satisfaction." Dueling scars were proudly borne "as a sign of academic rank." In like manner, aristocrats and army officers practiced dueling as a way of legitimating their ruling position in society, through their adherence to a highly demanding code of behavior. Kiernan has observed: "Liability to the ordeal of the duel was a burden imposed on itself by the elite as the gage of its right to be considered a higher order."[38] Dueling was an obligation of membership in a privileged group, an assertion of "corporate honor." For this reason army officers who refused a duel were reduced to common soldiers for disgracing the army.[39] Many viewed the dueling code as a crude throwback in modern Europe, where honor was understood more individualistically, as the ability to follow one's own conscience, to stand against the crowd, to measure up to rigorous internal standards of integrity. Moreover, the duel violated democratic sensibilities, since it measured people not by intrinsic worth, but by class membership. But for some Jews, being judged worthy of granting "satisfaction" was the ultimate cherished token of standing and gentile legitimation. Such standing meant that they belonged, fully and unconditionally. Status honor erased the taint of Jewishness. Herzl, who craved this belonging and acceptance, idealized the duel.

Herzl's Stereotype of the Jewish Parvenu

The plays Herzl wrote in the 1880s, such as *Wilddiebe* (*Poachers*) (1888), *Muttersöhnchen* (*Mother's Little Boy*) (1885), *Seine Hoheit* (*His Highness*) (1885), *Was wird man sagen?* (*What Will People Say?*) (1889), were light drawing-room comedies whose subject was bourgeois society. The theme in *What Will People Say?* was bourgeois social climbing and vulgar ostentation; love rendered cynical by dowry-chasing, aesthetic values cheapened by conspicuous consumption, conduct ruled by the tyranny of society. In *His Highness*, the sovereign's title refers to money, which buys honor, friendship, and love. A character in the play exclaims: "Everything can be bought—and everybody." In *The Poachers* a banker and stock speculator declares that he lives by the rule of "first business, then pleasure."[40]

Herzl's unflattering depictions of the bourgeoisie extended to a caricature-like view of the Jewish parvenu. Herzl did not see gentile vulgarity as a Christian or Austro-German trait, although Jewish vulgarity was part of the Jewish essence. Disparaging comments are to be found in his letters. In Berlin in November 1885, Herzl was invited to the home of Emil Treitel, a wealthy business friend of his father's and a patron of the arts. Describing the evening to his parents, he wrote: "Yesterday a grande soirée at Treitel's. Around thirty to forty ugly little Jews and Jewesses. No consoling sight." Writing to his parents from Ostende in that same year, he expressed disdain for well-off Jews: "Although there are many Budapest and Viennese Jews here, the rest of the vacationing population is very pleasing." A letter from Nice in 1891 was similarly disparaging: "Besides the really refined people who do not however create much of a noise, you see here a bunch of Jews from Pest, Vienna and Berlin."[41] Herzl's disdain, evident in this period, stayed with him for the rest of his life. It found its sharpest expression in nasty caricatures of Jewish parvenus in his play *The New Ghetto* and even in his later Zionist novel *Old-New Land*. Phrases used years before about the bourgeoisie were used again in later works and applied to Jews. In *Old-New Land*, portraying the Jewish nouveau riche of Vienna, Herzl has one character declare: "What care we for convictions? I know only two: Business and Pleasure!" In Herzl's depiction such Jews displayed cynicism, ascribing base motives to the noblest actions. The women were loudmouths, overweight, gaudily dressed, and dripping with jewels; "riff-raff," he called them.[42]

A class of nouveau riche—Gentile and Jewish—had emerged from the economic boom of the 1850s and 1860s. In visibility and notoriety, it overshadowed the older middle class, noteworthy for its austerity, modesty, and pride in its commoner descent. Critics fastened onto the worst traits of parvenus. The British journalist Henry Wickham Steed remarked on their mix of snobbishness and servility bred of insecurity, by turns arrogant to social inferiors while slavishly mimicking the nobility, their social superiors. Ilse Barea has described the penchant of the new class for "luxuriant exhibitionism." The wealthiest commissioned the fashionable painter Hans Makart, whose wall-size allegories of art, science, industry, and labor dominated their mansions. Hans Canon painted portraits of the new plutocracy to resemble nobility, in the manner of the new rich of mercantile Venice. Furniture styles went from the simplicity of the Biedermeier period to elaborately designed rococo, with inlaid mosaics in wood, ivory, or mother of pearl and heavy carved oak pieces. Apartments were virtual museums outfitted with heavy furniture, stained glass windows, thick tapestries and oversized paintings in the Renaissance style. Women dressed ostentatiously. Taste in food and wine was meant to impress. Conversation was sprinkled with French phrases.[43]

These were the most notorious marks of new wealth, and Herzl concentrated on them in appraising Jewish parvenus. The reality was far more complex. In Austria, still influenced by precapitalist social values, wealth as such conferred no status, which came instead from the ability to approximate an aristocratic life-style. But there were different ways of achieving this, and parvenus ran the gamut of human vice and virtue. Thus a few of the Jewish nouveau riche—those with considerable wealth—purchased a title and sometimes a landed estate, or an appointment to an order, which carried a state decoration or medal. Such a purchase was effected by munificent works of charity, such as founding an orphanage, as well as by well-placed payoffs to those with influence. Others simply copied the aristocratic life-style. Some imitated the drawling and protracted speech pattern favored by the aristocracy and high bureaucracy. For some, acquiring the externals of status meant taking part in hunts, raising horses, gambling, keeping a mistress. For some women it meant rubbing shoulders with aristocrats. Others were cultural dilettantes, inviting the academic, literary, or artistic celebrity of the day to their salons. But not all parvenus lived for the day they could boast of having played cards with a count, or relate what a baroness—referred to by her first name—had confided to her. Others, such as Josefine von Wertheimstein, admired for her subdued and polished manner, maintained an intellectual salon of high quality, while still others, having bought rural estates, lived up to a code of genuine *noblesse oblige* in fulfilling social and political responsibilities. Parvenus also endured tragedies particular to their success, sometimes having children who disdained their fathers and considered the fruit of their hard labors as nothing but ill-gotten, shady wealth.[44]

Jealousy from those below and social snobbery from those above conspired to reduce the parvenu to a caricature. The rise of the nouveau riche had marked the new-found power of money to buy social legitimacy. As a consequence, the old touchstones of status enjoyed by traditional classes— aristocratic birth, government and military service, Bürger respectability— were endangered. The high aristocracy closed ranks, refusing to accept the newly titled grand bourgeoisie as their social equals. The British ambassador to Vienna, Sir Horace Rumbold, described the ordeal of a Rothschild daughter in mid-century, snubbed and ignored at society dances.[45] If the power of money to acquire social legitimacy was threatening, the power of Jewish money to purchase status for recently despised outsiders was doubly threatening. Hence the parvenu, especially Jewish parvenus, were etched in caricature, their worst traits highlighted.

Contemporary descriptions of turn-of-the century Viennese society often singled out the Jewish nouveau riche. A typical account describes a scene at a fashionable cafe in the Prater: "A few yards away is seated the Baroness Z., whose annual dressmaker's bill alone would equal the salary of a Cabinet Minister. Red-faced and rotund in form, her figure is a striking contrast to that of the typical Viennese women of the higher classes, and her loud, harsh voice, no less than the splendour of her attire, her carriage, and the livery of her servants, betrays her Semitic origin." Another account describes " Jewish bankers' wives and millionaires," as "decked out like the show windows of a jeweller's shop." Jewish parvenus were stock characters in farces, where their genteel manners and refined French and German speech unraveled in a cascade of crude gestures and rapid guttural Yiddish in times of stress. Parvenus with incongruously Jewish aristocratic names such as Moritz Feigelstock beim Morgenkaffee, were featured in humor magazines.[46] The message was that for parvenu Jews, cultivation was only skin deep; scratch the surface and the loud, haggling trader was just underneath.

Hans Tietze has pointed out that Viennese Jews went to these farces and laughed at their parvenu coreligionists' awkward mimicry of gentility. In *The Baths of Lucca* Heinrich Heine had gently satirized the Jewish parvenu, the Marchese Gumpelino, whose attempts to mimic aristocratic refinement clashed comically with his Jewish trader's mannerisms.[47] Herzl's unforgiving caricatures in *The New Ghetto* and in *Old-New Land* were far more brutal than Viennese farces or Heine's gentle satire.

Why did Herzl single out these Jewish nouveau riche for his special contempt? The class of nouveau riche that emerged from Austria's industrial capitalist boom was after all hardly all Jewish. Many Gentiles were engaged in the shady investment practices that caused the stock-market crash. The new *haute bourgeoisie* came from every corner of the Habsburg Empire and was of every nationality. Jews may have been prominent among the newly rich out of proportion to their numbers, but they also made up an absolute minority of this class. In manufacturing, John Boyer notes that Jews made up a majority only in the ready-made clothing, shoe, and furniture industries. Most Viennese banks were managed by Jews. At the same time, their boards of directors were mostly Gentile. The parvenu mimicry of the aristocracy, the arrogance toward social inferiors, the vulgar ostentation, all to clothe new wealth with status and cover up feelings of inferiority, has been described by historians as a general social phenomenon linked to the rise of industrial capitalism. This did not stop an American traveler to Vienna from singling out Jewish bankers' wives, then declaring: "Who have built all those great [Ringstrasse] palaces . . . ? The Jews." She then repeated the canard: "Vienna has 18,398 banking houses, two of which are controlled by Christians."[48]

By the same token, were Jewish parvenus typical of Jewry? In the absence of comprehensive statistics on Jewish income levels or tax assessments in nineteenth-century Vienna, this question is difficult to answer precisely. John Boyer has judged the Viennese-Jewish community less prosperous overall than the Berlin-Jewish community. We know that the Jewish population of Vienna included a large proportion of poor Jews, usually recent immigrants from Hungary and Galicia. Vienna seems to have had a large number of poor Jews and a relatively small number of rich Jews. Sigmund Mayer pointed out that in 1880 Jewish capitalists represented a small strata of Viennese Jews and that in total there were at most a few hundred Jewish stock brokers. Similarly, though Jewish proportions in the free professions relative to Gentiles were exceptionally high—in 1888, well over half of Vienna's lawyers were Jews or 394 out of 681—this was a very small absolute number in a Jewish population of 118,495 (in 1890).[49]

We have to look elsewhere to explain this equation of Jews with parvenus. If self-made wealth carried no social legitimacy, unless expended to maintain a pseudoaristocratic life-style, Jewish self-made wealth seemed doubly illegitimate because in the gentile perception a pall of suspicion hung over Jewish economic practices. Moreover, Jews had ascended quickly from formerly despised outsiders to persons of substance, claiming their due place in the status hierarchy. Even more than gentile parvenus, the pretensions of Jewish parvenus were considered inappropriately arrogant and impudent. Gentile complaints about so-called Jewish immodesty, that Jews no longer knew their place, were legion. Jews may have enjoyed legal equality and economic success, but when they made a claim for status and acceptance, Gentiles sought to delegitimate Jewish success in order to ward off such claims. This was done by encapsulating Jewish success in the image of the parvenu, considered the embodiment of Jewish traits: opportunistic, materialistic, convinced that "everything is for sale," alternating chameleon-like between arrogance and obsequiousness. Herzl saw Jews through the eyes of the majority culture. For him too, the parvenu, not other Jews, seemed to epitomize the Jewish essence. In his novel *Old-New Land* Herzl was to observe: "Fops, upstarts, bejewelled women used to be regarded as representative Jews."[50] By himself, too, he could have added. Distancing himself from this image—for him reality, Herzl was drawn to its antithesis, idealizing the aristocracy as the embodiment of refinement, courage, sincerity, and spirituality. Both images, one base, one noble, were mythical, virtual caricatures, but it was their power over Herzl that led him eventually to Zionism.

There is a final reason Herzl was so disdainful of Jewish parvenus. The

Achilles heel of the parvenu was that he or she copied external forms of behavior and appropriated external marks of status while lacking the inward essence, the self-assured natural grace of the aristocrat. In the very act of copying or appropriating, the parvenu displayed the taint of commerce, for he or she seemed to believe that one could buy a way of life in one stroke. Unsubtle self-advertisement and conspicuous consumption made them the general butt of humor. The parvenu seemed "like a man in ill-fitting clothes." They were described as beribboned with their decorations "like parrots." One parvenu—it was said—displayed his certificate of nobility on his carriage; another built his house "not just to dazzle people, but to blind them."[51] Jewish parvenus were far more transparent and obvious, less successful in their effort to overcome their Jewish traits and achieve status than the cultured and poised Herzl, and were a grim and unwelcome reminder to him of his own origins and his kinship with other Jews.

Herzl's Stereotype of East European Jews

Herzl's scorn for the Jewish parvenu, a stereotype of the representative Jew, shows how much he had absorbed the negative image of the Jew, part of the ideology of emancipation. Such views also influenced his attitude to East European Jews, and to Viennese Jews of Polish origin. Sander Gilman has pointed to a psychological phenomenon whereby members of a minority transfer the negative traits attributed to them to a subgroup of their own kind. In so doing they strive to identify with the majority and distance themselves from defects attributed to the minority.[52] Gilman's analysis can be applied to Herzl's attitude to East European Jews.

To distance himself from these Jews, Herzl made the claim that he himself was of Sephardic origin, for Sephardic Jews were viewed differently from East European Jews. In his tract of 1881, *A Word about Our Jewry*, the German historian Heinrich von Treitschke had complained about the influx of Polish Jews into Germany. Treitschke insisted that French Jews, of Sephardic origin, were a different breed than the Ashkenazic Jews from Poland, far more easily assimilated, and with none of the negative Jewish traits of their coreligionists. Sephardic Jews in southern France would have agreed, for they proudly traced their lineage to a different tribe from that of the Ashkenazic Jews of Alsace. The image of the noble Jews of medieval Spain among romantic poets was a countermyth to that of the base Ashkenazic Jew. Sephardic origins erased the taint attached to Jewry.[53]

Even after Herzl became a Jewish statesman, he insisted that his own family originated in Spain. He told an early associate, Jacob de Haas, that his paternal great-grandfather Loebl, an orthodox rabbi, was a Spanish Jew who had been forced to convert to Christianity. He later fled to Constantinople, where he embraced Judaism again. A few months before his death in 1904, Herzl related a different version of the story to Reuben Brainin. He was descended from one of two brothers from Spain who rose high in monastic orders. Sent abroad on a mission, they escaped and re-embraced Judaism.[54]

These stories may have been family legends; obviously Herzl chose not to question them. Such claims were not unusual for assimilated German Jews. However, evidence for his Sephardic origins is nil, and it is hard to see how he could have been so certain of it. Herzl's paternal great-grandfather was from Semlin in Slovenia. The Herzls first settled there during an influx of Bohemian Jews in 1739, after the area was occupied by Austria. The family name was Loebl, which was of Bohemian-Jewish origin. When Jews were required to Germanize their names under Joseph II, the Hebrew *Lev* (Loeb), or "heart," became the German *Herz* along with the addition of the diminutive "l" from Loebl, to make *Herzl* or "little heart." Subsequent research has traced Herzl's lineage back five generations on his father's side to Bohemia, Moravia, and Silesia, and on his mother's side to Nikolsburg in Moravia.[55]

Herzl's need to distance himself from other Jews came out in other ways too. In one instance, Herzl's attitude to an East European Jew verged on cruelty. The case involved a comic impersonation Herzl and two lady friends inflicted upon the writer Joseph Ehrlich; "a shabby little Jew," Herzl called him. They met in the summer of 1883 (just four months after Herzl's indignant withdrawal from *Albia*) in Baden, a resort outside Vienna where Herzl's parents had a summer home. Ehrlich was a Galician Jew, born in Brody in 1842 and raised in a Hasidic family. He had published an autobiography in 1874, *The Path of My Life: Recollections of a Former Hasid*. Ehrlich had come to Vienna in 1863, where he established himself as a *feuilletonist* and as a popularizer of astronomy and German *Naturphilosophie*. He retained his Polish-Jewish appearance and mannerisms. Heinrich Gomperz, of an old Viennese-Jewish family, described him as a "wild-looking eastern Jew." Herzl and his friends introduced themselves to Ehrlich as aristocracy, Herzl as the elegant Baron Rittershausen, and proceeded to praise a comedy of Ehrlich's, *Cato the Wise*, and discuss literature with him in a mocking and condescending manner. Herzl described the incident in gleeful detail in a letter to his friend Heinrich Kana, recounting examples of Ehrlich's commonplace behavior, his lack of refinement. His description of Ehrlich reveals more about Herzl himself. He remarked: "To him poor Polish Jewesses must seem like princesses of fine bearing and grace." Two women friends with Herzl also treated Ehrlich disdainfully. So taken with the charade was the sham Baron

Rittershausen, that he proceeded to ask Ehrlich what he thought of the writer Theodor Herzl.[56] Herzl's behavior could not have been more transparent. Faced with his kinship with an Ehrlich, Herzl took on a gentile identity.

In other encounters, Herzl similarly recoiled and established distance, though he was not as cruel as with Ehrlich. But just as with Ehrlich and his father's Berlin acquaintance, Treitel, Herzl emphasized physical traits when describing Jews, like shortness, ugliness, and slovenliness, a sign that he saw Jews through a Germanic stereotype, as the antithesis of "Aryan" vigor, prowess, and erect bearing. In a letter to his parents in July 1883, only three months after resigning from *Albia*, he described meeting the grandfather of a friend of his: "an old Polish-Jewish bore with a dripping nose."[57] He again pointedly maintained his distance.

Herzl employed mockery to distance himself from other Jews. He laughed at Polish Jews' ineptitude with German; how they pronounced Vöslau as Wesslau and Feesloo. Herzl called them "Polish Jews from Polackei," a pejorative term for Poland, which was also termed the land of the "Polacks." Similarly, in the humorous epic cited earlier for a *Lesehalle* drinking session, Herzl had mocked the family names of fellow Jewish students. The poem was written to be read out loud. One of the names he mocked—Abeles—was the maiden name of his own maternal Hungarian grandmother.

> Schmelkes and Abeles, and the excellent Meisels
> Drops—not nit-wits [a pun: "Tropfen—nicht Tröpfe"],
> Scattered drops of the Hellenic spirit
> These three—known by the learned
> By their sonorous names,
> Especially with those Greek endings
> Schmelkes and Abeles!
> Has it not a well-nigh Homeric ring?

Later on, when he became a Zionist, Herzl was to castigate such mockery as "self-ridicule," a hallmark of Jewish self-disdain.[58]

Herzl's use of mockery to distance himself from other Jews was a trait of the native Viennese, famous for their wit. Mockery in polyglot Vienna was a way of establishing distance, setting up an ethnic hierarchy, and asserting status. In his memoir of Viennese Jewry, N. H. Tur-Sinai has described how the native Viennese mocked Croats, who were often peddlers; Czechs, for their speech and native foods; Italians, for being humble tinkers. Jews from different regions of the empire had gathered in Vienna, and Viennese Jews confirmed their cultural superiority over other Jews—for they alone had "entered the antechamber of European culture"—through mockery. Jokes abounded about the speech and dress of Galician Jews.[59]

Herzl's mockery was largely directed toward Polish Jews, a major source of discomfort for acculturated Viennese Jews. Who were these Jews and how were they typically viewed? Formerly Polish Galicia was the demographic heartland of the Habsburg Empire's Jewish population. In 1880, 68.2 percent of all Habsburg Jews, approximately 700,000, resided there.[60] A Germanized Jewish middle class—often semiacculturated—was to be found in the cities of Krakow, Brody, and Lemberg, but most Jews were Yiddish-speaking, traditionalist, and not acculturated.

From the 1860s on, the Jewish population of Vienna had increased by about thirty thousand per decade. But until the turn of the century Galician Jews made up a moderate, not a large, proportion of this immigration. The literature of the period has left the impression of a flood of immigrants from Galicia in the 1870s and 1880s, hardly congruent with the statistics and reflecting uneasiness over the presence of these Jews. Galician Jews who came to Vienna in those decades tended to be the better-off city dwellers. They were German-speaking but semiacculturated, with a strong sense of their Jewishness. As such, Galician Jews stood out. They formed a distinct Jewish community, built their own synagogues, and did not intermarry with other Jews. Austro-German Jews, in turn, often looked down on them. In their stubborn refusal to fully assimilate to Germandom, they were thought to hinder Jewish acceptance and integration. They were also a discomforting reminder to Viennese Jews of all the hapless Jewish "traits" they themselves had shed. In the 1870s, the Viennese-Jewish businessman Sigmund Mayer saw their orthodox religious observances as a temporary anomaly that modern progress would soon eliminate. It was in Goethe's writings that he found the inspiration for broad-minded toleration of these Jews. Had not Faust declared, "not what man believes, but that he believes, makes him blissful"? Mayer concluded that humans needed belief to engage their feelings. One had to recognize this and be forbearing "toward the right as well as toward the left."[61]

Views of Polish Jewry were also shaped by the Austro-German perception of living on the eastern frontier of the Germanic world. The German word *Oesterreich* meant, literally, the eastern kingdom, Europe's barrier to the encroachment of the semi-Asiatic Slavs. In that sense, Polish Jews bore a stigma common to all Slavs. Discussing East European Jewry in the 1880s, the Viennese-Jewish journalist Wilhelm Goldbaum saw them as "Asiatic." Pressburg, then in the Hungarian kingdom and near the Austro-Hungarian border, was considered by Wolf the dividing line between Europe and Asia, since it was the center of Hungarian Jewish orthodoxy. Civilization, moving from West to East, had left "its liberating and softening" mark in the West. By contrast, eastern Jewry had spawned, in the Bukovina, at the eastern edges of the Habsburg Empire, "filthy dens of sectarianism," Goldbaum's epithet for Hasidism.[62]

Viennese-Jewish attitudes to eastern Jews were not always that hostile. Karl Emil Franzos, the Austrian-Jewish writer and a journalistic colleague of Herzl, expressed a more common attitude in his famous collection of stories of East European ghetto life *From Semi-Asia*, published in 1876. Franzos characterized East European Jews as half-Asian, the redeeming European aspect grafted onto Asian backwardness and indolence. His attitude to them, perceptively analyzed by Steven Aschheim, combined "sympathy and distaste," solidarity and condescension. In keeping with the ideology of emancipation, Franzos considered East European Jewry more sinned against than sinning; their coarseness, shady business practices, and religious fanaticism were the result of centuries of persecution and forced isolation. German Jewry's mission was to transform and elevate their less fortunate coreligionists by helping them shed their traditional culture and by bringing them German culture and refinement.[63]

Herzl viewed Polish Jews from the vast distance of his Viennese bourgeois standards of gentility and cultivation. He himself spoke the pure German of the cultivated, without a trace of even the Viennese dialect. Even after having become a Jewish statesman, he referred to East European Jews as "semi-Asiatic."[64] For Herzl, Polish Jews were undifferentiated. He was a stranger to the vast differences between the elite Talmudic culture of Vilna and the more down-to-earth Hasidic communities of Galicia or the schools of Jewish enlightenment in Brody. What he saw was a stereotype, shaped by conceptions of Germanic enlightenment and Viennese refinement.

Herzl's remarks about Polish Jews were offensive, but except for the Ehrlich incident they were not usually vicious. After all, some Jews went so far as to blame the East European Jewish presence in central Europe for anti-semitism. In 1881–1882, when twenty thousand Jews from Czarist Russia fled pogroms and crowded into the Austrian border city of Brody, some Austrian Jews wished to bar their way.[65] Herzl never expressed such views. From his remarks on the Cologne ghetto described in chapter 1 and his response on visiting the Rome ghetto, described in our next section, we can draw some conclusions about his attitude to East European Jews, for they were seen as ghetto Jews par excellence. Like Franzos, Herzl would have considered them as more sinned against than sinning and their Jewish separatism the result of centuries of enforced isolation, their faults as due to persecution. Like Franzos, he would have favored their improvement through Germanization.

Herzl's Jewish Problem

If all Herzl had felt was the need to shed Jewish traits, he probably would never have ended up a Zionist. But he vacillated between Jewish pride and self-contempt, between wishing for the submergence of Jewry in Europe and loyalty to his Jewish origins, between feeling distance and kinship to Jews.

In Herzl's novel *Old-New Land*, Friedrich Loewenberg, a character modeled after him, reflects on the time before Zionism's advent: "What a degraded era that was . . . when the Jews had been ashamed of everything Jewish."[66] Herzl could well have been thinking of himself. During the 1880s his diaries and his letters to his parents were punctuated with disparaging remarks about Jews. The Treitel soirée, the writer Joseph Ehrlich, the Jewish vacationers in Ostende, all suffered the arrows of Herzl's disdain. More striking than Herzl's disdain, however, was that it coexisted with opposite feelings, not so much a conviction about the relevance of Judaism or Jewish culture in the modern world, but simply a sense of Jewish solidarity and loyalty.

About six months after his remark in November 1885 about "ugly little Jews," an incident occurred which evoked Herzl's Jewish loyalty. In recalling it much later in his Zionist diary, Herzl added that several times he had considered baptism, but insisted these were "only vague desires born of youthful weakness." What he says rings true. The period of his internship in the law courts, August 1884 to May 1885, would have been the time for Herzl to consider baptism, necessary for advancement if he was to choose a government career. No such thoughts were expressed that year. Not only did he never seriously consider baptism, he never considered changing his Jewish-sounding name. In 1886, as he recalled in his diary, Heinrich Friedjung, a Jew and a leading Austro-German nationalist, then editor of the *Deutsche Wochenschrift*, advised him to adopt a pen name that would not sound Jewish. He refused. He even offered Friedjung the option of not publishing an article of his, though Friedjung had already accepted it. Herzl was by no means stretching the truth in retrospect. His version is corroborated by an unpublished letter from Friedjung to Herzl. By Friedjung's account, his suggestion infuriated Herzl. Friedjung chided Herzl for making a "cabinet issue over a name," then mollified him by adding that he had no intention of suppressing his name and that there was no reason for Herzl to withdraw his article. He had reason to be taken aback by Herzl's emotional response, for Jewish writers in Austria often adopted non-Jewish sounding pen names.[67] Herzl's particular Jewish problem was the coexistence of Jewish self-disdain with an exacting sense of loyalty to his Jewish origins.

Herzl made disparaging remarks about Jews just months after he resigned from *Albia* over the issue of antisemitism, surely a sign of his ambivalence. Indeed, Herzl's attitude toward *Albia* exemplified this ambivalence. His behavior as a member was erratic, by turns ardent and quarrelsome, which suggests that his desire to shed Jewish traits evoked a deep though as yet unfocused inner conflict. On the one hand, he had joined a fraternity that demanded Jewish self-effacement; on the other hand, unlike *Albia*'s other Jewish members, Herzl seems to have alienated his brothers. Perhaps unlike his coreligionists in *Albia*, Herzl was of two minds about seeking the esteem of his fraternity brothers, since there was much condescension in *Albia*'s regard for those Jews who "felt German." Jacob Wassermann recounted in his autobiography that when a gentile acquaintance found out he was a Jew, he would make it clear that Wassermann had the good fortune to be considered an exception, not like "other" Jews.[68] Such longed-for acceptance carried a compliment that was insidious and patronizing. It may be that sheer pride made Herzl recoil from being treated as an "exceptional" Jew.

Even the manner of Herzl's resignation from *Albia* has all the signs of an overreaction, reflecting his tangled relationship both to his Jewishness and to assimilation. *Albia* rightly chastised him for resigning on the basis of a story he had read in a newspaper, without seeking an explanation from his brothers. Having resigned in this peremptory manner, Herzl then demanded that *Albia* sanction his act by formally acknowledging that he was being released honorably at his own request. Having acted highhandedly, Herzl expected special consideration in return, calling it a sign of "loyalty" to him. In fact, some members wanted him formally expelled. In the end his name was simply stricken from the membership list.[69]

Herzl's display of anger and demand that *Albia* turn the other cheek may have been a response to feelings of guilt. As a recruit he had been required to maintain a subservient attitude to his *Albia* mentor Gustav Staerk. He had additional reason to be indebted to Staerk, who had backed Herzl's membership in *Albia* over the objections of others. Staerk stood out in *Albia* for his militant pan-Germanism. After graduating he became a leading figure in Schönerer's pan-German movement, extremist in its racist antisemitism. Quite possibly by 1883 Staerk had already become an outspoken racist antisemite, moving as did Schönerer to a policy of total Jewish ostracism from German nationalist associations. That Herzl had once emulated the charismatic Staerk may have plagued him with guilt. His highhanded attitude to *Albia* may have been a way of erasing his sense of guilt.[70]

The *Albia* experience evoked Herzl's ambivalence because it marked one of the few personal relationships he had with Gentiles, up to that time and after. Surprisingly, this situation was common among Viennese Jews, who tended to associate with other Jews. In Vienna, the Herzl family first lived on an affluent residential street in the Leopoldstadt, the district with the highest concentration of Jews in the city, almost thirty percent in 1880, when Jews were about nine percent of the total Viennese population. In 1883, they moved to the elegant inner city (*Innere Stadt*) a favored area for affluent Jews. In 1880, this district was almost eighteen percent Jewish. From Herzl's letters it is clear that all his close relationships were with Jews. His intimate friends in Vienna—Heinrich Kana and Oswald Boxer—were Jews. He married a daughter of the Jewish upper bourgeoisie. Most of the writers and journalists he was associated with were Jews. In Budapest, where Herzl first came under the spell of German literature and high culture, the gymnasium he attended had a majority of Jewish students. Acculturation was, in this sense, a collective Jewish experience.[71]

While Herzl's primary relationships were with fellow Jews, Vienna provided points of contact where Austrians of different backgrounds encountered each other at close quarters; the university was one. As a member of the *Akademische Lesehalle* and later of *Albia*, Herzl found himself for the first time in his life in close contact with Gentiles, but it was close contact across a psychological abyss. Such relationships were not easy and spontaneous, but marred by swings between deference, pride, and oversensitivity on the part of Jews, and condescension on the part of Gentiles. Efforts at overcoming barriers between Jews and Gentiles only confirmed their distance from one another.

In some instances, when Herzl wrote about Jews, what stood out was a raw nerve of sympathy. An account by him in 1888 of the ghetto in Rome, which he visited during his travels to Italy, illustrates the complexity of affects we are dealing with. The visit left a deep impression: "What kind of stench is this and what kind of street? Countless open doors and windows, at which one spies pallid and abject faces. The ghetto! With what malicious and vile hatred did men persecute them, these poor people, whose huge iniquity was their loyalty to their faith"?[72] Herzl's description evinces both repulsion and sympathy in equal measure, a sense of distance and the consciousness of kinship, and not least the memory of a shared history of suffering.

Another *feuilleton* from his travels in 1891, on the Bishop of Meaux's visit to Lourdes, the place of Catholic pilgrimage, evoked an unforgettable image. Herzl described watching a wretched creature dowsing his diseased eyes over and over again with the holy water, with no result. Finally, with all hope gone, he gave up the effort: "He shrugged his shoulders and groped unsteadily for his cane. And while moving on he sighed, deeply and oppressively. He sighed like a Jew."[73] For Herzl, Jewish belief, knowledge, and values were benighted products of cultural isolation. Beyond that, his attitude to Jewry was one of shame and contempt tempered by sympathy, pity, indeed loyalty to a history—as he conceived it—of steadfastness in faith and unremitting victimization. When all the traces of Jewish culture and values had evaporated in him, the memory of Christian persecution and of the long and proud history of stubborn Jewish loyalty to their God, endured.

Herzl's view of Jewish history as a permanent state of siege was his way of explaining Jewish vices, Jewish "clannishness," Judaism's rigid legalism and insular hostility to external cultural influences, but it also elicited his loyalty and a strong identification with an imputed history of unremitting suffering. He described the burning of Jews at the stake with fierce indignation; he condemned Christianity, equating its ethical teaching with a "thirst for plunder." His Jewish pride was expressed through repeated references to Jewish steadfastness in faith, or "heroic loyalty . . . to its God."[74] Having abandoned belief in Judaism, indeed no longer respecting, let alone observing its practices, Herzl still celebrated Jewish martyrdom as a heroic struggle against insuperable odds and prided himself on the unparalleled history of Jewish survival and continuity amidst the wholesale disappearance of other ancient peoples. Pride in Jewish steadfastness was a counter-theme to the pervasive notion of Jewish cowardice.

Herzl's litany of Jewish suffering was wildly exaggerated, for he claimed that Jews were "always the carefully looked after and cultivated leeches or the . . . chamber serfs [servi camerae] of the powerful." In Herzl's view of Jewish history there were no periods of security or normality. Later this view was to become part of his Zionist conception of the Jewish dispersion as a two-thousand-year period of captivity and unfreedom.[75]

Herzl's writings yield one final element tying him to Jewry: blissful memories of a childhood bond to his father, through Judaism. Indications of this appear in the novel *Old-New Land* where the protagonist, modeled on Herzl, longingly recalls boyhood memories. This was his only link to Jewry, but it was a powerful one. Additional evidence appears in Herzl's reflections on changing his name, and on baptizing his son. In each case he cites filial loyalty as the force that dissuaded him.[76]

Herzl's childhood training in Judaism was not extensive. He seems to have been devoid of any Jewish interest during his adolescence. His tie to Jewry had nothing to do with Jewish knowledge or belief; it was maintained through a filial bond. Fathers and sons went to synagogue together, sitting separately from the women who went, in any case, much less frequently. The father-son bond linked males to powerful forefathers in a patriarchal religion. It was no coincidence that Herzl called Judaism the "God of his fathers" or spoke of the "faith of the fathers."[77] His wish to maintain and affirm his tie to his father preserved his residual attachment to Jewry.

Even before the successes of political antisemitism in Austria and the first stirrings of his own preoccupation with the Jewish question in the early 1890s, Herzl's attitude to Jewishness was ambivalent. So far, this condition was tolerable. But even during the 1880s, when he still believed that progress toward Jewish assimilation and acceptance was on an upward course, the rigorous terms for this acceptance set by the majority culture and ostensibly agreed to by Jews such as Herzl created inner strains. Feelings of Jewish inferiority, a self-surrendering craving for acceptance, provoked their opposites, Jewish pride, guilt, and anger.

Recently S. S. Prawer has brilliantly captured a similar tendency in Heinrich Heine. His private letters were full of "anti-Jewish abuse," displaying anti-Jewish stereotypes prevalent in Germany. Heine's literary portraits of Jews were shaped by these stereotypes, full of descriptions of Jewish physical clumsiness, of squalid Polish Jews, fast and loose business practices, the vulgar ostentation of Jewish parvenus, German speech barbarized by Yiddish inflections. Implied was that Jews themselves were to blame for anti-Jewish hostility. On the other hand, there were the "countercurrents," stirred in particular by anti-Jewish hatred. Heine's response to threats to Jews was instinctive solidarity, stemming from the consciousness of sharing a community of fate. Warm childhood memories of Jewish family life, festive sabbaths, nostalgia for Jewish cooking, reappear in his writings. There are admiring portraits of Jewish personalities, particularly of Sephardic Jews in medieval Spain. And again, as with Herzl, the belief that Jewish distinctiveness was no longer worthwhile or even tenable in modern Europe was undercut by admiration for "Jewish steadfastness in the face of persecution," the stubborn and heroic resolve to retain Judaism in the face of defeat and dispersion. Some have considered such ambivalence a pervasive modern Jewish trait. Jacob Wassermann observed in his autobiography: "The tragedy of the Jew's life is the union in his soul of a sense of superiority and a sense of inferiority." A modern psychologist has defined this condition as a "strange mix of Jewish pride and Jewish feelings of inferiority, of an appreciation for the Jewish consciousness and a hatred of typical Jewish behavior."[78]

Isaiah Berlin has provided us with a diagnosis of nineteenth-century European Jews caught in the middle, shifting uneasily, inwardly torn between their efforts at shedding Jewishness and "some unsurrendering quality in their temperament—sometimes against their conscious wills . . . incapable of the degree of accommodation which those who seek to alter their habits radically must achieve . . . tantalized but incapable of yielding." Such Jews ended up driven helter-skelter by opposite feelings: "Liable to waves of self-pity, aggressive arrogance, exaggerated pride in the very attributes which divided them from their fellows; with alternating bouts of self-contempt and self-hatred."[79] Berlin's sensitive portrait fits Herzl in every detail. This was the psychological price Herzl paid for identifying with a majority that required Jewish self-denial. When, in the 1890s, the dominant culture began to show itself unwilling even to grant acceptance in exchange for that self-denial, Herzl's accommodation to Austro-German assimilation unraveled.

PART II
Vienna in the 1890s

4

Herzl and Vienna, the New Capital of Antisemitism

How much pain does it [antisemitism] cause precisely the best Jews, those already emancipated from the ghetto, usury and money. A public promise to them has not been kept. They suffer.[1]

Introduction

THROUGHOUT THE 1880s and into the early 1890s, Herzl's attitude of mild vacillation between his Jewishness and assimilation remained constant. Then, in the space of several years, he experienced a gradual inner transformation that led him to Zionism. His Zionism was not, as many believe, the result of a single event, a prophetic response to the unexpected shock of the Dreyfus trial in France in December 1894. Rather, it was the culmination of a long-term inner struggle that began as early as 1892, as Herzl responded to the spectacular rise of antisemitism in Austria.

Since Herzl was the Paris correspondent of the Viennese *Neue Freie Presse* from the fall of 1891 to the spring of 1895, scholars have concentrated on his experience of French antisemitism in accounting for his conversion to Zionism. Consequently, the role of Austrian antisemitism and its impact on Herzl has not received the attention it deserves. Though based in Paris, Herzl was in no sense an expatriate from Vienna. His wife and children lived in Paris for about two-thirds of his stay there, and in Vienna for the balance of the time. He made regular visits to his home city, and he and his family took summer vacations in the Viennese countryside.[2] More important, though he witnessed and wrote about antisemitism in France, on a personal and emotional level, he was more deeply affected by the rise of antisemitism in Vienna.

When he recounted his odyssey to Zionism, Herzl described Paris as a city that had provided him with emotional distance, an opportunity to grasp the meaning of events in his Austrian homeland. In France he became an "observer" of politics: "Here too, I reached a higher, more disinterested view of anti-Semitism, from which at least I did not have to suffer directly," as in Austria or in Germany where he was recognized as a Jew and subjected to antisemitic taunts. Indeed, such direct experiences in Austria "went deeper" because they occurred on his "home soil."[3]

But it was not only his identification with Vienna that made him particularly sensitive to Austrian antisemitism. Herzl judged antisemitism in Austria as more powerful and threatening than its counterpart in France. He insisted in January 1893 that publicity campaigns against antisemitism in Austria were doomed to impotence, because of the "intensity" of the movement. On the other hand, some months earlier he had judged antisemitism in France to be an extremist movement, more marginal politically than elsewhere, a trend that would eventually pass. In Austria, he concluded, "they want to deliver them [Jews] over to the mob." By contrast, in France, he observed, "Here Jews are not thrown over to the mob."[4]

Though hardly sanguine over the suffering it was exacting on French Jewry, Herzl's assessment of antisemitism in France, as compared to that in Austria, was relatively hopeful. Indeed, nowhere else in Europe was the rise of political antisemitism so meteoric as in Austria; and nowhere else was the movement so mainstream and respectable. Moreover, in France antisemitism was centered in the antirepublican opposition and largely disavowed by liberal republicans, who remained the political allies of French Jewry. In Austria, on the contrary, antisemitism evoked latent anti-Jewish hostility among Liberals, who abandoned their former Jewish allies. By late 1892, Herzl no longer saw Austrian antisemitism as a fading residue of the past, as he had in the early 1880s, but as a powerful backlash against Jewish civil emancipation and assimilation, in a state where Jews had attained the rights of full citizenship by law.[5]

Herzl was unsparing in his denunciation of Austrian antisemitism; at no time did he play down its significance or impact. His rage was that of someone who had offered up so much on the alter of assimilation in Jewish self-effacement and in inner turmoil, only to be rebuffed and cast out by his co-citizens. His shock was that of an assimilated Jew who genuinely believed that Jews had found acceptance and a home in Austria. Our first task in this chapter will be to document the stunningly rapid rise of political antisemitism in Austria and examine its wide impact and its anticapitalist thrust. We shall then describe Herzl's response in detail.

The Rise of Political Antisemitism in Austria

Within the course of one decade, the mid-1880s through the mid-1890s, the political map of Austria underwent fundamental change. New mass parties emerged, the Social Democrats and the Christian Socials, the latter with a platform of political antisemitism; both parties realigned Austrian politics and pushed the Liberals out of political contention. Suffrage reforms in 1882 by the Clerical-Conservative Taaffe government, intended to weaken the still imposing Liberal opposition, unwittingly prepared the way for these changes. Taaffe had extended the suffrage to the lower levels of the middle class: small businessmen, artisans, and peasants with modest holdings, a stratum of the population ignored and disenfranchised during the period of Liberal hegemony. The weighted electoral system favoring the Liberals remained intact, for voters were still grouped in four separate curias on the basis of tax and occupational and educational levels; the curias of the privileged, with small numbers of voters, elected far more deputies than the curias of the less privileged, with far greater numbers of voters. But the reform substantially broadened the franchise. The impact of suffrage reform was even greater in Vienna, less weighted in favor of privilege in that each of its three curias elected the same number of municipal councillors, and one of the three was dominated by the lower middle class.[6]

With the expansion of the franchise, new political forces emerged. In elections in 1886, the first to be held under the widened suffrage, cooperation between Democrats, formerly allies of the Liberals, and the antisemitic artisanal associations gained them eighteen seats in the Viennese City Council. Several years later, the anti-Liberal coalition had expanded to include not only formerly anticlerical Democrats and the anticapitalist and antisemitic artisanal associations, but political Catholics and *völkisch* nationalists weary of Schönerer's counterproductive extremism. In subsequent city council elections in 1889, this coalition, now calling itself the United Christians and led by Karl Lueger, won 25 seats (out of 138), a substantial bloc. Even more important, though the coalition's electoral strength was concentrated in the Third Curia, dominated by the lower middle class, in overall numbers the United Christians captured slightly more votes than the Liberals (15,036 to 14,027). Thus, as early as 1889, only the curial voting system prevented the United Christians from governing Vienna.[7]

The initial successes of this anti-Liberal coalition in Vienna were matched by gains at other levels of government. In Lower Austrian Landtag elections in 1890, with the newly enfranchised, dubbed the five-gulden men, voting for the first time, the United Christians took half of Vienna's eighteen districts. Liberal Landtag seats declined from fifty-five to forty-one (out of seventy-two). Boyer calls the results "devastating" for the Liberals, for half of their seats were won in the two most privileged curias of the Chambers of Commerce and Industry and noble landowners, and Liberals gained the rest only by narrow margins.[8]

This trend was also evident in the Reichsrat elections of 1891, when the antisemitic United Christians captured seven of the fourteen seats in Vienna. Lueger, with twelve colleagues, now sat in the national parliament. In the Vienna City Council elections of that year, the United Christians, though

deeply disappointed by what they considered a modest result, almost doubled
their representation to forty-five seats, thirty-three of which were gained in
the Third Curia of the lower middle class.[9] In subsequent Viennese elections
the United Christian coalition (which became the Christian Social party in
1893) continued to make gains, though Liberal manipulation of the electoral
laws warded off a Christian Social majority until the elections of 1895. To
gain a majority, the Christian Socials had to attract middle-class voters in the
Second and First Curias, outside their artisan and small-shopkeeper political
base: civil servants, the lower clergy, schoolteachers, owners of real estate in
the city. This they gradually did, until, in November 1895, the Christian Socials gained a solid majority in city council elections. After almost three decades of Liberal rule, Vienna became the first city in Europe governed by a
self-declared antisemitic administration.

In the early years, to anchor itself firmly in its artisan and small-shopkeeper base, the United Christians appealed to radical anticapitalism and, in
Boyer's words, to "popular religion and histrionic antisemitism." The party
was able to move on to attract the more conservative strata of the middle
class because Karl Lueger, its leader, was a supreme pragmatist or opportunist, a master of political ambiguity. Adam Wandruszka has characterized the
party as embracing opposing tendencies: "Political realism that sometimes
bordered on opportunism, along with political romanticism and intense ideological traditionalism; conservative views on defending private property, and
social reformist, indeed almost social-revolutionary tendencies; monarchist
and democratic-republican; patriotic Austrian and pan-German annexation-
ist." From radical anticapitalism, the party moved handily to support the salary and pension demands of teachers, white collar employees, and lower- and
middle-level state officials and to back protests over high property taxes by
owners of rental property. Appeals to this clientele were couched in more
moderate rhetoric than were appeals to the lower middle class. Concrete economic issues and the socialist threat to private property were emphasized over
antisemitism.[10]

Common denominators patched together the diverse tendencies singled
out by Wandruszka. According to Boyer, Christian Social supporters represented traditional Bürger culture, income, and status, in a common front
of retrenchment against new wealth, new claims to status, new cultural
modes. Christian Socials mounted an offensive against the new bourgeois
elite—many of whom were Jews—who had come to the fore with late-
nineteenth-century commercialization and industrialization. The new elite
was the "second" society, distinct from the titled aristocracy, a parvenu elite
of wealthy entrepreneurs, bankers, merchants, as well as high state officials,
artists, academics, and prominent members of the free professions. Resentment was directed against this "second" society and against upwardly mobile

recent outsiders in general, largely Jews, whether university-trained professionals seeking government posts or employees of the new large commercial and insurance bureaucracies. Under the Christian Social banner, the self-proclaimed traditional Bürgertum united in a political offensive furthering its own social, economic, and cultural supremacy.[11]

In addition, the Christian Social coalition was inspired by the Catholic revival. The Christian Social program has been called a "restoration ideology," aiming for the "rechristianization of society." The movement had started out, in the words of the antisemitic priest and Christian Social supporter, Father Kannengieser, as "an alliance of priest and worker on the terrain of the social question," and had transformed Vienna into "one of the most pious cities in Austria." Lower-middle-class economic distress provided the lower clergy with a political lever to advance religious interests. For decades, clerical politics had been controlled by a Josephist church hierarchy conciliatory to the state and bowing to the constraints of the constitutional era, which had ousted them from their political and societal leadership role. Lower-order clergy, especially, found in the Christian Social movement a way of reasserting their role in Austrian society. This was to be done by reestablishing the relevance of Catholic social and economic corporatism in an overall program that sought to reinfuse Austrian politics and society with Catholic values. Such values reinforced anticapitalist radicalism but could also support what Boyer aptly calls "hierarchic paternalism" when Christian Socials wished to emphasize their economic conservatism as a bulwark against Social Democratic egalitarianism. The Catholic revival thus softened the movement's radicalism and unified rather than polarized its Bürger clientele.[12]

The Christian Social ideal was of a nonpluralist society pervaded by Catholic piety. As such, Christian Socials only grudgingly accepted the Jewish presence in Vienna, considering it alien and undermining. The platform of the United Christians in 1889 had called for the reintroduction of denominational schools. In the meantime, Jews were to be barred from teaching Christian pupils in the primary schools. The United Christians also insisted that the University of Vienna, supported by Catholic endowments, be a full-fledged Catholic institution, giving precedence to Catholics and to Catholic teachings. Christian Socials were hostile to the Liberal press and the cosmopolitan artistic and literary culture patronized by the new high bourgeoisie, both realms in which Jews were prominent. Lueger referred to the Liberal press as the "Jewish press," accusing it of ridiculing Christianity, thus robbing the Viennese of their "moral footing." He went on to charge the "Jewish press" with promoting literature and drama that would corrupt the native Viennese character, importing alien political concepts from France, and through its advocacy of capitalism, perpetrating "robberies and thefts . . . against the Christian people." Jews subverted the Catholic resurgence not only because they pushed for the primacy of talent and achievement, but also because as Liberals they defended the values of cultural pluralism.[13]

One can thus observe Christian Socialism replacing Liberalism as the party of the Viennese middle class. Just as universalist as Liberalism in its pretensions, Christian Socialism could claim to be more democratic and far more representative of the Bürgertum in its widest possible range. By the same token, Christian Social antisemitism, sparked by Catholic corporatist anticapitalism, by the antipluralism of the Catholic revival, and by the nativism of the self-styled traditional Bürgertum, was popular, respectable, and mainline.[14]

The Impact of Christian Social Antisemitism

One effect of the new political alignment was to create a widely permissive climate for verbal and physical abuse against Jews. By the early 1890s, Christian Social anti-Jewish slanders at electoral meetings and even in parliamentary bodies were everyday occurrences, tolerated by other political parties and by the authorities. After the elections of 1891, antisemitic rhetoric became even more strident and extremist. Lueger and his colleagues were disgruntled with their capture of just under a third of city council seats. They believed Liberal electoral manipulation in 1890 had robbed them of victory and endangered their future prospects. To maintain impetus, Lueger allowed extremist figures in the party free rein. Although antisemitic zealots were squeezed out of the party elite after 1895, when the Christian Socials attained a majority on the Vienna City Council, from 1891 to 1895 their coarse, violent, street-corner-style rabble-rousing inflamed the Austrian political atmosphere. To cite one example among many: In May 1893 in the Lower Austrian Landtag, Ernst Schneider of the Christian Social artisan wing declared that the party's aim was to win a majority in the Reichsrat that would enable them to repeal Jewish emancipation, expropriate Jewish property, and expel the Jews from Austria. In September, an even more inflammatory Schneider made a statement that *Die Neuzeit*, the weekly of the Jewish communal establishment, called "an incitement to the murder of Austrian citizens." Jews, he declared, should be hunted down like the Mongol invaders of Europe once were, a "bounty per head" placed on them. Schneider was not ejected for this utterance.[15]

Few Jews were entirely sheltered from verbal harassment and humiliation. *Die Neuzeit* reported that insults directed against Jews were common in public places, such as trains, trams, and eating and drinking establishments. This climate extended to the schools: the *Oesterreichische Wochenschrift* reported regular complaints of teachers making "gestures, grimaces, mimicking Jews [Jüdeln], making malicious remarks, mocking the names and occupations of the fathers [of Jewish pupils]." Mockery included addressing Jewish children sneeringly with Yiddish diminutives such as "Schmul," "Haschl," "Kobi." A child reported his teacher as saying: "You're a nice lad; it's a pity you're a Jew."[16]

In addition, anti-Jewish libels were once again common. In a debate in the Lower Austrian Landtag in September 1892, the Christian Socials opposed smallpox vaccination as a swindle engineered by Jewish physicians. Ernst Schneider charged that Jewish doctors sent their Christian patients to the hospital to die, so they could appropriate their bodies for dissection. These modern renditions of medieval blood libel charges soon gave way to a more literal version. In 1893, Father Joseph Deckert, a Viennese parish priest, published a book on the fifteenth-century case of Simon of Trent, claiming to have found new evidence that Jews murdered the boy to acquire his blood for ritual purposes. Deckert went on to charge: "such ritual murders are still perpetrated today; the blood ritual is handed down as a secret tradition among the Chassidim, which is found also in the Caballa." Deckert's charges were widely reported in the press, and his book was distributed at church doors in Vienna. The public prosecutor did not move against the parish priest, and the Liberal Ernst von Plener, then in the cabinet, thought a court trial risky, "since antisemitism was very widespread not only in the jury-box but among the younger members of the judiciary." Finally, the intrepid Jewish militant Dr. Joseph Bloch successfully sued Father Deckert for libel. Deckert ended up paying a fine.[17]

The permissive climate for Jew-baiting encouraged random violence. On 8 April 1890, rampaging mobs in Ottakring and Neulerchenfeld, working-class districts in the Viennese suburbs, destroyed and looted the brandy shops of poor Galician Jews, who had settled in these districts. As the *Neue Freie Presse* reported, rowdy elements had been drawn to the area by labor unrest, after striking workers had gathered to hurl insults at strike-breakers. By evening a crowd of several thousand suddenly materialized, overwhelming the police. Attempts by the police to disperse the crowd led to stone-throwing, then to a rampage, mostly aimed at Jewish brandy and grocery shops and accompanied by cries of "Down with the Jews" and "Beat the Jew down." Christian store-owners speedily put up placards identifying their shops as Christian. Jewish shops were looted, windows were smashed, several shops were razed to the ground by fire, and family members were injured by rock-throwers. By late evening the army arrived on the scene and restored order. The *Neue Freie Presse* recalled that a similar riot had occurred the year before, on the occasion of a tramway strike, when labor unrest had attracted a mob of rowdies to the scene.[18]

Some elements of the Jewish population, such as Galician shopkeepers in working-class districts and Jewish peddlers soliciting in eating and drinking places in the evening, were especially vulnerable to violence. But violence was more random and thus more general. Arthur von Suttner, president of the Defense Association against Antisemitism, singled out other cases: soldiers had knocked down an old Jew on the street, a schoolboy had stuck a knife in a Jewish boy's eye.[19]

It must be said that law and order and property rights were strongly upheld under Habsburg rule. Perpetrators of violence against Jews were punished. Moreover, as some have pointed out, much of the anti-Jewish verbal abuse was hyperbole. Words and action did not neatly correspond in Austrian politics; the Viennese were well known for their theatricality and easygoing inconsequence. Still, verbal abuse and slander and unremitting anti-Jewish agitation, from street corners to the halls of Parliament, were tolerated by the authorities and fostered random violence. By the early 1890s, the government considered Lueger's expanding Bürger coalition too close to the social and political mainstream to suppress. Though disquieted by its populist character, the government also realized that it faced a Bürger reaction which might usefully serve as a counterforce to both Liberal influence and socialist incursions. The government still largely accorded Jews patrimonial protection; constitutionally, they continued to enjoy legal equality. All believed that the age of massacres had passed in nineteenth-century Europe, and Viennese Jews hardly feared for their lives. But Jews were being forced into a condition of political impotence and social disparagement; they were being "put in their place" and had become once more objects of unrelenting and widespread contempt and abuse.[20]

The Social Question and the Jewish Question

Before we record and explain Herzl's response to the new anti-Jewish climate in Austria, the economic basis of Christian Social antisemitism needs to be highlighted. Radical and ideological anticapitalism, which went hand in hand with antisemitism, shaped the United Christian movement in the early years, when artisans and small shopkeepers were its chief clientele. When the movement widened its middle-class base and abandoned principled anticapitalism, the shift was masked by unrelenting rhetorical attacks on Jewish capitalist exploiters. Though mainline Austrian antisemitism was multifaceted and religiously and culturally based as well, economic antisemitism stood out as its main motif. Christian Socials concentrated on what was widely called "the social question," the distress caused by laissez-faire capitalism, or "Judeo-liberalism."[21] Anticapitalism and antisemitism were thus synonymous in Austria and shaped Herzl's understanding of the causes of anti-Jewish hostility.

Anticapitalism arose as a response to the Habsburg state's free market policies and the capitalist modernization of the 1850s and 1860s, which exacted a heavy toll among artisans, small shopkeepers, and peasants. The rise of light industry, particularly mechanization in the textile, shoe, and furniture industries, intruded on formerly secure artisan domains, the railroads easing the cheap transport in bulk of raw materials and finished goods. The rise of the small general store and large department store took retail selling, and consequently control over the selling price of his product, out of the artisan's hands. Master artisans lacking capital and easy credit were exceptionally hard hit by the stock market collapse of 1873, which triggered a general economic depression lasting some seven years. Many of those remaining found themselves reduced to doing piece-work and repairs on commission for manufacturers. Artisans who switched to mechanization found themselves entangled in debts. Those who could not or would not adapt often ended up in the ranks of the new industrial proletariat.[22]

Capitalism was thus a novel phenomenon in Austria. Until 1848, government policies had hindered industrial expansion and innovation and had inhibited economic growth through trade protectionism. Only in the 1850s, the period of neo-absolutism, did the government both free up trade and stimulate economic growth through a great railway expansion program. Even then the government's new policy of economic liberalism was imposed from above by a modernizing regime, and not deeply rooted in Austrian culture and ideologies. Indeed, after an economic upswing during the 1850s and 1860s, the 1873 stock market collapse, which led to an economic depression lasting some seven years, produced an anticapitalist resurgence.[23]

Hans Rosenberg has called the 1880s an era of "neomercantilism." Responding to this new mood, the government embarked on a limited program of guild protectionism, regulation of factory labor, industrial accident and sickness insurance schemes that exempted small workshops, high taxes on joint-stock companies, and nationalization of the railroads.[24]

But in spite of such policies, the government basically stayed the course of economic liberalism by balancing the budget and going on the gold standard, moves which benefited large-scale capitalists over small producers. With its credit requirements and military needs, the government could not afford to resist modernization. Capitalist development in Austria thus came to be shadowed by ambiguity. Interests of state required its encouragement, while public opinion viewed capitalism as socially destructive and ethically repugnant.[25]

Popular opposition to commercial and industrial capitalism stemmed from widely held attitudes shaped by still recent precapitalist economic practices. When guild corporatism and paternalism were juxtaposed to the impersonal power of the stock exchange, when "productive" capital was contrasted to "unproductive" capital (profits derived from labor versus profits derived from investment and speculation), many Austrians insisted upon the ethical superiority—even the greater social and economic efficacy—of the former. Such Austrians distinguished between "rapacious" ("raffendem") and "productive" ("schaffendem") capital. As a result, the Christian Social belief that capitalism was a symptom of "spiritual and moral anarchy" carried enormous weight. In his novel *Big City Jews*, the Austrian-Jewish writer Adolf Dessauer had one of his characters say that Austria was very different from Great Britain or the United States, where self-made men of wealth enjoyed moral approval. Many Austrians doubted that profit seeking and the pursuit of economic self-interest benefited the general good.[26]

Anticapitalism was widely considered not only unethical, but un-Christian, and thus was anchored in mainline Catholic social teachings. Christian Social ideologues Karl Vogelsang, editor of the newspaper *Vaterland*, and Prince Alois Liechtenstein had come from the social reform wing of the Clerical-Conservative party. Both spoke to the distress of small artisans and tradesmen and developed an anticapitalist social and economic program with roots in Catholic corporatism and patriarchalism. Both framed utopian schemes. Guilds were to be reestablished in each branch of industry. Liechtenstein favored giving guilds bank credits to run factories, prohibiting usury, heavily taxing stock-exchange transactions, and abolishing the ready-made manufacturing sector. Vogelsang called for patriarchal "industrial families" of both workers and proprietors to form guilds in every branch of industry.[27]

In reality, Christian Socials pared down their anticapitalist program to demands for cheap credit, tax relief, and tariffs, while sustaining their politically radical tone by condemnations of "the Jewish exploiters of the people." For example, in 1889 the board of the Vienna stock exchange complained that Prince Liechtenstein's attacks at a Catholic congress on the stock exchange and produce exchange would retard economic progress. However, at that same congress Karl Lueger pleaded that a resolution condemning interest and usury not be passed, so as not to alienate party adherents who clipped coupons. Equally, party platforms were often hedged in generalities. The platform of 1894 stipulated, "We want to restore the social and economic order in great measure destroyed by atheism and materialism, and the capitalism that has arisen from them."[28]

Christian Social antisemitism helped mask the widening gap between anticapitalist cultural preferences and relentless capitalist realities. The task of the Christian Socials, in the words of Prince Liechtenstein, was to "rescue the Mittelstand from the clutches of capitalism and Jewry." As Karl Vogelsang explained, Jews, through their control of the Liberal press and party, had introduced economic liberalism into Austria, bringing untold social distress, while creating opportunities for themselves. He contrasted the spirit of

Christianity, which based society and economics on "mutuality and righteousness," to the spirit of Judaism, which made "the inferior spirit of individualism" its ruling socioeconomic principle. Jews, according to this stereotype, were uninterested in honest labor, pride in work, and a well-made product. They were, instead, "specialists in vile profit, accumulators of the property of others." This equation between anticapitalism and antisemitism became so automatic and widespread that the Jewish Liberal deputy Heinrich Jaques called antisemitism a "disguised formula" for anticapitalism.[29]

It must be said that blaming Jews for capitalism seemed plausible to many, for such blame rested on partial, if superficial, evidence. After all, Jews in Vienna benefited from exactly those developments that undercut the lower-middle-class economy. The trade regulations of 1859, which destroyed guild monopolies, opened up industry and trade to Jews. As a result, most of the ready-made clothing, shoe, and furniture industries were pioneered by Jews. Capitalism fostered the Jewish entrance into the Viennese middle class.

Herzl and Christian Social Antisemitism

The first sign of Herzl's growing concern with antisemitism was in the summer of 1891, coinciding with the early years of United Christian electoral gains. For the very first time, he wished to express himself publicly on the Jewish question. He wrote a draft for "a Jewish novel," depicting antisemitism as the fault of rich Jews, while its victims were "the suffering, despised and decent mass of poor Jews." Herzl seems to have partly accepted the United Christian indictment of Jewish capitalists, though he was indignant that all Jews were equally condemned. In October of that year the *Neue Freie Presse* offered him a position as its correspondent in Paris, and his new responsibilities forced him to set the novel aside. Signs of his concern during 1892 appeared in a discussion of the Jewish question in June and in a broad survey of French antisemitism in September, both for the *Neue Freie Presse*. Such signs were as yet scanty, but in December/January 1892/1893, assessing Austrian antisemitism in private notes and in letters to his publisher and to Baron Friedrich Leitenberger, honorary president of the Austrian Defense Association against Antisemitism, Herzl's concern had turned to alarm. Reacting to steady Christian Social electoral gains, he now considered antisemitism a "movement," or an organized force, too powerful to "suppress." Once the "hate speeches of a few agitators," antisemitism now enjoyed popular support. These remarks signal a change in Herzl's view of antisemitism. He no longer saw it as a stubborn survival of medievalism, destined to fade away with growing enlightenment, but as a powerful and ongoing political force.[30]

To Leitenberger, Herzl described Austrian Jews in no uncertain terms as "outcasts of society," "driven into a corner." In spare, graphic words packed with fury, Herzl detailed the range of Christian Social anti-Jewish harassment: "coarse speech . . . hate literature . . . brutal acts." Later he was to remember his own dread of being the butt of anti-Jewish insults in Austria. In an apparent reference to the 1890 anti-Jewish riots in Ottakring and Neulerchenfeld, he recalled the smashing of Jewish windowpanes and concluded with stark fury, "If you ask the antisemites: what do you want? We certainly won't kill Jews [they'll answer]. Absurd. They'll murder Gittel Rubin and loot her brandy shop—that's all."[31]

Herzl was all the more devastated by antisemitism in Vienna because of his ambivalence toward both assimilation and his Jewishness. Jews were Viennese to their fingertips; they were "natives" who had "shared in the sorrows and joys of the nation." Now they were being cast out. In shock and rage, Herzl recoiled from assimilation, one pole of his ambivalence, even hastily declaring Jewish emancipation a "failure."[32] But there was nowhere else for him to turn, for Jewishness too, the other pole of his ambivalence, was no option. Herzl's predicament was to lead to a conflicted, indeed self-contradictory assessment of the antisemitic crisis in Austria.

Explaining the causes of Austrian antisemitism, Herzl insisted that a new force was shaping Austrian politics, the "lower instincts of the masses" marshaled by political demagogues. Though riding a tide of genuine distress, politicians like Lueger and von Liechtenstein were "dealers in snake oil," manipulating mass resentment with simplistic slogans and miracle cures.[33]

Shaped by Austro-Liberalism, an elitist governing party, whose power was based on a privileged and restricted suffrage, Herzl shared its defensive view of the irrational, instinctual nature of the masses. His attitude was only clarified and deepened during his years in France. Covering the Chamber of Deputies on the heels of the Panama scandal and the volatile election campaign in the summer of 1893, he later recalled: "I . . . stood amazed at the phenomenon of the crowd." Nineteenth-century France was Europe's laboratory in mass politics: convulsed by periodic revolutions and workers' uprisings, inaugurating universal manhood suffrage in 1848 and parliamentary democracy in the 1870s. Herzl observed that accelerated development in France foretold Austria's future as well.[34]

Herzl's view of modern mass politics was pessimistic. Universal manhood suffrage—which he believed was the wave of the future—led to the rule of demagogues, for the masses were "jealous and . . . ungrateful," impatient with genuine talent and merit.[35] He singled out the potential for instability of parliamentary democracy: governments were hostage to the intrigues of ambitious parliamentary deputies who toppled cabinets at will, hence "everything hangs in the air." Political instability, popular agitation for the leveling of privileges and property, the backlash to this on the part of the possessing classes, all invited the trials of Caeserist dictatorship.[36] Finally, Herzl described the masses, now conscious of their collective might through universal manhood suffrage, as "fickle, unthinking."[37] Mass empowerment unleashed the reign of instinct: "The uneducated, that is to say the primitive man . . . wants to destroy, because he does not comprehend. The centuries have passed him by; a stranger, fearful, savage, he immediately reaches for his weapon." Hence the masses were easily seduced by demagogues feeding on monumental resentments, preaching class hatred, and trading on utopian dreams of prosperity and perfect equality.[38]

The new age of mass politics posed special dangers for Jews. Herzl considered the rise of the Christian Socials a rebellion of the "little man" against economic and social distress, caused by capitalism and its cyclical "crises of production." But the "social question," the issue of mass distress, had quickly become transformed into the "Jewish question." After all, Herzl declared: "Jew-baiting is the old box-office hit of world history . . . a diversion with minimal risks." In France, the Marxist politician Paul Lafargue's appeal to antisemitism had increased his disquiet. Herzl's French experience only added to his apprehension about the coming of mass politics to Austria, where, if anything, popular antisemitism was far more deeply entrenched.[39]

Herzl insisted that the unleashing of mass instinct was a new factor in European politics, bringing ominous dangers, not least to Jewry. But then he seemed to reverse his course, almost rationalizing antisemitism by narrowing its cause to economic distress. Herzl seems to have accepted Christian Social avowals that they harbored no hatred for Jews or Judaism as such, just of "oppressive big business that finds itself in the hands of the Jews."[40] If this was so, economic distress could be remedied and antisemitism eliminated. He made this categorical assessment in 1893. Herzl found it strange that Reichsrat deputies—among them von Liechtenstein—were debating about whether Christ and the Apostles should be considered Jews:

> If the Jewish question is on the agenda today, then none of the above gentlemen have spoken to it . . . It is both funny and sad to watch such cultivated, dignified, sedate and mature gentlemen play blind-man's bluff with each other in public.
>
> No, the Jewish question . . . has nothing to do with theology and religious worship. The times are past when men beat each others' heads bloody over the ritual of Holy Communion. The issue today is no longer the Lord's Supper, but daily bread. The Jewish question is neither a national nor a confessional one, it is social. It is a branch, early canalized, of the great river called the social question. But great rivers cannot be artificially diverted, and when the snow melts in springtime, floods dig, burrow, and force their own passage.

Herzl's image of the "social question's" unleashing uncontrollable floods was one of ominous dangers. Of equal importance was Herzl's view of anti-semitism as a reaction to social distress. He was denying its other facets—religious, cultural, nationalistic, racial—and besides, seeing it not as Europe's mass pathology, but as a response to genuine suffering and thus potentially eradicable.[41]

Herzl's assessment of Austrian antisemitism leaned in two different directions: one full of foreboding, the second more optimistic. Austrian anti-semitism, he decided, could be combated by addressing the "social question." Through the early 1890s, Herzl envisioned several solutions to mass distress. One was technological: electricity, generated by the power of rivers, would replace steam power. Electrical power was cheap, capable of being widely dispersed, accessible to small units of production. Society could then dispense with massive units of production; oppressive factories could be dismantled. Herzl held to the belief that human invention would bring social peace, in his words: "technology would reconcile labor and capital."[42]

Herzl also insisted that Austro-Liberals could outflank the Christian Socials and restore their fortunes, by addressing economic distress through a social reformist program. To his editor, Eduard Bacher, in December 1891, he proposed that the Liberal party adopt a platform of universal manhood suffrage to regain popular support. To the Liberal notable Baron von Chlumecky in July 1893, he proposed a scheme of work-relief that he had seen operating in France, something like the National Workshops of 1848, though privately funded, offering temporary work to the unemployed. Work-relief would tide workers over the cyclical crises of capitalism. Writing of this scheme in the *Neue Freie Presse*, Herzl concluded that if applied on a vast scale, it provided a "Liberal solution to the social question." He wrote to Chlumecky that Liberals had to move aggressively in the area of social reform, till now abandoned to the "seduction" of Karl Lueger and von Liechtenstein. The work-relief scheme was "suited to affect the popular imagination" and could boost Liberal fortunes against the Christian Socials.[43]

Herzl hardly met Austrian antisemitism with denial; he was devastated by it. Antisemitism's success, he believed, was due to the political advent of the masses, creatures of instinct, seduced by appeals to the irrational. At the same time, he sometimes rationalized antisemitism, attributing it to the "social question," a problem amenable to technological, economic, and political remedies. Thus he opened up the prospect of the Austro-Liberal return to power and the withering away of antisemitism. Herzl's thinking moved on two separate tracks. On one, a historic watershed had been crossed, emancipation and assimilation were failures, and Jews had to radically rethink their stance. On the other track, Herzl continued to believe that the crisis was not deep and would pass. Devastated by antisemitism, he continued to think like an Austro-Liberal, wedded to European civilization as the home of enlightenment and progress.

Herzl's Response to German Nationalist and Liberal Antisemitism

If Christian Social antisemitism was all that Austrian Jews had to face, Herzl probably would not have questioned his assimilationist stance, simply combated antisemitism side by side with other Austrians. But the antisemitic crisis went far deeper, affecting wide sectors of Austrian society, including Jewry's allies the Liberals. Jews experienced not only abuse from those they could easily despise, but ostracism and betrayal from those they respected. Herzl's 1894 play *The New Ghetto* was about this ostracism and betrayal.

The experience of ostracism and betrayal had a particularly strong impact on Herzl, for he had believed in the promise of assimilation. Fulfillment of this promise meant enabling Jews to shed Jewish traits, escape the social and occupational ghetto, and gain legitimacy within gentile society. Besides its other transgressions, antisemitism was thwarting the goals of assimilation. Accordingly, Herzl became preoccupied with the devastating effect of antisemitism on assimilated Jews. Herzl wrote in 1892 that antisemitism had a beneficial side, for it would educate monied Jews about their faults. But unhappily, such lessons were purchased "through the injury of precisely the better [Jews], by crippling those deserving to rise upward." These, whom Herzl also termed "the best Jews," were the ones "emancipated from the ghetto, usury, and money."[44]

These "better" Jews, "emancipated from . . . money" were professionals, making their way in gentile society. Herzl highlighted their plight in *The New Ghetto.* Jacob Samuel, the young lawyer protagonist, fails to gain a gentile clientele. Needing money, he must resort to the help of his brother-in-law, a stock promoter, and becomes entangled in his shady dealings. This theme continued to touch a raw edge in Herzl after he became a Zionist; it reappeared in Herzl's utopian novel of 1902, *Old-New Land.* There Herzl described the Jewish entry into the professions in the 1870s and 1880s as a flight from the taint of money, concluding that such flight had become futile. He was speaking of his own generation and telling his own story. Herzl described the Jewish lawyer Friedrich Loewenberg's predicament: not only were government posts closed to him, but "Christian society and a Christian clientèle were the most unattainable things in the world." Left for him as clients were Jewish parvenus with "low ideals" for whom "money was all." Jewish professionals, making their way in gentile society, were being thrust back into the ghetto.[45]

Herzl's lament was justified, for after a decade of rising expectations, Jewish professionals were particularly hard hit by the antisemitic backlash of the 1890s. In the 1880s, the Taaffe government had begun to recruit Jews into the lower levels of the civil service. By 1891, Christian Socials and pan-Germans were demanding a law excluding Jews from all government posts. Though no such law was passed, government policy became exclusionist in practice, while Jews already in government service found prospects for promotion barred. The same held true for academic appointments, subject to government policy and approval. Jews were finding it increasingly difficult to become *Dozenten*, the very bottom of the academic ladder. Those who had become *Dozenten* in better times remained frozen in that position. The *Oesterreichische Wochenschrift* pondered the fact that the previous generation of Jews had been more fortunate in its access to professional opportunities, while Jews were now being pushed back into the ghetto.[46]

Career difficulties were an aspect of a wider rebuff directed against assimilated Jews, those who had practiced Jewish self-denial, identified with Germanic culture and Austro-German Liberalism, and who sought thereby acceptance and validation—in Herzl's words—as "fellow human beings not to speak of fellow citizens." To those Jews, who had shed the ghetto and the preoccupation with money, Herzl insisted: "a public promise has not been kept. They suffer." The promise referred to the terms of emancipation: Jewish acceptance in return for their shedding Jewish traits and Jewish self-effacement. Such Jews were now rejected by former allies, Austro-German nationalists and Liberals.[47]

This rejection too was a central theme of *The New Ghetto*. To shed his Jewish traits, the protagonist, Jacob Samuel, models himself on his gentile friend Franz Wurzlechner. But with growing antisemitism in Vienna, Franz breaks off their friendship, not only for opportunistic reasons, for he plans a political career, but because the new climate has brought his own latent antisemitism to the surface. Jacob is devastated by this rejection, which leads him ultimately to abandon Austro-German assimilation and to identify with a new ideal of Jewishness. Wurzlechner stood for all those Austro-Germans tested by growing antisemitism, who betrayed their former Jewish associates and allies.[48]

Thus what Herzl encapsulated in the breakup of a Jewish-gentile friendship once marked by deep mutual affection was Jewry's rejection by its former allies, rather than by antisemitic demagogues. Such rejection was both abrupt and wide-ranging, a traumatic turnaround in the growing acceptance Austrian Jews had experienced in previous decades. Herzl's preoccupation in *The New Ghetto* with the theme of rejection and its psychic toll on assimilated Jews, poignantly seeking acceptance and validation and plagued by Jewish self-contempt, reflected this trauma.

Here too, Herzl's lament was justified. Many examples can be cited, beginning with Jewish ostracism from Liberal and from German nationalist social and political associations. Sigmund Mayer described how Jews and Gentiles had gathered together in Liberal electoral assemblies, places of "lively mutual contact" in an earlier era. Now Gentiles began avoiding electoral meetings where Jews were present, till de facto segregation came to be practiced, with Jewish and gentile Liberals meeting in separate branches. By then, only Social Democratic party meetings still regularly brought Jews and Gentiles together. Jews saw exclusionary walls going up again; now, as aspiring members of the Austro-German Bürgertum, this social reghettoization was a thousandfold more painful.[49]

Concurrently, Jews—who Herzl described as having "shared in the sorrows and joys of the nation"—were being banished from the Germanic people of Austria as nationalist associations moved from accepting Jews to sanctioning their exclusion. In the early 1880s, most German nationalists still emphasized an assimilatory, cultural version of *Deutschtum*. Eventually, as the nationalities conflict heated up, radical nationalism took on an integral and racist tone. This led to Jewish exclusionism, a policy that liberal nationalists resisted weakly.

One example was the *German School Association (Deutscher Schulverein)*, a defense league launched in 1880 by a coalition of liberal and radical nationalists. The association's aim was to subsidize schools in Bohemia and Moravia, in localities where Germans were a minority, and to employ teachers who would maintain a nationalist tone in the classroom, to ensure that no German child was denied a German education. In these predominantly Czech lands, Jews were considered allies in the struggle for *Deutschtum*. In 1881, the 120,000-member association was subsidizing eight German-Jewish denominational schools, a number that grew to twelve by 1883. In the mid-1880s, the association began to divide on its policy toward Jews. The struggle continued through the 1890s. In 1899, the association resolved its internal differences by allowing local branches to make their own policies, excluding Jews if they wished.[50]

The *Deutscher Klub*, a radical nationalist parliamentary caucus, followed a like path. Though opposed to Schönerer's racism, the *Deutscher Klub* split in 1887, not least over its Jewish policy. At issue was a quarrel over whether to retain Heinrich Friedjung, of Jewish origin, as editor of its party newspaper, the *Deutsche Zeitung*. Aggrieved, Friedjung resigned, his publicist career effectively destroyed. While some radicals returned to the Liberal fold, others went on to form the *German National Union (Deutschnationale Vereinigung)*, which rejected a single line on the Jewish question and allowed each member to define his own position "according to his view of his duties to the German *Volk*."[51]

Herzl was well aware of the Friedjung incident. Friedjung had written him about his forthcoming appointment, and Herzl thought he might be asked to join the editorial staff. Several years later, Herzl planned a novel about Friedjung's rebuff. Its hero "who turns Germanic," sinks his fortune into a crusading nationalist newspaper. The paper collapses when Germans "refuse to be led by a Jew." The hero is "dishonored." He had once scorned Jewish nationalists "as peculiar Asiatics." He now turns to Zionism. The transition from rejection by fellow Germans to wounded pride and then to Jewish pride, Herzl's own experience, could not have been traced more clearly.[52]

The trend line of change was also reflected in the nationalist student fraternities, the first Germanic associations to exclude Jews in the mid-1880s. During the 1890s, this policy spread to the liberal *Korps* and the *Landsmann-schaften* (student associations from the same home region in the empire). By 1900, the ghettoization of Jews at the University of Vienna was complete.

The first nationalist fraternity to stop admitting Jews was *Libertas*, as early as 1878. *Libertas* kept its policy quiet, in deference to the still-prevailing liberal mood. By late 1883, all but one of the pan-German dueling fraternities had stopped admitting Jews. The one fraternity to resist this trend, *Arminia*, dissolved in 1887, after finding itself unable to attract gentile recruits. By the end of the 1880s, all but two fraternities, *Albia* and *Silesia*, had even forced out their Jewish "old-boys," members of their alumni unions. "Old-boys" were an integral part of the fraternities, attending fraternity functions, main-taining contact, tendering reciprocal favors.[53]

What sealed Jewish exclusion from even the liberal *Korps*, was the refusal announced in 1890 by a cartel of German nationalist fraternities, the *Waid-hofener Union (Waidhofener Verband)*, to duel with Jews. Initially, the principle was not uniformly observed, in part because many students served a year as reserve officers, and army regulations prohibited refusal on the basis of an opponent's religious origin. In addition, not all students approved of such a sweeping ban. What finally made the boycott effective was the large number of challenges from affronted Jews. In 1891, fully fifty-seven of 151 challenges to members of the *Waidhofener* cartel were from Jews. This trend continued in the following years as Jewish students organized their own dueling frater-nities in response to ostracism.[54]

Faced with duel challenges from Jews, the German nationalist fraternities closed ranks, adopting the *Waidhofener* declaration of 11 March 1896. It is worth quoting at length:

> In fullest recognition of the fact that a profound moral and psychological difference exists between Aryans and Jews and that our character has al-ready suffered so much from Jewish troublemaking; in view of the abun-dant evidence that Jewish students have given of their absence of a sense of honor and principle, and their total lack of honor according to our German

conceptions, the present assembly of German able-bodied student fraternities adopts the resolution: "to no longer grant satisfaction to a Jew with any weapon, since he is unworthy of it."[55]

Seven of the eleven affiliated fraternities in Vienna adopted the resolution and broke off relations with the liberal *Korps* and *Landmannschaften*, still accepting Jews. These associations then failed to attract gentile recruits; some proceeded to bar Jewish recruits, others simply dissolved.[56]

Our final, perhaps most painful example of rejection or, more accurately, betrayal of the Jews, was the Austro-German Liberals. The Liberals had always been strong advocates of Jewish civil emancipation, and Jews had always been loyal Liberals. As late as July 1893 Herzl professed his devotion to the Liberal Party.[57] By the 1890s, the Liberal party was on a steep political decline. Lueger was uniting the Austrian middle classes in a broad anti-Liberal coalition.

In this situation, expediency played a large role in the Liberal abandonment of the Jews. Till 1885 radical and liberal German nationalists had been allied in the United Left. They had long split by the 1890s, and radical nationalists had adopted a stance of uncompromising opposition to the government. Since Liberals and radical nationalists competed for the same constituency, the new "sharper key" adopted by the radicals affected the Liberals. Particularly in their Sudetenland stronghold, Liberals became hostages to the more outspoken nationalism and antisemitism of the radicals. Ernst von Plener, the leading Liberal politician of the 1890s, insisted that the mood of lower-middle-class voters made it "plainly impossible" for Liberal deputies to mount a campaign against antisemitism. The party could do no more than "denounce open violations of the law and violent acts," if it was to survive as a political force. Reflecting this strategy, while the Liberal platform in 1885 denounced antisemitism, the platform of 1891 did not.[58]

Similarly, Viennese Liberals sought to ensure their continued rule in the city by neutralizing the political potential of antisemitism. The tactic employed was to maintain a low profile on the issue; instances of this were legion. A historian of the period noted that whenever the Jewish question was raised in city council deliberations, "The Liberal elements, unnerved to their marrow, timidly stepped out of the way." When Sigmund Mayer, Jewish city councillor and Liberal stalwart, raised the issue of antisemitism in the public schools, documented by him with abundant examples, he was denounced by the Liberal mayor, Dr. Prix. Faced with schoolteacher dissatisfaction over salaries and Christian Social competition for their votes, Liberals were not going to risk alienating teachers on the issue of antisemitism.[59]

Sound electoral strategy may have required a Liberal retreat on the issue of antisemitism. What the retreat brought home was that Jews had always been considered dispensable when Liberal political fortunes were at stake. During their years in power, Liberals had balked at admitting Jews to state service or to the professoriat and had been parsimonious in nominating Jewish Liberal candidates for representative bodies. Such Liberal lapses in the benign atmosphere of the 1860s and 1870s could be overlooked, not so in the menacing atmosphere of the 1890s. Now it seemed that the Liberal retreat came too easily, too painlessly, according with deep-seated Liberal antipathies toward Jews, rising to the surface in a time of crisis. Sigmund Mayer certainly thought so, observing that the Christian Social deputies in the Lower Austrian Landtag were able to intimidate the assembly and set the agenda on the Jewish question, not because of their real power—they had only twelve deputies—but because of the "feeble convictions" of Liberals about antisemitism.[60]

Liberal politicians seem to have considered antisemitism primarily a Jewish concern and opposition to it a favor to Jews. The Liberal leader Ernst von Plener complained that Liberals suffered insults from the antisemites without "receiving proper thanks from the Jews." Far from being embarrassed by their opportunism, Liberals seemed to blame Jews for saddling them with difficulties. In the spring of 1894, when Jews appeared reluctant to support the Liberal nominee for a parliamentary seat, because they had wanted a Jewish candidate to succeed the deceased Jewish incumbent, they were warned by the deputy Karl Wrabetz that Liberals would have to reconsider whether they would continue to open themselves to being called "Jewish stooges." Jews responded that opposition to antisemitism went to the heart of liberalism's commitment to "legal equality for all citizens," while Wrabetz was saying, in effect, that Liberals were sick and tired of "enduring so much hostility on account of the Jews."[61] Liberals even suggested that Jews were to blame for antisemitism. Professor Eduard Suess, Reichsrat deputy for the Leopoldstadt, depended upon the support of Jewish voters, making up fully thirty percent of the district. This did not prevent him from declaring in a speech to Liberals: "Jews could best cut the ground out from under antisemitism by exercising strict control over themselves and their actions, living moral lives and showing the populace that in Jewry too, a certain honest self-confidence prevails." Jews in the audience accused Suess of saying that antisemitism had a real basis. In another case, a Liberal Reichsrat deputy, in an attack on antisemitism, concluded: "After all, the worst Jews are to be found among Christians." Few could shake off the connotations carried by the word "Jew" in the Vienna of the 1890s.[62]

During their period of hegemony in Austria in the 1860s and 1870s, Liberals regarded Jewish integration as both right in principle and beneficial to the empire. But Liberal devotion to the rule of law, pluralism, and toleration, to careers open to talent and economic modernization, inhibited their anti-

Jewish antipathies only so long as the challenge to Jewish rights came from marginal political groups. When tested by political adversity, their anti-Jewish antipathies surfaced. Herzl seemed to reflect the disillusionment this created in Jews when he distinguished between Austrian antisemitism "of the tumultuous sort that makes [entering] taverns unsafe," and the antisemitism of "the educated and well-bred for whom antisemitism is neither a business nor a sport. . . . The prejudice against Jews is there but it is overcome in certain instances."[63] It was exactly this prejudice Herzl described in *The New Ghetto*, in Wurzlechner's mercurial attitude to his Jewish friend.

Even those opposed to antisemitism could harbor antipathy toward Jews. Friedrich Nietzsche, master prober of the psyche, had explained this apparent paradox in *Beyond Good and Evil*. Opposition to antisemitism, he observed, was "not directed against the species of this feeling itself but only against its dangerous immoderation, especially against the insipid and shameful expression of this immoderate feeling." Similarly, the German-Jewish philosopher Fritz Mauthner remarked that only "the barbaric fighting style of the antisemites . . . inhibited the anti-Jewish utterances of the liberally, i.e. reasonably minded." The same seems to have held true in Austria. For the Austro-German nationalist Engelbert Pernersdorfer, the only meaningful distinction in Austrian attitudes toward Jews was between "personal antisemitism of feeling" and the more drastic "political antisemitism." He believed no one could be blamed for the first, while "political antisemitism" he considered "by no means acceptable."[64]

Herzl's concern about the ravages of antisemitism ran the gamut of Jewish distress in Vienna as well as elsewhere: poverty, violence, humiliations, balked careers. He later recalled that during this era he wanted to write a book on the "undeserved misfortune" of the Jews in all the lands where they lived.[65] Still, he was particularly sensitive to the rejection experienced by assimilated Jews, the theme of his first comprehensive treatment of the Jewish question in *The New Ghetto*. After seeking gentile acceptance by shedding his Jewish traits, by Jewish self-effacement, Jacob is cast out of gentile society. Jacob's story was a paradigm of the Jewish condition, seen from Herzl's perspective. He too had sought acceptance and belonging as an Austro-German: through a professional career, as a devotee of Vienna's aesthetic culture, by joining a German nationalist fraternity, by asserting the caste privilege of dueling, by idealizing the Austrian aristocracy, and not least by molding himself against the Jewish stereotype and distancing himself from unassimilated Jews. As a liberal, he had identified with the German nationality, the most urbanized, educated, and wealthy nationality in the empire, its predominant ruling stratum, the trustee of its high culture.

To call Herzl a social climber would be to trivialize the impulses behind his yearning for acceptance and belonging, for an added spur was his negative image of Jews as society's perpetual wanderers, emblematic pariahs, despised aliens. Through assimilation, Herzl had sought to terminate what to him was the inferior condition of Jewish marginality.

Friedrich Nietzsche best captured the sources of these Jewish cravings for recognition and standing in *Beyond Good and Evil*: "they long to be fixed, permitted, respected somewhere at long last, putting an end to the nomads' life, to the " 'Wandering Jew.' " For Herzl Jews were the *"Ahasveras* people." The name came from the Christian legend of the Jew *Ahasveras*, cursed to wander forever because he had rebuffed Christ. The pride Jews had once drawn from their condition of exile as God's chosen people was no longer available to Jews like Herzl. While some secular Jews turned their marginality into a new source of pride, celebrating their role as social critics, rebels, and innovators in cultural modernism, Herzl loathed the condition of the outsider, believing it evoked shame and self-contempt in those who endured it.[66]

Herzl described the connection between marginality and self-contempt in *The New Ghetto*, in Jacob Samuel's sense of Jewish inferiority and his flight from his Jewishness. This too was a theme to which he kept returning. In a striking *feuilleton* written in 1896, "Frühling im Elend," about a charity hospital, Herzl conveyed the Jewish experience through the leper-like ostracism endured by charity patients. He pointed out that the word *Elend*, the German for misery, combined the Greek word *alius*, meaning "different or strange," and the German word *land*. *Elend* was the land of the banished or ostracized. Misery and ostracism were one and the same. Herzl theorized that the word originated in an era when human beings feared the different or strange. In the Middle Ages, he observed, strangers were lodged in a special section of town called *Elend*. Such strangers would slink about timidly, thus provoking suspicion; they "became ugly in the sight of others." Similarly, the patients in the charity hospital were shunned. In response, they saw their hospital garb as a sign of shame, walking about timidly with eyes lowered. Herzl's parable of the Jewish condition concluded with the observation that people were now consigning "certain groups" to "*Elend*," through "organized agitation."[67]

In his novel *Old-New Land*, Herzl was to make *Elend* the central theme in Jewish history. For centuries, he wrote, Jews had lived in "the limbo of the banished." "The Jews had thus fallen always lower, as much by their own fault as by the fault of others. Elend . . . Golus [Hebrew for exile] Ghetto. Words in different languages for the same thing. Being despised, and finally despising yourself." Herzl could not have put more clearly the connection he saw between marginality and self-contempt. Being an outcast is, after all, a state of mind. As the Russian Zionist Ahad Ha-Am once insisted: "When the Jew in the Middle Ages bowed to the masters of the land, it was only the body which did so." But for Herzl, outcasts were ugly in the sight of others and became ugly in their own eyes as well.[68]

Herzl's special identification with the plight of assimilated Jews in Vienna explains his approach to the Jewish question. Judging assimilation in its traditional mode a failure, Herzl sought other paths to end Jewish marginality and reintegrate Jews into gentile society.

PART III

Herzl in the 1890s

5

The Reabsorption of the Jews

I wished to gain access to the Pope . . . and say to him: 'Help us against the anti-semites and I will start a great movement for the free and honorable conversion of Jews to Christianity.'[1]

The Self-Transformation of Jewry

IN JANUARY 1893 Herzl was invited to contribute to the weekly newspaper of the Viennese Defense Association against Antisemitism, of which Baron Friedrich Leitenberger was an honorary president. Herzl declined. Antisemitism, he insisted, could no longer be fought with the written word; more drastic means were necessary. He then unleashed a flood of radical proposals for solving the Jewish question. Antisemitism had destroyed the promise of Austro-German assimilation. Yet Jews had to end their debilitating condition of marginality. Still a devotee of Austria, Herzl sought new paths to Jewish integration and acceptance. He advanced several plans, one of which was nothing less than the conversion of Austrian Jewry to Catholicism.[2]

Leitenberger met this proposal with sarcastic disbelief. What would Herzl think of next? he wrote back. His ideas were nothing more than "charming salon-chatter." Herzl's head had been turned by his years in jaded Paris, where only solutions accompanied by "a thousand festering sores or a thousand balls of fire" were able to command attention. Leitenberger then showed Herzl's letter to Professor Hermann Nothnagel, a world-famous specialist in internal medicine, devout Catholic, and like him an honorary president of the Defense Association. Nothnagel was horrified by the conversionist proposal.[3]

Leitenberger and Nothnagel may have been shocked by Herzl's proposal advanced in a decade of rising antisemitism, but conversion had often been advocated, especially in more hopeful times, as the perfect consummation of assimilation. Ten years earlier, at the high tide of his optimism over the prospects of assimilation, Herzl himself had called for conversion.

The logical force of the conversionist position was best articulated by the assimilated Viennese Jew Theodor Gomperz, when he lamented that religious differences drove a wedge between human beings: In Gomperz's view: "Whatever differentiates men, also divides them." Modern culture, he observed, rested on Christian foundations, for Europe's literary classics and its historical memories were intertwined with the history of Christianity. Consequently, Jews should seek "union and fraternity" with the majority through conversion. After all, Jewry's historic contribution to culture belonged to the distant past. Judaism was now "worn-out and out of date," and persistent "isolation and separatism" on behalf of it was "pure folly."[4]

Conversion to the majority religion was thus considered by some the logical end-point of full assimilation. Herzl's biographers have accordingly either judged his proposal as the last gasp of his old assimilationist viewpoint or dismissed it as a wildly far-fetched, theatrical fantasy. But the idea was not a throwback to a past phase. It flowed from a radical idea he expressed to his editor Moriz Benedikt: heightened antisemitism must call forth "a saving act" on behalf of the Jews.[5]

This notion of "a saving act" marked a change in Herzl's thinking. He had once believed that emancipation and assimilation into European society would transform Jews; now he believed that Jews would have to transform themselves, and that this self-transformation would eliminate antisemitism. By bold acts in response to antisemitism Jews could transform themselves, rid themselves of their faults, and gain self-respect and the esteem of their Christian compatriots.

Surprisingly enough, Herzl's proposal for the mass conversion of Jewry represented, for him, just such a bold act. The event would occur "in broad daylight . . . with festive processions," in the vast square before St. Stephen's Cathedral in Vienna. It would be sealed by a historic alliance with the Pope, binding the Church to eradicate antisemitism. Clearly, Herzl still conceived of full assimilation as the ultimate goal of Jewry, and he viewed Judaism as an outmoded faith, an unnecessary barrier to submergence in the majority culture. He confessed to Benedikt: "I am not in the least resistant to formal conversion to Christianity."[6] But his initial solutions to antisemitism pointed not just in one direction but in two opposite ones: both to the total submergence of Jewishness, and—still dimly perceived—to a new kind of Jewish self-assertion. Herzl moved confusedly between these two poles, wanting both, caught in the middle between the quest for total assimilation and on the other hand, for Jewish self-respect.

Herzl's contradictory goals can be explained by his heightened Jewish ambivalence brought on by the strong upsurge of antisemitism. Throughout the 1880s, when he was still optimistic about the prospects of Jewish integration, Herzl's conflicts about his Jewishness were troubling but bearable. But now the situation had changed. Antisemitism unleashed in him abrupt swings of conflicting feelings: rage at Gentiles, wounded Jewish pride, heightened Jewish self-disdain leading him to blame Jews for antisemitism, calls for Jewish self-assertion and renewed wishes for radical assimilation, for a Jewish "submergence into the nation."[7] How far Herzl blamed Jews for Christian Social economic antisemitism comes out in a letter to Moriz Benedikt. He confessed: "I do not consider the antisemitic movement entirely harmful. It will break the arrogance of the ostentatious rich, the unscrupulousness and cynicism of Jewish financial wire-pullers, and contribute much to the education of the Jews." On the other hand, his rage at antisemitism is best captured in an unpublished outburst: "Antisemitism is a reprimand for the Jews, but it's enough by now! I will have quiet! Otherwise . . . " Rage and humiliation led him to insist that if Jews were "pushed too hard," they would retaliate.[8]

Herzl's confused and self-contradictory mood was evident in his attitude to the Defense Association against Antisemitism. Before examining his attitude, a few words must be said about this organization, founded in Vienna in May 1891 by Christian notables: members of the upper aristocracy, industrialists, Reichsrat deputies, and academics. The Defense Association combated antisemitism through its publications and public meetings. In October 1892, it held a protest meeting that passed a resolution calling on Parliament to make antisemitic agitation in its chamber illegal. The tone taken by the Defense Association was hardly circumspect or diplomatic. At the meeting, attended by 2,000, Baron Gundaccar von Suttner, the association's president, called for the "total uprooting" of antisemitism; Dr. Hermann Nothnagel predicted that, if not stopped, antisemitic rhetoric would culminate in "horrible deeds." In December 1892, the association sent a public letter to the president of the lower house of the Reichsrat, calling on him to stop Jew-baiting in Parliament. At its height the association attained a membership of approximately 5,000. But by 1896 demoralization had set in, for the organization had failed to attain the support and influence it sought. Publication of its newspaper was then suspended, though the Defense Association remained in existence.[9]

Herzl's view of the association, expressed in his letters to Baron Leitenberger, came at a time when hopes were high and membership was climbing. The tone he took was patronizing and belligerent. He considered it "magnificent that there were human beings who do not care a hang what people think and take an interest in . . . the despised, hated, weak Jews." However, "he [Baron Leitenberger] and the eminent men" in the association were too late; they should have done something ten or twelve years ago, when the "first stirrings of antisemitism" had occurred. Herzl's belligerence was uncalled for. Almost everyone, including himself, had seen the antisemitism of the early 1880s as a fading residue of the past. Herzl said as much in early 1893, when he observed that antisemitism "ten or fifteen years ago . . . existed among isolated agitators . . . and the people showed no sympathy for this agitation." However, it is not difficult to explain Herzl's belligerence. The Defense Association had only a few Jewish members. It was founded and led by non-Jews and thus entailed gentile intervention on behalf of Jews. For Herzl, such intervention could only undermine efforts at Jewish self-assertion. The association actually wished to spur an equivalent Jewish militancy and self-defense; it showed no sign of a condescending attitude toward Jewry. But for Herzl all gentile initiatives now conjured up sensitivities about inherent Jewish cowardice and timidity.[10] In his letters to Leitenberger, Herzl could both express resentment at gentile intervention on behalf of Jews and call for the conversion of Jews to Christianity.

Groping for a solution, Herzl sought both Jewish assimilation and self-assertion, a search that culminated in Zionism. As unlikely as it may sound, there are similarities between Herzl's proposal for mass conversion to Christianity and his later plan for Jewish sovereignty; the earlier proposal was not at all anomalous to his Zionism. Indeed, a common thread extends from the reflections of 1892/1893, continuing on through Herzl's play *The New Ghetto*, written in October/November 1894, to the idea of a Jewish state, conceived in May 1895. In all these phases, Herzl was thinking of a bold act that would transform Jews and gain them self-respect, but also realize Jewish assimilation and win them gentile acceptance. At first, still ambivalent about his Jewishness, he saw mass conversion as the answer. With time, his notion of this act became less self-contradictory, as he found a way to resolve his Jewish ambivalence. By the fall of 1894, when he wrote *The New Ghetto*, Herzl, increasingly radical, had abandoned his old mode of assimilation involving submergence into European culture and created a new one based on a positive reinterpretation of Jewishness. By the spring of 1895, Herzl carried this new understanding of assimilation even further, by redefining Jewishness in national terms. With this he achieved his quest both for Jewish pride and self-respect, and for gentile acceptance.

All these phases represent stages in which Herzl gained increasing clarity in his quest for a new mode of Jewish assimilation that would eliminate Jewish self-disdain, along with servile dependence on gentile acceptance, and enhance the self-respect of Jews. Redefining Jewishness in national terms was a way of resolving his own Jewish ambivalence. His charisma as a Jewish leader derived from this transformative breakthrough to a new kind of Jewish self-affirmation.

Mass Baptism

There may have been considerable logical force to the idea of Jews converting to Christianity, since blending into the majority culture was the goal of assimilation, and for some Jews at least, Judaism was defunct. But Herzl fully realized that the history of Jewish persecution at the hands of Christians, not to speak of nineteenth-century antisemitism, made conversion a far more complicated act. To take the example of Theodor Gomperz, it was not surprising, in spite of his impeccable arguments, that Gomperz did not convert; he was prevented, as he put it, by "motives of a not ignoble kind." Residual Jewish bonds, a sense that conversion was disloyal, a craven act, morally repugnant in a period of heightened antisemitism, inhibited him. To add to the stigma of conversion, most Viennese Jews who chose this path were professionals or civil servants, seeking to advance their careers. Hence conversion was considered just another manifestation of Jewish opportunism and social climbing. Some nasty Viennese anecdotes recalled by Max Grünwald illustrate how widespread this notion of Jewish opportunism was. In one display of wit, a Viennese Jew claimed that it was his *Germanic* sense of loyalty and pride that prevented him from converting to Christianity. In another, baptism was described as typical "Jewish nonsense."[11]

For these reasons, some who would not convert themselves, thought instead of having their sons baptized, before their Jewish loyalties crystallized. This was Gomperz's recourse; he wanted his eldest son to apply for unaffiliated religious status at eighteen as a transitional stage, then later convert, and his two younger sons to convert to Protestantism at fourteen. From Todd Endelman's recent account of Jewish conversions in nineteenth-century central Europe, there is reason to believe such hesitations and expedients were typical. The view that conversion was ignoble would keep even Walther Rathenau, the Weimar cabinet minister whose Jewish self-contempt was notorious, a nominal Jew.[12]

Herzl was aware that conversion was considered an act of disloyalty, cowardice, and opportunism. Thus, his scheme for the conversion of the Jews was meant to transform it from an act of cowardice to one of pride and self-assertion. The act would occur as a grand public ceremony. Jews would convene in St. Stephen's square and convert "not in shame," as occurred when individuals converted, "but with proud gestures." Herzl continued: "Because the Jewish leaders [with Herzl at their head] would remain Jews, escorting the people only to the threshold of the church and themselves staying outside, the whole performance was to be elevated by a touch of great candor." The leaders of Jewry, including Herzl, would remain the "last generation" of "steadfast" Jews. Herzl conceived of a strategy that would accomplish two contradictory ends: assimilation or the "mingling of the races," and Jewish self-affirmation. The act by which Jews sealed their immanent disappearance, considered by many a characteristically insidious Jewish act, motivated by "cowardice or careerism," would be candid, honorable, and audacious.[13] Jews would overcome their cautious and timid ways, thus gaining self-respect as well as the respect of Gentiles. They would break their old habits and adopt a Prussian-like bluntness, openness, and boldness, *Albia's* ideal. Herzl was intent on remolding Jews in this image.

Why would Herzl, along with the Jewish leaders, not convert? The answer can be found in Herzl's letters to Benedikt and Leitenberger. What hindered his conversion was neither belief in nor regard for Judaism, but other reasons altogether. First, "devotion and gratitude" to his father, who would be devastated by his apostasy, and second, "a matter of self-respect," for "one must not abandon Judaism when it is being persecuted." Herzl would remain one of the last of the Jews, not out of conviction, but out of filial loyalty and manly pride. In one account of his scheme, *only* the sons would be converted, while *all* the fathers would remain Jews. Jewish fathers, to spare their sons the "mortifications and slights" suffered by Jews, would have their sons baptized, but they themselves would remain proud, even defiant Jews, the last of the Jews. Thus Herzl could, at one and the same time, recommend the baptism of young Jewish sons and then equally insist that if his son grew to manhood unbaptized, he hoped he would be "too proud to abjure his faith." (In the event, Herzl equivocated in the case of his son Hans, born in 1891. He was not baptized, but neither was he circumcised.)[14]

Herzl had transformed conversion from an individual to a collective Jewish act, for individual converts were still considered Jews. Conversion, as such, did not necessarily lead to Jewish assimilation. To Benedikt, Herzl cited the medieval example of Spanish Jews, discriminated against and prevented from intermarrying, even after their conversion. Individual conversion did not alter the stereotype of Jewry. Prejudice was a collective judgment; overcoming it required a collective act. The question was whether Jews could promote a "climate of toleration," as a prelude to conversion. This required, he believed, a radical act on the part of the Jews.[15]

Herzl envisaged conversion as a radical act, virtually an act of Jewish realpolitik involving "a diplomatic peace treaty" negotiated with the pope. He noted that the greatest "hindrance" to conversion had been the absence of "reciprocity." But now, a quid pro quo would be involved, for the pope, in return, would be persuaded to launch a campaign against antisemitism. Herzl discussed this plan with his editors because he wished to offer the pope an additional inducement: the *Neue Freie Presse* would adopt a pro-papal line. Jews would not act as individuals but as a solid collective, intent on serving their own interests. Herzl was summoning up resources for Jews wherever he could find them, which would enable them to deal with Gentiles on a basis of equality. Only in this way could they gain gentile respect, thereby promoting a climate of toleration. By contrast, Herzl referred to a recent incident to argue that a climate of toleration could not be achieved by soliciting the mighty, as German Jews had just done in appealing to the kaiser for aid against antisemitism. He found this even more "laughable than contemptible." Herzl chided German Jews for appealing for patrimonial protection. If antisemitism spurred Herzl's desire for total Jewish absorption in Austrian society, ending Jewish marginality, it also awakened his desire for a new Jewish self-assertiveness. The notion that it was up to Jews to command gentile respect was already germinating in him, if confusedly.[16]

Mass Jewish Enlistment in Socialism

Mass baptism was not the only scheme brewing in Herzl; he also proposed as another possibility that Jews as a body turn to socialism.[17] Herzl was not wedded to one solution to the problem of antisemitism. He was still groping for some form of Jewish collective action, seeking total assimilation, but achieved in a manner that was open, defiant, heroic, transforming Jews, enhancing their self-respect, and making them esteemed, even feared. The problem remained one of altering Jewry and consequently gentile attitudes to Jewry, thus eliminating antisemitism as a prelude to Jewish assimilation.

Just as with mass conversion to Catholicism, the turn to socialism ensured Jewry's total disappearance as a distinct entity. The Austrian Social Democrats, as Herzl well knew, stood for internationalism and cosmopolitanism and were hostile to all forms of Jewish distinctiveness. Socialists upheld the primacy of German culture as the universalistic culture of central Europe. Though equivocal about combating antisemitism, they nevertheless believed that with the elimination of capitalism, which had pushed Jews to the foreground as exploiters, and with the ebbing of Jewish distinctiveness through socialist and Germanic assimilation, antisemitism would disappear. Jews were prominent in the Social Democratic party apparatus, particularly in party journalism, youth work, and cultural and education activities. Socialism was an alternative form of Jewish assimilation, promising the total absorption of Jewry in an era when Austro-German nationalism, even in its liberal version, excluded Jews from the German nation.[18]

Nevertheless, Herzl's recommendation that Jews turn to socialism is puzzling at first glance, for he was a paternalist Austrian Liberal and despised socialism. In his articles on the French parliamentary elections of August/September 1893, he expressed opposition to universal suffrage and distrust of parliamentary democracy. In the first draft of his 1894 play, initially titled *The Ghetto*, Herzl expressed his suspicion of socialism through the views of Jacob Samuel, his alter ego: "It seems to me it [socialism] would set up a new form of oppression in place of the old. And perhaps the new one would be still worse."[19]

Behind Herzl's proposal lay several as yet unclarified ideas, none of which had to do with democratic or socialist goals. Least of all was he interested in developing an independent Jewish electoral strategy, as was the Jewish defense organization, the Austrian-Israelite Union, when it calculated the prospects of a Jewish-socialist alliance. Herzl was attracted to socialism, just as he had been drawn to radical German nationalism, for its political style, not its political goals. In proposing that Jews turn to socialism he mentioned, indifferent to their goals, parties reformist in action and revolutionary in rhetoric, like the Austrian and German Social Democrats, and terrorist groups like the violent wing of French anarchism. In unpublished notes, he called socialism the answer to antisemitism in Germany, and baptism the answer in Austria, evidence that he was thinking more of the method and style of Jewish action, rather than of its ideological content.[20]

Herzl's rage and wounded pride over antisemitism was more evident in his flirtation with socialism than in that with Catholicism. Pushed back into pariah status, Jews, by turning to socialism, would respond by becoming pariahs with a vengeance. Enemies of society, they would join other marginal groups in overturning society. He wrote to Baron Leitenberger: "From outcasts of society they will become enemies of society. Ah, they are not protected in their civic honor, they are permitted to be insulted, scorned and on occasion also a bit plundered and maimed—what prevents them from going over to the side of anarchy?" Feelings of helplessness, anger, and injured pride found relief in fantasies of violent retaliatory action, candidly expressed only in Herzl's unpublished notes: Jews "no longer have a stake in the state. They will join the revolutionary parties, supplying or sharpening their weapons. They want to turn the Jews over to the mob—good, they themselves will go over to the people. Beware, they are at their limit, do not go too far." Jews would no longer seek acceptance by Gentiles: they would more independently endeavor to command respect, even fear. Herzl called for Jews to respond with "pistol bullets when their window-panes were broken."[21]

For Herzl, revolutionary action as an expression of rage and wounded pride was not an end in itself but linked to his germinating notion of Jewish self-transformation. Reporting on the French elections of August/September 1893, Herzl saw a similarity between the French proletariat and Jewry: right now both "were in a bad way"; eventually both would see better days. Both Jews and proletarians were powerless outcasts ground down by the status quo, but the similarity did not end there. Herzl had been profoundly impressed by the transformative effect of radical politics on its working-class adherents and now sought to apply what he had learned to Jewry.[22]

Herzl's Paris years coincided with a period of anarchist terrorism, beginning in 1892 and petering out in 1894, after the spectacular assassination of the president of the republic, Sadi Carnot. In April and June 1892, Herzl covered the first and second trials of the anarchist Ravachol, where he saw the transformative power of radical politics at first hand. Ravachol was an enigmatic figure, who had been a common criminal prior to his anarchist exploits. In March 1892, explosions had destroyed the homes of the law-court president Benoît and the advocate-general Bulot, both of whom had been involved in passing harsh sentences on anarchists after a workers' demonstration in Clichy in 1891 had turned violent. Benoît had been the judge in the trial and Bulot had been the prosecutor. Neither was killed, but their official standing made the act of terrorism particularly notorious. Ravachol was soon arrested and tried for these bombings.

Ravachol's first trial ended with a sentence of life imprisonment, much to the consternation of public opinion. A second trial took place for crimes Ravachol had committed before he avowed anarchism, including a murder charge, and this time he was sentenced to death. He was soon virtually canonized by some anarchists as a martyr to the cause, raised to the level of a Socrates or of Jesus Christ.

Ravachol's deed and his behavior in court both fascinated and frightened the public and turned anarchism, still a subject of only marginal interest, into front-page news. The prisoner was cool and unruffled during his trial, seemingly indifferent to his fate, fearless, impassive, even proffering a friendly smile to the witness who had informed on him.

Herzl was fascinated with Ravachol and, in addition to his daily dispatches, devoted two *feuilletons* to the trial. In one, Herzl described how Ravachol had assumed the role of judge, calling down punishment on those who had committed crimes against the downtrodden. Herzl queried whether Ravachol was a "visionary or a scoundrel? Benefactor of the poor and destitute—and therefore a robber or murderer?" He then offered this gripping evaluation of Ravachol: "There is something impersonal about this man. He speaks quietly. Firmly and serenely he asserts that we must alter the present state of affairs, and when he describes the better epoch to come, when the weak will enjoy the protection of all, his voice sounds tender. His path is marked with blood—he knows this. . . . Today he believes in himself and his mission. He has become honest through his crimes. The common murderer rushes to the brothel with his loot. Ravachol has discovered another kind of lust: the voluptuousness of a great idea and of martyrdom."[23]

In a second *feuilleton*, a series of scenes, Herzl described how fear of Ravachol shadowed the daily lives, even the private fantasies, of all strata of French society. A good bourgeois accosted by a beggar hastily hands money over to him, fearful that the beggar may be Ravachol in disguise; the wealthy high-born guests at a first-class hotel prepare to leave Paris out of fear of Ravachol; a mother threatens her child that she will fetch Ravachol if the child does not behave; a woman confesses that she fantasizes sexually about the terrorist. Ravachol had become a mythical figure, a collective phantom.[24]

As Carl Schorske has pointed out, it was the "voluptuousness" or transformative power of "the great idea" that fascinated Herzl in Ravachol, a power he also saw at work in socialism. He observed a number of socialist electoral meetings during the French parliamentary elections of August/September 1893. One in Lille, a socialist stronghold, was addressed by Paul Lafargue, the son-in-law of Karl Marx. Herzl was profoundly stirred by the spontaneous discipline and powerful feeling of solidarity among the workers. He noted that "each drew solace and confidence" when addressed as comrade. The power of the socialist idea filled them with dignity and self-respect. Herzl reported: "I have never seen such an audience. They drank in his [Lafargue's] words as if they were evangelical, a gospel in which they still believed. They stared at him, entranced, all motionless, tightly packed, sitting, standing, and their direct glance was so staunch, artless, dutiful, of such a holy simplicity." Herzl contrasted this virtual epiphany with the shabbiness of the meeting hall, the dulled, careworn appearance of the workers. The socialist idea had transformed its wretched adherents. Herzl was swept up by an almost "physical presentiment of their [the workers'] might . . . united they are like a great beast, just beginning to stretch its limbs, still half unaware of its power."[25]

In one of his letters to Leitenberger, Herzl had described Jews as "harmless, contemptible fellow human beings, not to say fellow citizens, lacking honor and thus bent on profit, become crafty through prolonged oppression."[26] In proposing that Jews turn to socialism, Herzl was saying that like the proletariat, touching bottom, the limits of extreme dehumanization, Jews would, through a radical act, transform themselves. The "voluptuousness of a great idea" would transform the love of profit into a yearning for heroic self-sacrifice, turn craftiness into courage. Just like Lafargue's words, Herzl's language was evangelical; he was thinking in terms of Jewish self-transcendence.

Duels with Antisemites

Herzl considered one more proposal during this key period of ferment. He mentioned it only in passing to Baron Leitenberger but later described it in detail in his Zionist diary, where he called it more a "dream" than an idea. He would challenge a foremost Austrian antisemite to a duel, either Baron von Liechtenstein, Georg von Schönerer or Karl Lueger. If he were shot, outrage would be unleashed against antisemitism for bringing about such a senseless loss of life. If his opponent were shot, Herzl would graciously express his sorrow at his trial and eloquently expound on the Jewish question, moving the awed jury to acquittal. This would be followed by another honorable gesture, for Jews would offer to elect him a member of Parliament, but he would nobly decline, not wishing to advance himself at the expense of someone's death.[27]

Once more Herzl was seeking to realize his goal of Jewish assimilation through Jewish self-transformation. Dueling, the code of honor of aristocrats, officers, and university students, carried high status. As we saw earlier, by the early 1890s in Austria, sentiment was building against accepting Jews as equal and honorable foes in the duel. It is inconceivable that Schönerer or Baron Liechtenstein would have even condescended to duel with a Jew, while Lueger disdained the duel. Herzl's fantasy expressed his quest for both Austrian social legitimacy and Jewish pride. To Leitenberger he wrote that "half a dozen duels would raise immensely the social standing of the Jews."[28] Jewish pride was to be attained by abandoning calculating prudence, timidity, and cowardice, seen by Herzl as Jewish traits, and by acting Germanic, or boldly and directly, in a Jewish cause. Only through the self-transformative act of dueling would Jews gain self-respect and the respect of Gentiles, and hence make assimilation a reality.

Once more, his experiences in France spurred this idea. Herzl's fantasy replicated the duel in Paris in June 1892 between the Marquis de Morès, an associate of Edouard Drumont, and a Jewish army officer, Captain Armand Mayer. The affair was the result of publicity-seeking accusations of treason against Jewish army officers by Drumont's antisemitic newspaper, *La Libre Parole*. Captain Mayer had responded to this slur by seeking a duel. Herzl wrote about the incident in the *Neue Freie Presse*. He had been deeply moved by Mayer's "noble demeanor and impeccable gallantry." Apparently Mayer had an injured arm, and it was difficult for him to wield the heavy sabre, but he was "too proud" to reveal this. Herzl well understood that as a Jew Captain Mayer could not afford to leave himself open to the reproach of cowardice, from Gentiles or even in his own eyes. He was stabbed within three seconds. Herzl's speech to the jury in the case of his own fantasized duel, expressing his regrets at "the death of an honorable man," were exactly the words the Marquis de Morès had used at his trial after stabbing Captain Mayer.[29]

The significance of the Mayer-Morès duel went far beyond the public acknowledgment by Morès that his opponent was a man of honor and courage. In Michael Marrus's account of the aftermath of the duel, Captain Mayer became a national hero, his death a standing reproach to antisemitism for causing divisions in the French nation. As someone whose family had left Alsace after its annexation by Germany in 1871, Mayer was widely recognized as "a symbol of Jewish devotion to the nation." His funeral was the occasion for a great outpouring of patriotic fervor; somewhere between 20,000 and 100,000 Parisians lined the streets for the funeral cortège. The casket was accompanied by senior military officers and resplendent troops of soldiers.

In Parliament, the minister of war declared that the army recognized no differences between Frenchmen, while the Paris newspapers condemned antisemitism for sowing national discord. Jewish spokesmen responded by reaffirming their devotion to—and faith in—France. The Mayer *affaire* ended as a decisive defeat for antisemitism and as a strong vindication of Jewish assimilation.[30]

This outcome could not have been far from Herzl's mind when he dreamed of combat with an Austrian counterpart of the Marquis de Morès. The Mayer *affaire* and its aftermath fulfilled Herzl's dual goals, expressed both in the proposals for mass conversion and those for revolutionary agitation: to realize assimilation, dissolving antisemitism by introducing new modes of Jewish self-assertion, audacious, heroic modes breaking with old Jewish habits. In virtually contradictory fashion, having transformed themselves, Jews would both merge into Europe and create a new basis for Jewish self-respect.

Jews as Recent Freedmen

Reacting to mounting antisemitism, Viennese Jewish militants called for Jewish self-assertiveness and pride, which entailed pride in Judaism. With his categorical view of Jewish faults, Herzl aimed at a far more radical, even utopian goal: a transformation of the Jews. Analyzing the Jewish question in a period of rising antisemitism, Herzl turned back to the explanatory myths of liberal emancipationism. The past ten years had only confirmed for him that the Jewish character was deformed by centuries of persecution and ghetto incarceration. Restricted to commercial occupations and squeezed for booty, Jews had found their only security and outlet for ambition in the acquisition of money. Their power drive and resentment at their persecutors could only find expression by outsmarting Gentiles in commercial dealings. Persecuted and regularly expelled from their homes, they developed the surreptitious and submissive habits of a powerless minority. Incarcerated in ghettos, ostracized by the gentile world, and unable to share in its intellectual progress, Jews were plagued by a sense of inferiority and self-disdain. Herzl wrote to Moriz Benedikt in December 1892 that Jews were "a people debased through oppression, emasculated, distracted by money, tamed in numerous corrals."[31] Herzl's view of Jewish faults had not changed over ten years; he explained these faults historically and attributed them to gentile persecution. They remained defects nonetheless.

Thus, one reason Herzl sought the transformation of the Jews was that he viewed antisemitism as an understandable reaction to Jewish defects. Antisemitism was an exaggerated, even unfair response to Jewish faults, for gentile persecution had created these defects; it was a comprehensible response, nonetheless. To Leitenberger he insisted: "I do not deny all good to anti-semitism. . . . it will educate the Jews," in that it will spur them to overcome their centuries-old faults.[32] Other concerned Jews did not share this view. Articles in *Die Neuzeit* (the Viennese-Jewish weekly that reflected the posi-tion of the official Jewish community) argued that there was no causal rela-tionship between antisemitism and Jewish behavior. The author of one insisted that wealthy Jews were denounced not because they were wealthy nor because of how they had gained their wealth, but simply because they were Jews. Why have none of the other English plutocrats, as wealthy or wealthier than Rothschild, become a notorious household name, the writer asked? Why are *they* not envied, hated? Why is their fortune legitimate, but not Roths-child's? Because Rothschild is a Jew. The Jewish weekly, the *Oesterreichische Wochenschrift*, wondered why the era of the Hansa League in Germany or the more recent British supremacy in trade, were celebrated as glorious achievements, while Jewish wealth was derided. What was the difference, ex-cept that "solely in regard to Jews was wealth branded a crime."[33]

But if Herzl emphasized Jewish faults, in another respect his views had changed drastically over the past ten years. He now had an added purpose: to show that persecution and the deformations it had created in Jews ham-pered them in combating antisemitism. The issue had shifted for him; per-secution, he insisted, had robbed Jews of self-respect and the capacity for self-assertion, preventing the bold action that would end antisemitism. Herzl's critique of Jewish existence now concentrated on issues of Jewish self-asser-tion and pride.

Out of this preoccupation, Herzl layered a new element onto the old emancipationist image of the Jews: the Jewish experience as recent freedmen, a people recently freed from a submissive condition akin to slavery. With this notion, Herzl believed he could explain Jewish inadequacies in combating antisemitism.

Herzl's review of a satirical French play, *Prince Aurec*, by Henri Lavedan, shows us where his new analysis was taking him. The play was about the high French aristocracy in sordid decline. Herzl described one of them as "a match for any Jewish second-hand peddler." Lavedan was exposing corruption in the French high aristocracy, stripped by now of any useful social or po-litical function, selling access to its circles in an effort to maintain its profli-gate lifestyle, making marriages of convenience with the daughters of wealthy parvenus. There is a Jewish character in the play, the wealthy parvenu Baron Horn, who yearns to mix socially with these aristocrats, gain entrance to their exclusive clubs, and climb into bed with the wife of Prince Aurec. To ingratiate himself with the prince, Horn has lent him a large sum of money

so he can pay off his gambling debts. Eventually Baron Horn is thrown out
of the prince's house for the advances he has made to the princess, who has
nothing against adultery but is offended at being propositioned by a Jew.

Herzl's observations about Baron Horn are worth quoting at length. He
insisted that Lavedan's portrait of Horn showed a lack of understanding of
Jewish parvenus:

> In the play Horn is no more than a nabob, not unduly clumsy and not
> at all ridiculous. It is a pity! The clarity of a greater comedy would have
> required drawing a contrast between the contemptibleness of Aurec who
> trades on his exclusivity, and the ridiculousness of the snob. Horn does not
> boast enough to his distinguished acquaintances, he feels himself too little
> honored, he does not stammer with glee when he speaks with duchesses.
> The insecurity of the Jew is not shown. Yet this is part of Horn's very
> being, his most striking feature, showing itself in abrupt swings between
> arrogance and obsequiousness. A more charitable insight would certainly
> understand that this insecurity is a product of age-old wrongs, which con-
> tinue to this day.[34]

Herzl's comments moved automatically from Jewish parvenus to Jews in
general. For him, the parvenu was the representative Jew, the insecure former
pariah all too obviously and all too vulnerably yearning for acceptance and
recognition. This was the Jewish condition in the postemancipation era:
grateful when they were treated decently, feeling inferior when they were
disdained by those whose respect and recognition they yearned for, swinging
from fawning servility to intervals of self-inflated arrogance and barely disguised aggressiveness, even hostility, in overcompensation for centuries of
long-endured humiliations. What Jews lacked was settled self-esteem.

How far Herzl came to generalize this plight to all Jews can be seen
from another review, of a play by Dumas the Younger, *Femme de Claude*. A
Jewish character in the play wishes to lead the Jews back to Palestine. Herzl
commented that Jews were no longer a nation; once in Palestine they would
only discover that they no longer "belonged together". He went on to describe the modern Jewish condition:

> For centuries they have been rooted in new homelands, become nationals,
> different from one another, preserving a similar character only through the
> oppression that everywhere surrounds them. All subjugated peoples have
> Jewish characteristics, and when the oppression lifts they act like freedmen.
> Who has the historical insight to discern in the presumptuousness of the
> freedman a reproach to the slaveholder? This presumptuousness is indeed
> swiftly put down again.[35]

Similar to freed slaves, Jews were still denied genuine equality. As such, they swung between timidity, feelings of inferiority, and self-disdain and, on the other hand, avid desire for success and recognition; they also showed presumptuousness expressed through ostentatious display, petty vanity, crude arrogance, resentful hostility, all to conjure away the memory of felt humiliations. Still denied status, Jews continued to seek security and power in acquiring money. They continued to meet hostility with timidity and apprehension. Trapped in their old habits, Jews lacked secure self-respect.

Complaints about Jewish presumptuousness were legion in late-nineteenth-century Vienna. A contemporary commentator spoke of Jewish parvenus as "usurping a position to which nothing entitled them but their possessions." Such Jews, he went on, "affronted" Gentiles through "the provocative manner in which they paraded their wealth, as well as through their lack of genuine taste and their arrogant mode of behaviour." Their message to society was that "everything is for sale."[36] Profoundly influenced by Austrian stereotypes of Jews, Herzl too had once seen Jewish parvenus as embodying Jewish materialism. But now his analysis of what moved them was far more sympathetic. They manifested, just more obviously, more nakedly, a Jewish tendency, as insecure recent freedmen still denied status, to yearn servilely for acceptance and to swing between self-disdain and an overcompensating presumptuousness.

With the rise of antisemitism, Herzl abandoned the hope that Jews would become transformed through their assimilation into gentile society. But antisemitism, which had closed off one road to the improvement of the Jews, had opened another. Victimized, rejected, betrayed, dehumanized by the society around them, Jews were thrown back on themselves, only on themselves, for their pride and self-respect. At this stage Herzl believed that Jews could recover their self-esteem through the very means they used to combat antisemitism. Bold self-assertion—negotiating with the pope, socialist radicalism, dueling—would transform Jews, lay antisemitism to rest forever, and command the respect of Gentiles. Jews would then be "reabsorbed" into European society. Though Herzl now spoke of the need for Jewish pride and self-assertion, such categories were not anchored in a conception of Jewishness. Heightened Jewish self-assertion was still tied in somewhat illogical fashion to his long-held goal of full assimilation into gentile society. Herzl was soon to move beyond this position and link Jewish pride to a new conception of Jewishness.

6

The New Ghetto

Jews, my brothers, they will not let you live again, until you learn
how to die.[1]

Herzl's First Conversion Experience

IN OCTOBER 1894, Herzl experienced a sudden illumination that unleashed feverish creativity. In just "three blessed weeks of ardor and labor," he finished a play, *The New Ghetto*. He described the illumination to a friend in spectacular tones: "I was aglow with the blaze of a great eruption. When I left, the whole piece shot up in me like a block of basalt." The revelation had come during a heated conversation with his friend the sculptor Samuel Beer, who was making a bust of Herzl. While walking home, he saw the whole play in his mind's eye. For three weeks this highly charged mood took possession of him. The handwritten first draft of the play ended with the words: "Written while deeply gripped, at one stretch, while laughing and weeping."[2]

Herzl had broken through to a new understanding of the Jewish question. To a friend he called the play "a Jewish sermon" with "redeeming effect." Even more ambitiously, he considered it "a piece of Jewish politics," that "sets the necessary tone to solve the Jewish question and lead Jews out of the ghetto."[3] Herzl had concluded in 1893 that antisemitism foreclosed Jewish improvement and acceptance through assimilation. Rejected by Gentiles, Jews would have to transform themselves, both rid themselves of their faults and find sources of pride and self-respect in themselves. In shedding their faults and becoming more self-assertive, far less dependent on Gentiles, Jews would win—almost command—admiration and acceptance. Only then would they be "reabsorbed" in Europe. But Herzl's initial ideas had foundered on contradictions, as he tried to join Jewish self-assertion to Catholic and socialist assimilation. He was seeking to pry Jews loose from their subordinate and dependent position in the gentile world, so they could rejoin it on more favorable, even equal terms. Distant from—and even averse to—existing modes of Jewishness, Herzl had difficulty giving Jewish substance to his call for pride and self-assertion. But now he had made a breakthrough, for he had discovered in the biblical history of the Jewish kingdoms an alternative model of Jewishness and a countermyth to the history of Jewish materialism and timidity.

A dawning realization of this had come a few months before his illumination when he told his friend Ludwig Speidel: "Our character . . . had in earlier times been proud and magnificent. After all, we once were men who knew how to defend the state in time of war." The Jewish character had been deformed during the dispersion, but this was an accident of history. By peeling off layers of skin, as it were, the original Jewish character would emerge. Herzl had discovered a source of pride in Jewishness, and with this both a new Jewish possibility and a new autonomous mode of assimilation.

Herzl's breakthrough was both a modification and an extension of the program of assimilation. He was turning to an idea central to Dohm's classic case for Jewish emancipation and assimilation: that Jews had deteriorated because they were oppressed, restricted in their occupations, and excluded from participation in the state. Dohm had observed that when Jews possessed a kingdom in biblical times, they had enjoyed a "golden age," displayed physical courage in war, and valued honor and patriotic loyalty. Once brought into full participation in the modern state, Jews would rediscover their original character. Herzl was merely insisting that the terms of such full participation be more equal.[4]

Herzl's discovery of a new Jewish possibility went hand in hand with another realization first intimated by him in analyzing the Jewish inferiority complex as recent freedmen. The second pillar of *The New Ghetto* was Herzl's insight into the psychic price Jews paid by assimilating. Embracing the majority culture, they had internalized its Jewish stereotypes. Assimilation had bred Jewish self-contempt and an idealization of Gentiles, persuaded them that Jewishness carried a taint of materialism and cowardice, and robbed them of self-respect. For this reason, Jews themselves had to alter the terms of gentile acceptance.

The milieu of *The New Ghetto* is the Viennese-Jewish upper middle class. For Herzl in 1894, the Jewish question and its resolution had little to do with pogroms, nor with the poverty-stricken masses of Eastern Europe. Of course it had to do with antisemitism, but the kind that aroused what Felix Salten called the "drawing room anguish" of Viennese Jews, not the kind that culminated in massacres.[5] *The New Ghetto* is about a member of the assimilated Viennese-Jewish middle class overcoming gentile rejection and Jewish self-contempt. Its drama is inward, psychological, centering upon issues of Jewish psychic dependence and self-esteem. The story is Herzl's own, as he worked through the contradictions of his earlier proposals and arrived at a new understanding of Jewishness.

We can even go further and say that telescoped within an evening's drama was the fruit of an inner process stretching over the previous two years. The evidence for this is the thought that triggered his feverish state in Beer's studio in October 1894. Herzl had exclaimed: "It does a Jew no good to become an artist and free himself from the taint of money. The curse still clings. We cannot get out of the Ghetto." It is easy to be baffled by the importance Herzl attributed to this insight, for he had recognized this state of affairs long before. But the personal reference is significant. Herzl himself was the artist who had shed the taint of money to no avail. Nothing had changed on the political scene immediately prior to this insight, no momentous antisemitic incident had occurred. Something had changed, however, inside of Herzl. He wrote Schnitzler that the play "had been stirring within me for a long time and so intensely." He told Teweles that the play was the final fruit of a lengthy process working in his "unconscious." *The New Ghetto* documents Herzl's own Jewish ambivalence and the beginning of its resolution through the creation of a new understanding of Jewishness.[6]

Herzl could not have written *The Jewish State* without first having undergone this inner transformation, but his later conversion to Zionism has served to overshadow *The New Ghetto*. Herzl himself bears some responsibility for this. The play was staged in 1898 in Berlin, Vienna, and Prague. Reviews were mixed. A number were highly laudatory, but the Berlin critics, in his words, "demolished" the play. Deeply stung by criticism, still regarding himself as a potentially great playwright, Herzl now considered the play a closed chapter in his career. In a letter to the Hungarian-Jewish writer Adolf Agai, forgetting the epiphany of 1894, he minimized the play. He insisted that only one thing needed to be said: "This play was the young fruit of *The Jewish State*." Accordingly, Herzl's interpreters viewed the play less in its own right than as a prelude to his Zionism. This it certainly was, but *The New Ghetto* marked a key turning point between Herzl's initial solutions to the Jewish problem and *The Jewish State*, and as such requires a fuller interpretation than it has received so far.[7]

A Summary of the Play

The story of the play can be briefly told. It opens minutes before a lavish wedding reception for Dr. Jacob Samuel, an attorney, and Hermine Hellmann, the daughter of a wealthy textile manufacturer. Jacob's new brother-in-law is Fritz Rheinberg, a stock-market speculator and promoter, married to Charlotte, Hermine's sister. We meet another promoter, Emmanuel Wasserstein, who has lost his fortune on the stock exchange and is reduced to working for Rheinberg.

Two key incidents occur at the wedding reception. Jacob is upset over encountering Count von Schramm, a retired cavalry captain who has business with Rheinberg. He informs his close friend, Franz Wurzlechner, a Gentile, that he once had an argument with von Schramm that culminated in a challenge to a duel. Jacob's father was seriously ill at the time, and Jacob lost heart and called off the affair with an apology to von Schramm's seconds. Several scenes later, the second incident occurs. Franz informs Jacob that he must break off contact with him. Franz plans to go into politics, and now that Jacob is associating with stock-exchange Jews, Franz runs the risk of being labeled a "Jewish stooge."[8] Jacob is stunned by Franz's rejection.

We then learn why von Schramm has come to see Fritz Rheinberg. Von Schramm and his brother-in-law Count Wulkenau share the ownership of a coal mine, whose profits have gone to maintain their profligate life-style. Rheinberg has interested him in a scheme for incorporating the mine. As there is a bull market in coal stocks, von Schramm will make a tidy profit by selling his portion of the shares. Rheinberg, in turn, would have an option to buy one-third of the shares. Rheinberg asks Jacob to draw up the papers for the deal, and Jacob agrees.

Soon after, Jacob is visited by Peter Vednik, who happens to work in the von Schramm mine. Jacob has established a reputation as a workers' advocate, and Vednik has been sent by his fellow miners to enlist Jacob's aid. The workers fear for their lives. The mine is unsafe; no money has been put into maintenance and repairs. Jacob goes to the mine to investigate. Before leaving he returns money he had borrowed from Rheinberg for his wife's wardrobe. In view of conditions at the mine, he now considers the money tainted.

Six weeks pass. A disastrous accident has occurred at the mine, and many miners have been killed. Two weeks after Jacob investigated the workers' complaints, the miners had gone out on strike. They had held out for three weeks, then returned to work. During the weeks of inactivity water had backed up in the mine, causing its already weak foundations to collapse when work was resumed.

The mine disaster has ruined von Schramm. To pay off debts incurred by their improvident ways, Count von Schramm and his brother-in-law had secured a large bank loan, with their mining shares as collateral. After the accident, the mine shares had plummeted. When the stock fell, the bank called in von Schramm's note. He was forced to sell his stock when it was at its nadir and now, in addition, owes money to the bank. By contrast, Wasserstein, Rheinberg's agent, had managed to sell the shares he acquired in the deal just before the collapse, thereby restoring his personal fortunes. Rheinberg however, was in great difficulty. He had sold mine shares short, planning to acquire them when prices leveled off. Suddenly no shares were to be had. He now had to produce the shares or risk being debarred from the stock exchange. Unknown to Rheinberg, Wasserstein had bought up the shares when prices fell. Wasserstein saves Rheinberg's skin by selling him the shares at a modest price.

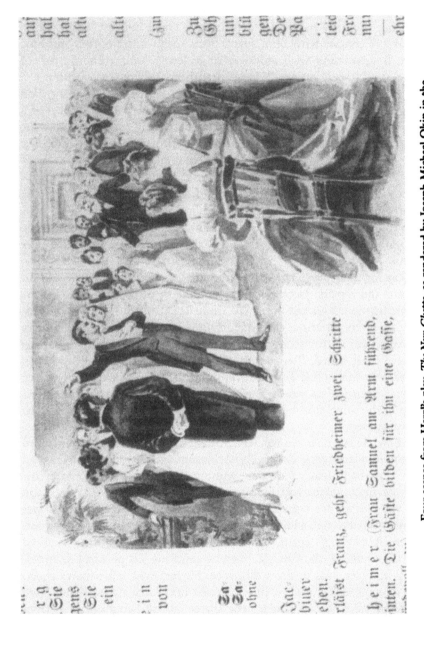

Four scenes from Herzl's play, *The New Ghetto*, as rendered by Joseph Michael Okin in the Zionist weekly *Die Welt*, 1898, nos. 9, 11, and 12. The wedding reception of Jacob Samuel and Hermine Hellmann. Jacob and Rabbi Friedheimer argue about the Jewish condition.

Jacob Samuel and Count von Schramm just prior to von Schramm's challenge to a duel.

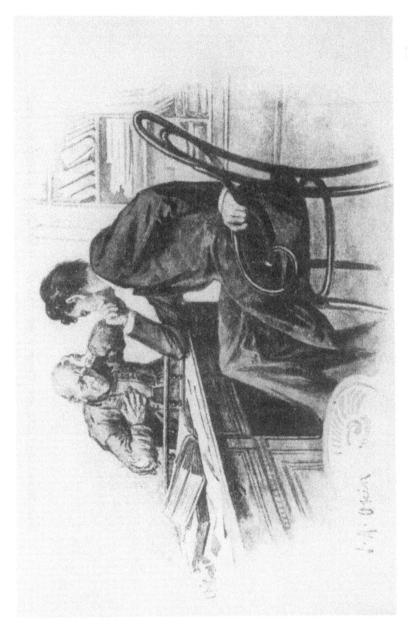

Peter Vednik, a miner, tells Jacob, the workers' advocate, of unsafe conditions in the mine owned by Count von Schramm.

Jacob and Hermine with Jacob's parents. Frau Samuel comforts her son after learning that Jacob's closest friend, a Gentile, has broken off contact with him.

While these events unfold, the ruined von Schramm accuses Jacob of being in cahoots with Rheinberg and of instigating the miners' strike in order to drive down the price of shares. He is sure the Jews have conspired to ruin him. Von Schramm calls Jacob "Jewish rabble"; in a fury he strikes von Schramm in the face. A duel ensues, and Jacob is shot dead by the count.[9]

Herzl's Critique of Assimilation

In *The New Ghetto*, Herzl developed his ideas about the Jew as recent freedman into a full-scale critique of assimilation. Jacob is the archetypal assimilated Jew. But while assimilation into gentile society has eliminated his Jewish faults and improved him, it has also divested him of self-respect and plagued him with Jewish self-contempt and self-recrimination. After he is shattered by gentile rejection, Jacob realizes that he lacks settled self-esteem, and this is the beginning of his transformation.

The other characters in the play are emblematic distasteful Jews; their faults stand out, a product of the Jewish historical experience. Thus Herzl continued to view Jews through the ideology of assimilation, even continued to see Jewish faults as evoking antisemitism. But in addition, he now saw these faults as hindrances to Jewish self-assertion. Moreover, one of the characters, Wasserstein, still close to his East European origins, carries the germs of Jewish redemption. Not only is he acutely aware of the Jewish condition, but he harbors the memory of ancient Jewish greatness.

We saw in earlier chapters that the image of the Jew embraced by Herzl—deteriorated prior to emancipation and assimilation, perfected after— was the common coin of nineteenth-century emancipationist novels. Jacob Samuel, the protagonist in the play, is the typical good Jew described in these novels. He believes that it is up to Jews to remove the "invisible barriers" that separate them from gentile society, to shed Jewish distinctiveness, clannishness, and the base traits acquired through oppression. He has done this through his friendship with the Gentile Franz Wurzlechner. Franz is Jacob's model, for his forbears "have been free citizens for several hundred years," while Jews have been kept in "slavery" so long that they are not yet "inwardly free." Jacob imitates Franz, "speaking his language, thinking his thoughts." From Franz, Jacob declares: "[I learned] both great and small things. Accents, looks, gestures, how to bow without being servile and how to stand erect without swaggering—and more!"[10]

Jacob is noble, lofty, and idealistic, a sign of his distance from the taint of money. He wishes to further progress and justice and to labor in the name of all humanity. He regularly defends socialists in court, waiving his attorney's fees. Though Jacob himself favors capitalism, he is not an uncritical defender of the profit motive and speaks of the need for a new economic morality, one that will limit profits. Jacob also possesses an exacting sense of honor, another indication that he has shed Jewish traits. He frequently declares: "There is something else too [besides money]—Honor!"[11]

Jacob has fulfilled all the prescriptions for assimilation found in proemancipationist novels and favored by Herzl himself throughout the 1880s. Like Bernhard Ehrenthal in Gustav Freytag's *Debit and Credit*, Jacob is a paragon of rectitude, ashamed of the materialism of his coreligionists. He aspires to integrate fully into the gentile milieu and has gained the affection of a gentile friend. Like Miriam and Isaac, in Dahn's *Fight for Rome*, Jacob's association with Gentiles has enobled him.[12] Freytag's purpose had been to contrast the good Jew with the archetypal Jew, whose character was unmodified by contact with the gentile milieu. By contrast, Herzl now wished to point to the ambiguities of assimilation, for while improving Jews, they were now rendered both inwardly and outwardly defenseless in the face of antisemitism.

Jacob measures his humanity by his distance from the ghetto. He is ashamed of being a Jew. He is more at ease with Gentiles than he is with Jews. When the rabbi who officiated at the wedding declares, "we have survived with our ancient virtues intact," Jacob counters, "And our ancient vices." Jacob's mother informs Hermine that she abandoned Yiddish and learned to speak German so Jacob would not be ashamed of her (though she still calls him by the Yiddish diminutive *Kobi*). Even more telling, in the first draft of the play, Herzl has Jacob say that Hermine will add "a new infusion to our blood . . . she looks Christian. I hope our children resemble her." Jacob's ideal of physical beauty is Germanic; Jewish features he considers ugly, outward signs of the stigma of Jewishness. All these attitudes Herzl would once have considered acceptable. Now he was to show how they divested Jacob of his self-respect. Jacob seems more and more like a recent freedman than an exemplary Jew. Grateful to have a Gentile accept him as a friend, he displays the same servility to Gentiles that Herzl saw in Baron Horn, only on a more lofty level.[13]

A turning point in the play comes with Franz's announcement to Jacob, sudden and devastating, that he wishes to make a clean break of their relationship. Franz's decision shatters Jacob. "They cast me out, they want nothing to do with me!" he exclaims. "He was the best of the lot, and look what he did to me! Oh, one could laugh—or weep. Get away from me, Jew! Back to the ghetto!" Franz's rejection is a blow time will not soften or dim: "Sometimes when one suffers a blow, one knows one will get over it. But this wound will never heal."[14]

But though the sting of rejection brings pain, it also leads Jacob to the hard-won insight that assimilation has made Jews incapable of an autonomous act of self-definition and self-affirmation. Instead, Jews measured their standing in spoonfuls of gentile acceptance; they depended on others for a confirmation of their worth. Accordingly, Jacob's mother declares when he tells her of Franz's betrayal: "If you haven't been true to yourself, my boy, you can't complain when others are faithless." To which Jacob replies: "You're right, Mother, right, as always."[15]

After his rejection by Franz, Jacob comes to realize that the desire to model himself on his friend stemmed from feelings of servility and inferiority: "It was quite flattering—there's a bit of the Ghetto left in all of us. We're grateful when we're treated like human beings. I tried to show my gratitude by modelling myself after him."[16] Jacob now sees his behavior as no different from the parvenu's ostentation and social toadying, just more subtle and veiled.

Herzl's critique of Jewish assimilation expressed through Jacob's self-insight turns equally on a second event, the story of his withdrawal from a duel. Jacob is shaken when he sees von Schramm come to pay a call on Rheinberg, for he had encountered him once before. Several years prior, a quarrel in a cafe over a newspaper had led von Schramm to challenge Jacob to a duel. Jacob's father was ill at the time, and when he returned home his father was worse, seemingly near death. Jacob had no heart for the duel and apologized the next day. Since then, he has suffered endless torments, considering himself a coward. Von Schramm, Jacob laments, "has the right to hold me in contempt!"[17] It is clear that Jacob is no coward; on the contrary he is brash, even impertinent in his initial encounter with von Schramm, courageous in defense of the downtrodden, foolhardy in slapping von Schramm later on in the play. However, Herzl now believed that assimilation made it impossible for Jews to drain the cup of self-contempt. Holding a negative view of Jewish traits and an idealized image of gentile traits, Jews started out with a presumption of their own inferiority. Hence serene self-confidence was forever unattainable; self-doubt and inner recriminations were ever present.

Jacob is aware that all Jewish actions are suspect. Jews had to be doubly honest just to earn the distinction of being patronizingly considered exceptional, not like other Jews. Jews, too, measured each other's behavior by the same yardstick, aware that what each Jew did reflected on them all. Jacob exclaims: "We're not even permitted to have everyday human foibles."[18]

Racked by the fear that his Jewishness has tainted him permanently, Jacob transforms the virtues attributed to his Jewishness to faults. He explains to Franz: "I haven't been able to forget it [the duel]. Not I—you see, I'm a Jew! You and your kind can take that thing in stride. When you, Franz Wurzlechner, settle such a run-in peaceably, that makes you a solid, clear-headed chap. Me—me, Jacob Samuel—it makes me a coward!" Jacob had interpreted his filial love and devotion, which prevented him from dueling and which was admired by Wurzlechner, as an act of Jewish cowardice. Herzl was clearly underlining Jacob's tendency to turn Jewish virtues into defects, since in the play Herzl had emphasized that intense mutual devotion in Jewish family-life was a particular Jewish virtue.[19]

It is noteworthy that by the 1890s Herzl was not alone in pointing to the inner costs of assimilation; the problem had become a major theme in some widely read Jewish novels. One such novel was Ludwig Jacobowski's *Werther the Jew*, published in Germany in 1892. Jacobowski, like Herzl, was fully assimilated, a fervent, patriotic German, and a tireless and militant opponent of antisemitism, serving on the board of the German Defense Association against Antisemitism. Leo Wolff, the novel's protagonist, is a university student and a member of a German nationalist student fraternity. His Germanic outlook has made him virtuous, but also ashamed of Jewish faults. As Georg Brandes, the famous literary critic, described Leo: "He loathed the defects and vices of his own breed; he wished to be, in Goethe's words, 'noble, benevolent and good' "[20] Leo seeks out the company of Gentiles and avoids Jews.

Leo's family are all archetypal Jews untouched by gentile influences. His boorish cousin Siegmund Königsberger, a newcomer from a Polish *shtetl*, is a reincarnation of Veitel Itzig from *Debit and Credit*. Persecuted in his youth, Siegmund, a master at calculated obsequiousness, retaliates by taking commercial advantage of the *"Goy."* Leo's father, a banker, is no better. His profitable stock-market speculations in league with Siegmund, lead to the ruin of Leo's gentile friends. Leo feels disgraced and pleads with his father to make good their losses; his father refuses. Leo's self-torment causes him to become ill and take to his bed. His gentile sweetheart, pregnant, believes herself abandoned by him and commits suicide. An antisemitic newspaper reports her death, charging that she was seduced and abandoned by a Jew whose father had swindled gentile stockholders. Leo is expelled from his fraternity for dishonorable behavior. He then kills himself, dying in the arms of a gentile friend. (Jacob Samuel will also die in the arms of a gentile friend.)

In highlighting Jewish defects, and in contrasting the ideal fully assimilated Jew to the archetypal Jew, Jacobowski's novel repeated and upheld the theme of earlier emancipationist literature. But in addition, a major theme in the novel was the ambiguity of assimilation in a period of rising antisemitism. Leo is a tormented personality, for assimilation has plagued him with Jewish self-hate. He lives by a double standard, idealizing Gentiles while being harsh toward Jews, wildly exaggerating their faults. He knows that he harbors a hatred toward Jews indistinguishable from that of the most vicious antisemite. This is a source of torment to him because antisemitism has awakened his Jewish loyalties and his identification with the history of Jewish victimization, as well as warm memories of his Jewish childhood. He considers it an act of cowardliness to abandon his people in their moment of need. As a result, self-reproach has brought him to the verge of psychic collapse.

Another novel dealing with the psychic costs of assimilation was Adolf Dessauer's *Big City Jews*, set in Vienna. Dessauer's assimilated Jews see Jewish traits as tainted by definition; they idealize gentile virtues. One character comments on this syndrome: "They [the younger generation of Jews] consider even virtues to be defects, simply because they are our virtues." Dessauer's assimilated Jews are eaten up by self-contempt. Leopold Kastner (né Kohn) hates "Jewish emotional excessiveness" and is flattered when accused of being "hard and unfeeling," traits he associates with "Aryan spit and polish." Like Jacob Samuel, he is devastated when his father's illness overwhelms him with worry, for he sees this state not as a sign of filial love, but of the free-floating anxiety bred in a weak and persecuted minority. By the same token, Leopold considers "everything intelligent, diligent or keen on business in him," a Jewish defect. A bank clerk, "he became downright angry with himself when he understood a complicated piece of business better than some of his [gentile] colleagues." Clearly Herzl's play was part of a larger trend, as antisemitism spurred assimilated Jews to reexamine their assumptions.[21]

If Herzl was articulating a critique of assimilationism, he still believed that the Jewish character needed to be transformed, both because it evoked antisemitism and because it paralyzed Jewish self-assertion. This part of his message is embodied in the characters of Fritz Rheinberg, Hermine Samuel, Rabbi Friedheimer, and Emmanuel Wasserstein.

Fritz Rheinberg was the archetypal Jew. As hostages of power, profit had become the sole means of Jewish survival. Excluded from the enjoyment of honor and status, only money gave Jews a semblance of security and a taste of power. Insecure, and hounded from place to place, caution and guile became their only weapons against the hostile outside world. Rheinberg was the living embodiment of this historical ordeal.

The New Ghetto thus marked no break from Herzl's stereotyped view of Jewry; indeed, its message of Jewish transformation presupposed these stereotypes. Indeed, shortly after completing the play, he attended services in the main synagogue for the first time since his arrival in Paris three years before. "I took a look at the Paris Jews," he commented, "and saw a family likeness in their faces: bold misshapen noses; furtive and cunning eyes."[22] Not courage, but deviousness and avarice were etched on the Jewish physiognomy.

Rheinberg is cynical; appeals to rectitude evoke his sneers. "Earn and let earn" is his motto.[23] He is peeved that his agent Wasserstein abruptly left the wedding service at the temple, for he wished to instruct him during prayer on what to buy and sell for him on the stock exchange. There is nothing sacred for Rheinberg; he reveres only money. In Rheinberg's drawing room, a valuable painting is conspicuously displayed on an easel. Art is just another commodity for him. When the mining disaster occurs, he feels no responsibility, even though a speed-up in production, ordered to drive up the price of the mine shares, helped bring about the disaster. Herzl endowed Rheinberg with other features of the Jewish stereotype, familiar to us from his discussion of Baron Horn. Rheinberg swings between arrogance and obsequiousness. He is abjectly proud that von Schramm deigns to be seen with him, but arrogant and abusive to Wasserstein, when the latter's fortunes are in eclipse. When Wasserstein scores a sudden coup, and Rheinberg now in financial difficulties needs him, he is all flattery and groveling humility. He sends his sister-in-law Hermine to Wasserstein, knowing Wasserstein was once her suitor, to plead on his behalf for mercy. In short, he crawls. When von Schramm comes to confront him about his financial loss, Rheinberg, a miserable coward, flees.

Rheinberg's female counterpart is Jacob's wife, Hermine, a spoiled Jewish "princess," preoccupied with the vanities of her wardrobe. Hermine had been "brought up to marry millionaires." Affectedly, she addresses Jacob with the French, "Jacques." She coaxes him into putting aside his feelings of honor in order to solicit a loan from Rheinberg for her wardrobe. Her character too is a result of oppression, and ghetto confinement. Her craving for honor and status has become diverted into vanity and ostentation. Hermine is like a famished person at a banquet, avid and insatiable. As Herzl wrote to Schnitzler: She was necessary to the play "as an illustration of what was repressed in the ghetto."[24]

Rabbi Friedheimer, who had performed the wedding ceremony, is no different from Rheinberg or Hermine. Herzl was demonstrating how deeply Jewish deformations penetrated Judaism itself. Overhearing him discuss the stock market with Rheinberg, Jacob and Franz are astounded that the rabbi plays the stock exchange. The impression is not softened by the rabbi's self-satisfied explanation that the returns from what might well be unethical stock promotion went to aid Russian Jews in distress.[25]

Devoid of spirituality, Rabbi Friedheimer is the unctuous cleric and the embodiment of Jewish passivity and fatalism. The rabbi responds to Jacob's pained indignation at the mine disaster with soothing banalities: "My son, no one suffers more than he can bear. God in his wisdom has so ordained it. Whoever goes barefoot grows callouses on his soles." Even rising anti-semitism merely evokes trust in the Divine: "Our God always delivers us from bondage."[26] Passivity has been given a Divine cachet. Accordingly, Rabbi Friedheimer disapproves of Jacob's intervention on the side of the miners and his resolve to confront von Schramm. The Rabbi wants Rheinberg to make good von Schramm's loss, not because he believes Rheinberg swindled the count, but to ward off any possibility of the case being exploited by antisemites. The way to deal with antisemitism, it seems, is for Jews to be doubly honest.

But there is another reason why Rabbi Friedheimer opposes Jacob's social activism. He scolds Jacob: "By what right do you meddle in the affairs of the miners?" He considers Jews too weak and vulnerable to participate in the universal struggle for freedom and justice. Persecution had limited Jewish concerns to their own kind. "Be glad they're leaving you alone!" he tells Jacob. The rabbi proceeds to recount a story to Jacob, recorded in a Hebrew chronicle of the Middle Ages, of an incident in fifteenth-century Mainz at the time of the expulsion of the Jews from the Rhineland. The story concerns one Moses ben Abraham, a noble and high-minded scholar. Late one night while at his studies, he heard "cries for succour" coming from outside the ghetto. They "grew more and more desperate." Moses felt impelled to respond. His mother asked him where he was going so late. "Mother, I hear someone cry for help," he said, and vanished. Hours later he had not returned. His mother was frantic and ran out of the ghetto to search for him. The next morning he was found, stabbed to death "just outside the open gate of the ghetto." His mother was by his side, gone insane from grief. The rabbi's message was crystal clear. Jews "meddled" in wider human concerns at their peril.[27]

Herzl's portrait of Rabbi Friedheimer seems a product of his assimilationist assumptions about Judaism and the Jewish character. The Viennese reality was different. The first two chief rabbis in Vienna, Isaak Noah Mannheimer and Adolf Jellinek, were strong advocates of liberal universalism. Mannheimer sat in the constituent assembly of 1848. A recent work calls him "among the first modern Jewish religious leaders to speak out openly for social justice." Jellinek's successor, Moriz Güdemann, was an early supporter of the militant Joseph Bloch and the work of the Austrian-Israelite Union. Appeals in the *Oesterreichische Wochenschrift* during the 1890s for intensified Jewish militancy in combating antisemitism often originated with rabbis.[28]

Of all the characters in the play, Emmanuel Wasserstein, the stock-exchange speculator and promoter, was Herzl's only endearing creation. Wasserstein has all the vices of the archetypal Jew. He is the most abject character in the play, but at the same time shows signs of latent nobility. Wasserstein carries memories of an ancient time before the dispersion, when Jews had been "proud and magnificent."[29]

Wasserstein was drawn, in part, from a stock character in nineteenth-century German literature, the good-natured, sympathetic Jew. He is, in some ways, similar to *Schmock* in Gustav Freytag's 1853 comedy, *The Journalists*. Schmock is a hack journalist, seeking a modest niche in the world. He is opportunistic and unprincipled, disloyal when it suits him, and plays the toady when necessary. What redeems him is his naiveté, simplicity, and tenderheartedness. He too possesses the stigma of Jewish traits, but he is also portrayed as a victim of centuries of persecution, more an object of sympathy because of his basic humanity than an object of scorn. Charlene Lea, in her study of Jewish characters in the nineteenth-century German and Austrian drama, discusses a number of such creations found in the *Posse*, a genre akin to the English farce. In these farces, authors often toyed with paradoxes; in several, Jews are victimized by Gentiles, far surpassing them in guile and deception. Though these Jews remained stereotypes, they elicited sympathy.[30]

Like most of the Jewish characters in the play, Wasserstein's life turns around money. He cannot look at an object of art without estimating how much it would fetch. He participates in Rheinberg's stock-promotion scheme and is equally unscrupulous in the pursuit of gain. At the nadir of his fortunes at the start of the play, he is obsequious when Rheinberg abuses him.

What marks Wasserstein as different from Rheinberg or Hermine is that he lacks their veneer of Germanic gentility. Unpolished, bereft of social graces, a *Fresser* or glutton, his awkward German comically inverted and sprinkled with Yiddishisms, Wasserstein still bears the stamp of the East European ghetto. He is endearing in his lack of pretense, his painful insecurity, and his self-effacing manner. The world holds him in contempt and so he holds himself. As he explains: "If people hadn't always wiped their boots on me—perhaps I would have been a different man. . . . I have to buy everything—for money. I have to pay for friendship, love. I even have to pay to have people treat me decently, as though I was always in a restaurant." Wasserstein knows that money can buy him at most polite condescension. To borrow a Marxian term, he lacks the "false consciousness" of Rheinberg or Hermine who believe assimilation and wealth will bring them status and acceptance. Finally, he can rise above considerations of profit. Having made a fortune on the stock exchange, he magnanimously saves Rheinberg from ruin.[31]

In the character of Wasserstein, Herzl portrayed the archetypal Jew, possessed of all the defects brought about by oppression. Close to his ghetto origins, less entangled in the delusions of assimilationism, possessed of sparks of nobility, by the end of the play Wasserstein—along with Jacob—breaks through to a new mode of Jewishness. Herzl had finally abandoned his old equation: Jews would not need to convert to Christianity or become socialists to be assimilated. The seeds of Jewish transformation existed in the Jewish character itself.

The New Jew

The turning point in the play is Jacob Samuel's transformation after recoiling from Franz Wurzlechner's rejection. His transformation issues in a duel with von Schramm on behalf of Jewish honor, a declaration of solidarity with Wasserstein, and a call for reconciliation with the Gentile Wurzlechner. We shall take these up in order.

After his financial ruin, von Schramm returns for a showdown with Rheinberg. Rheinberg flees, and it is Jacob who confronts him. Jacob no longer feels as he did before, that Rheinberg must compensate von Schramm for his loss, to raise his opinion of Jews. Instead, he upbraids him for having neglected the mine, leading to the death of the miners. Von Schramm is incensed at Jacob's Jewish insolence, preaching to a cavalry officer and member of the gentry about financial scruples. He accuses Jacob of having fomented the miners' strike to assure his brother-in-law a quick profit, and ruin him, then sneers at Jacob: "Jewish rabble!" When Jacob demands he take back his words, von Schramm refers to their first encounter: "If I don't—you'll soon grovel as you did that other time." At this Jacob blanches, and strikes von Schramm in the face. A duel ensues with pistols, and von Schramm fatally shoots Jacob. With his last breath Jacob utters a message to his fellow Jews: "Jews, my brothers—they will not let you live again, until you learn how to die. . . . I want to get out! Out of-the-ghetto!"[32]

Jacob has realized that seeking acceptance from Gentiles only exacerbated Jewish self-contempt. Jews would have to gain self-respect by their own efforts: "The visible walls had to be destroyed from the outside—but we must pull down the invisible barriers ourselves. We ourselves! Out, we must break out!" Jews had been deformed by history, but they possessed within themselves the capacity for self-transformation. "Morality begins only later, with self-awareness! By overcoming instinct." All the virtues Jacob had aspired to, that once marked his distance from Jewishness—pride, honor, rectitude, courage, manliness—were now to be redefined as a Jewish possibility. Jewishness itself was to be recast into something noble and good. Wasserstein calls Jacob, "another kind of Jew." Jacob reminds him of the Maccabees.[33]

We have seen that in Austria dueling was a corporate act, meant to uphold the status and honor of the group as well as of its individual members. Thus, Jacob's duel with von Schramm was fought on behalf of Jewish honor, not just his own. His last words to Jews was that they did not know how to die. They had to learn how to die, both to rid themselves of minority habits of fearful apprehension and to learn to count something higher than survival and personal advantage. In seeking a moral reformation of the Jews, Herzl was moving into uncharted territory. His new ideal, emphasizing courage, honor, forthrightness, was derived from the Prussian virtues he had admired in *Albia* and the aristocracy he had idealized in his youthful novel *Hagenau*. Both models were absorbed into the conception of a Maccabean revival, a myth of former Jewish greatness.

Jacob's next act is his declaration of solidarity with Wasserstein, made to Franz Wurzlechner in response to his betrayal: "Even if you pressed me now to choose between you and Wasserstein, I would choose him. I belong with Wasserstein, through thick and thin."[34] Of all the Jewish characters in the play, it is with Wasserstein, bearing the traces of his Galician origins, that Jacob chooses to identify. Wasserstein was the Jew speaking clumsy German with a Yiddish accent, a stock comic character on the German stage. Indeed, in Sander Gilman's words, a Yiddish accent was "the hallmark of the comic Jews." Not only was the accent believed to express the base and exotic mentality of Jews, but it showed up the impossibility of genuine assimilation, its superficial, surface-like quality. Accordingly, in one play seemingly cultivated German Jews inadvertently lapse into frenetic Yiddish when excited or upset. Jews such as Wasserstein reminded assimilated Jews of their own lowly origins and accentuated the vast, perhaps insurmountable, distance between Jews and Gentiles. Steven Aschheim has described German-Jewish views of Yiddish: "The *Jargon* [Yiddish. Often used pejoratively] seemed to embody all the negative Jewish qualities of the past. Its association with coarse Jewish behaviour made it the very antithesis of *Bildung* [culture]. More and more the traditional ghetto Jew—the language he spoke, the habits he retained— became synonymous with *Unbildung*, counter-example of what the new German Jew had to become." As we saw, Herzl had once kept his distance from Jews such as Wasserstein. Now for the first time he insisted that distancing and ambivalence had to be overcome, making way for solidarity with all Jews.[35]

Herzl underlined Wasserstein's noble side, his admiration for Jacob's defense of the workers and his devotion to honor. "Yes, I buy and I sell— everything revolves around money. But there is something else too—honour!" His greatest enthusiasm is reserved for Jacob's blow to von Schramm, as if the deed had relieved him of a lifetime of bottled-up resentment toward his persecutors. His speech to Hermine in the first draft of the play, toned down in the published version, is a kind of epiphany. "No Frau Doctor—you do not know how much that thrilled me. A Jew striking back hard, that is great, that is beautiful. He reminded me of the Maccabees. We weren't always such dish-rags. Sometimes I think that I too once lived to see this, in past history, but I don't know when it was. It must have been a long time ago. Or when one dreams of something—yes, that's what it was. I've dreamed that we too are men who don't allow themselves to be stepped on." Wasserstein concluded: "I cannot fly, and he cannot crawl. . . . God, if I could say what he did to the antisemites!"[36]

Though Wasserstein harbors the memory of former Jewish greatness, history has made of him, he readily admits, "an uncouth, ignoble Jew." The writer and early Zionist colleague of Herzl's, Max Nordau, was to capture the essence of Wasserstein. He wrote to Herzl: "I must give you great credit for interweaving compassionate humor in the base, degraded Jewish usurer Wasserstein, whose character has been pulverized by a two-thousand year old Jewish fate, but who lets us see, under all the dust, the original and abiding nobility of our race." Disdain was still there in Herzl's portrait of Wasserstein, but now it was overshadowed by identification and sympathy.[37]

Our final theme is Jacob's wish for the restoration of harmony with the gentile world. Dying, Jacob calls for his gentile friend Franz and almost with his last breath, tells him he seeks "reconciliation." He then caresses Franz's hand.[38] Jacob has realized that seeking gentile acceptance will not gain self-respect for Jews, quite the contrary, it breeds contempt. Jews were to abandon the supplicant's quest to be counted by Gentiles as compatriots, to be confirmed by others. The relationship between Jews and Gentiles was to be placed on a new footing. Jews were to achieve respect on their own, but in so doing, they would gain the respect of others. Asserting Jewish pride was evidently done with one eye on Gentiles, to win their respect. In this sense Jacob, like Herzl, still appraised himself in the mirror of gentile society. Jews still sought gentile confirmation, though their manner of seeking it was now far more dignified than before.

The New Ghetto as Autobiography

I have argued in a previous chapter that Wurzlechner's rejection of Jacob, his long-time and intimate friend, stood for the betrayal of Vienna's assimilated Jewry by their Liberal and German nationalist allies, indeed for all the broken promises of assimilation. Not dyed-in-the-wool antisemitism in the person of von Schramm, but Wurzlechner's betrayal transforms Jacob. Herzl was responding to the shattered promise of assimilation. Some parts of the play are more deeply personal, but no less a reflection of Herzl's vision of the Viennese-Jewish experience. Herzl had come to see his personal history as a paradigm of the Jewish experience.

Herzl put his struggle with his own Jewish ambivalence into *The New Ghetto*. His exhilaration when conceiving the play came from a feeling of hard-won liberation from inner pretense, from being untrue to oneself, aping others, as he now judged assimilation. Herzl experienced an inner breakthrough from Jewish self-effacement to pride, solidarity, and self-affirmation. One might ask, pride in what? Only later would Herzl find a conduit for Jewish autonomy and achievement in the idea of a Jewish state. His play articulated as yet no political program, only his personal breakthrough.

Felix Salten remarked about *The New Ghetto* that its author was constantly "pushing his figures aside in order to speak himself." The play was full of set speeches through which Herzl "forcefully vented his rage, humiliation and indignation."[39] Salten's shrewd observation does not go far enough. Even characters and incidents in the play were taken from Herzl's life.

Jacob Samuel, with his handsome bearing, resembled Herzl. Herzl's exceptionally self-possessed and gracious demeanor has been described by a Zionist associate Erwin Rosenberger: "He always held his well-proportioned body erect, yet relaxed. His movements were controlled; he was not given to

exaggerated gestures." Jacob acquired his dignified bearing by mimicking his
gentile friend. We can assume that Herzl was acknowledging his own mimicry of gentile manners, perhaps going back to his fraternity mentor Franz
Staerk. Yet Herzl also saw himself as bearing a permanent physical mark of
his Jewishness. The gentile servants mock Jacob's Jewish nose. Surprisingly,
Herzl believed he had a "Jewish nose," claiming this as the reason he had
endured antisemitic insults in the summer of 1894. Descriptions of him by
others do not indicate so. Erwin Rosenberger mentioned this disparity of
perceptions, describing Herzl's nose as "well-formed, slightly curved and
fairly prominent, but not 'fleshy' . . . not a 'Jewish nose,' " as Herzl himself
believed.[40]

Perhaps the most important trait common to Jacob and Herzl was pride.
In the first draft of the play Jacob's mother describes this trait as "a great
failing, which is also his greatest virtue . . . an unnatural pride."[41] Pride is a
key element in the play, evident in Jacob's exacting sense of honor and me-
ticulously upright behavior, his wounded pride at Franz's rejection, and the
shameful memory of his withdrawal from the duel. For Herzl, questions of
pride and honor were fundamental to the Jewish problem and to its resolution. In part, these issues were so central because of his own unusually sensitive pride, expressed in the demand to be treated with all due dignity, even
in a characteristic conceit and arrogance, but also in a tendency to easily
succumb to the opposite, a crushing sense of shame and humiliation.

Those who knew Herzl during his early years in Vienna, Heinrich Kana,
Arthur Schnitzler, and Hermann Bahr, drew attention to these traits. Heinrich Kana, a frank and sympathetic confidante, captured Herzl's mood swings
graphically in a letter. We do not have Herzl's letter to Kana, to which his
friend was responding, but it appears to have been a moody declaration of
wounded narcissism. Herzl was downcast because he had given one of his
plays to some people to read, and they were yet not furthering its production
on the stage. Kana chided his friend: "The young man becomes embittered
. . . he sees shit! shit! shit! everywhere, and he feels disgust. Foolish or hyperegoistic! Not foolish, because he's written a basically clever play. Thus
hyperegoistic. The world contains 1,300 million people—1,300 million central
points in the world. And a single small 1/1,300 millionth demands that all
others cease functioning."[42]

Arthur Schnitzler and Hermann Bahr have described the sense of superiority Herzl projected to others. Schnitzler recounted how he once felt put
down by Herzl's "ironic smile." In another incident, Herzl shattered him:
"With a composed, superior look you inspected my tie—and—crushed me.
Do you know what you said—? 'And I took you for a—Beau Brummel!!!' "
Herman Bahr, later a leading Austrian writer, was a fellow member of *Albia*
and recorded his impression of the young Herzl: "It was not only by his

appearance that he dominated his fellow students—his gallant nature, his ironic superior spirit, his easy masterfulness were irresistible." Bahr would hardly have guessed that around the same time Herzl was suffering paroxysms of despair over his future as a writer. In his diary he recorded "the peculiar feeling of impotence, the humiliating consciousness of being incapable! Eunuch, away!—And so dreams of success and happiness gradually scatter."[43]

If pride and self-disdain were especially salient emotions for Herzl, if he swung uneasily between the two, he was also highly vulnerable on the issue of physical cowardice. The story of the canceled duel with von Schramm, described with such anguish by Jacob, matches in every detail Herzl's withdrawal from the duel in 1885, described in chapter 3. Herzl simply reproduced his own story in the play: his own sick father, his mother insisting he take a break from his bedside vigil, the quarrel at a table with a gentile stranger, the exchange of cards, and the challenge to a duel. In both cases, distraction over a father's illness made dueling out of the question, an apology was made, the duel was called off, and what followed was self-flagellation over the issue of physical courage. Herzl, too, did not feel he had made a free choice between the demands of Jewish filial devotion and the dueling code of honor, shadowed as he was by the conviction of an innate Jewish cowardice.

Herzl's concern with Jewish inhibitions in combating antisemitism stemmed, in part, from self-doubts over the issue of physical courage. These doubts may have been exacerbated by his reaction to two antisemitic incidents. The first incident occurred when Herzl was passing though Mainz in 1888, returning from a trip to England. When antisemitic taunts were flung at him, Herzl did not respond. He was just leaving "a cheap nightclub" when someone shouted "Hep hep" after him. The patrons erupted in "a chorus of horse-laughs." Herzl swallowed his feelings and silently continued on his way. The second occurred in the summer of 1894; he was in a carriage passing through Baden just outside Vienna, returning from Speidel's summer home. Coincidentally, he had just discussed his evolving thoughts on antisemitism with his journalist colleague. Someone called out to him, "saujud" ["sow-Jew"]. This insult affected him more deeply than the first, for he was now on his Viennese "home soil." Again he silently proceeded on his way. Herzl's personal conflicts coincided remarkably with wider Jewish dilemmas. In dealing with the Jewish plight, Herzl also sought to resolve these personal issues.[44]

The portrait of Hermine, Jacob's wife, is further evidence that Herzl wrote himself into the play. Hermine resembled Herzl's own wife Julie, or rather Herzl's embittered appraisal of her. Schnitzler had considered Hermine

a caricature and the marriage between her and Jacob an implausible mis-
match.[45] Consequently, Herzl toned down his portrait of Hermine in the
final version of the play. Hermine, in the first draft, is selfish, spoiled, and
distant, even icy to Jacob's parents. She and Jacob bicker from the start, for
he cannot keep her in the latest Paris fashions, which she craves and expects.
Hermine is uncomprehending of Jacob's dedication to humanity, for it is all
time and energy diverted from her needs.

Like Hermine Hellmann, Julie Naschauer's family was very rich. Her father was a millionaire, with holdings in oil fields, factories, and Danube river
shipping. From the start of her marriage to Herzl in 1889, major differences
surfaced. Just like Hermine, Herzl's wife was accustomed to an extravagant
lifestyle and jealous of the time her husband devoted to his work. Less than
a year after their marriage, Herzl asked his wife for a divorce, which she
refused. Herzl could have sued for divorce but did not want to expose the
family to legal proceedings. The following years were marked by extended
periods apart, reconciliations for the sake of their children, and renewed efforts by Herzl to persuade his wife to agree to a divorce. In April 1892,
Herzl's wife and children joined him in Paris—three children had been born
by then—and a joint household was established, which included Herzl's parents. In accord with his wife's lavish tastes, they lived in a fashionable district
and maintained four servants. All this was beyond Herzl's means, and they
drew on his wife's dowry. Herzl's wife had not wanted Herzl's parents to
move in, but gave in to his insistence. (In the play, Jacob makes the very
same request of Hermine). Tensions between Herzl and his wife came to a
head once more in the fall of 1894, just when he was writing The New Ghetto.
In November 1894, around the time he completed the play, Herzl's wife took
their children back to Vienna and moved in with her parents.[46]

The portrayal of Hermine was a caricature, skewed by Herzl's own bitterness over his marriage. Herzl played his part in the failed marriage. Elon
describes him as totally self-absorbed, preoccupied with work day and night,
and an inadequate husband who had never separated emotionally from his
parents. Most accounts describe Herzl's mother as possessive and imperious,
interfering in the lives of those around her. Herzl, of course, portrays Jacob
as saintly, his mother as warm, doting, and self-effacing. The play records
and reflects not reality, but Herzl's perception of reality. As such, the play
served as an emotional catharsis, a conduit and release for his feelings toward
his wife.

In Herzl's depiction—or caricature—of the Jewish "princess" Hermine,
and by extension his wife, Jewish issues were not far from his mind. Hermine
was the female counterpart of Rheinberg. Extravagance was the female version of the Jewish male's tireless quest for financial gain. Herzl had come to

view Jewish faults sympathetically, as the outcome of historical circumstances. His depiction of Hermine was far more hostile than understanding
or sympathetic.

This hostility remained unabated even after Herzl became a Zionist
statesman. In his utopian novel *Old-New Land*, he was to depict a circle of
Viennese-Jewish parvenus who move to the new Jewish commonwealth but
still cling to their old habits. The women were decked out in "ostrich feather
hats . . . gaudy silk dresses," "bejewelled and overdressed." Herzl underlined
their superficiality and their fundamental coarseness beneath the veneer of
fashion. In an early scene still in Vienna, at a social gathering heatedly discussing anti-Jewish riots in Moravia, one woman interrupts her husband by
screaming over the conversation: "Moriz! You must take me to the Bürg
Theatre the day after tomorrow!"[47] Herzl's portrayal of Hermine carried over
into his depiction of the wives of Jewish parvenus in *Old-New Land*. In both
cases historical empathy gave way to intense hostility.

It cannot be said that Herzl simply wanted the Hermines of this world
to have more genuine pride, settled self-esteem, and be more altruistic. The
likeness between Hermine and his wife Julie suggests that Herzl's Jewish self-
contempt extended to his own spouse. Herzl's distaste for Jews as they were
shadowed his personal life and helped motivate his vision of Jewish self-transcendence.

The Immediate Aftermath of *The New Ghetto*: Jewish Objections

Herzl completed *The New Ghetto* on 8 November 1894 and immediately
wrote to Arthur Schnitzler, by then a noted playwright, seeking his help in
getting the play on the stage. But Herzl's request was ambiguous: "Along
with the passionate desire to communicate my work to the world, I have a
far more passionate desire to hide and to bury myself. It may be pride, cowardice or shame, or whatever you wish." He was finding it difficult to publicly proclaim his adherence to the Jewish cause: "In the special instance of
this play, I want to hide my genitals even more than any other time."[48]
Showing his circumcised penis, as it were, still evoked shame and feelings of
vulnerability.

Herzl implored Schnitzler to aid him in a strategem. Schnitzler was to
choose an intermediary, a lawyer who would circulate the play to theater
companies on behalf of its author, to be called Albert Schnabel. Only
Schnitzler would know who the real author was; the lawyer would pass on
all correspondence to him, and he would communicate with Herzl. One can
only speculate on why Herzl chose the name Schnabel, the word for a bird's
beak, and a colloquialism for mouth, equivalent to "trap." Paranoid projec-
tions showed in the details of Herzl's scheme, evidence of his anxiety. Herzl

asked Schnitzler to have the play typed in Vienna. He would mail the revisions, in installments, from Paris. He feared discovery if the play was typed
in Paris. Herzl pleaded with Schnitzler not to leave the typed copy at the
bindery too long, fearing that the binder would read the play and reveal its
contents.[49]

By April 1895, Herzl's play had been rejected by two theaters in Berlin
and one in Vienna. From the start, and more insistently each time it was
rejected, Schnitzler advised Herzl that the play's chances of acceptance would
be enhanced if Herzl were known to be its author. There was no reason not
to trade on his name, for he was recognized as a master of the *feuilleton*,
while two of his comedies, *Der Flüchtling* and *Tabarin*, were in the repertory
of Vienna's Burgtheater. Plays required more than sheer merit to be accepted,
Schnitzler argued. Theater managers shied away from anything risky. Moreover, Herzl was sabotaging the play's acceptance by insisting on a speedy
production. Herzl's response was lame. If he were known to be the author,
people would conclude the play was accepted to gain the favor of the *Neue
Freie Presse*. When he sent the play in May 1895 to his friend Heinrich
Teweles, director of the Deutsches Landestheater in Prague, he still insisted
his name not be revealed, though his letter to Teweles was not as anxiety-
ridden as his earlier letters to Schnitzler. In May 1895, Herzl conceived the
idea of the Jewish state; after that his energies were no longer concentrated
on the play. He next communicated with Teweles in November, proposing
revisions to the play. Now he was ready to attach his name to it; he had long
since burned his bridges. He had had the famous interview with Baron
Hirsch and had spoken before the Maccabean Club in London about his idea
of a Jewish state.[50]

How did Herzl's contemporaries respond to the play? In addition to
Schnitzler's appraisal, we possess a wide range of responses to the play from
both Jews and Gentiles: from theatrical producers and those whose advice
they sought; from numerous reviews of the play in the Vienna, Berlin, and
Prague press when it was finally produced in early 1898, some penned by
leading writers such as Felix Salten, Karl Kraus, and the socialist leader Engelbert Pernersdorfer; and from Habsburg officials who had to give the play
their imprimatur prior to its staging. For some, Herzl's play helped clarify
their own hazier insights, some understood but objected to his message, but
the play was more often misunderstood, particularly by Jewish readers. These
misconceptions only highlight the striking novelty and path-breaking quality
of Herzl's achievement.

Let us begin with its first Jewish reception, Schnitzler's appreciative, but
highly critical response to the play. Schnitzler praised Herzl for his boldness
and courage in having created characters with the "breadth of life" that no
one had dared put on the stage before. He also singled out the play's stylistic

weakness: light and shade in characterization was too often sacrificed for a message; Wasserstein and Jacob delivered too many set speeches, explaining themselves too overtly. The play was marred by Herzl's ill-concealed desire to hammer home his points.[51] When revising, Herzl removed some of the speeches, but some of Schnitzler's advice Herzl could not and did not take.

For one, Schnitzler was offended by Herzl's one-sidedly negative depiction of Jews. "There are more sympathetic figures," he chided Herzl, "even in the circles depicted by the author." He missed in particular a sympathetic young woman. "There are some too," he lectured Herzl. Instead of the caricatured Hermine, Herzl could have shown "how an initially highly talented young woman is ruined by her Hellmann upbringing." In addition, Schnitzler criticized Herzl's image of centuries-long endemic Jewish timidity and passivity. What he missed in the play was "strong Jews." He insisted: "It is not at all true that in the ghetto, as you suppose, all Jews ran about oppressed or inwardly base. There were others—and precisely these were most deeply hated by the antisemites." Herzl's play was "bold," but Schnitzler regretted it was not more "defiant."[52]

What Schnitzler found of value in the play was its depiction of the ravages of antisemitism: "This poor devil and noble human being must let himself be shot down by a pitiful scoundrel—simply because he was born a Jew!" In this vein, he advised Herzl to add two more characters: "A Jewish fraternity student who after thirty duels is expelled because he is a Jew." The second was to be a Catholic student who refuses to duel out of religious conviction, "and is much revered for this!" Schnitzler clearly would have preferred a different play, a ringing protest against antisemitism. Accordingly, he failed to see why Herzl depicted Wurzlechner so sympathetically, or why he didn't have Jacob simply "throw the fellow out, the way he squirms and wiggles." He preferred a Jewish second for the duel, not Wurzlechner. Schnitzler kept his most trenchant observation to himself, recalling it only fifteen years later when he wrote his Jewish novel, *The Road to the Open*. There one of his Jewish characters exclaims: "I myself have only succeeded up to the present in making the acquaintance of one genuine antisemite. I'm afraid I am bound to admit . . . that it was a well-known Zionist leader."[53]

Schnitzler's penetrating observations certainly had more truth on their side than Herzl's one-dimensional image of Viennese-Jewish society and of Jewish history, but this only highlights the nature of Herzl's achievement. What Schnitzler judged to be lack of defiance missed the point. Herzl was engaged, without knowing it, in political myth-making. His ideologically foreshortened portrait of Jewry reflected assimilationist self-disdain, the trauma of Jewish defenselessness, the vision of a new Jewish possibility, and hopes for Jewish reconciliation with Gentiles. Schnitzler, more nuanced in his thinking, not prone to ideological simplification, saw only the gross distortions in Herzl's image of Jewry.

Schnitzler's response to the play goes far to explain why it was rejected by theater producers and only staged three years later, when Herzl's prominence as Zionist leader quelled troubling reservations about the play's depiction of Jews. Before then, Jewish opposition torpedoed the play's chances of being staged.

Few Jewish readers responded like Heinrich Teweles who was gripped by the play and wanted to produce it in his theater in Prague. He sought the advice of his stage manager, a Christian, who felt no hesitation himself but thought that Jews might be offended and reminded Teweles that Jews made up a large part of the theater-going public. Teweles agreed that some of the Jewish characterizations were "unsparingly critical," though he, as a Jew, did not feel offended and believed he understood Herzl's intent. Both sought the opinion of Dr. Arnold Rosenbacher, the president of the Jewish religious community in Prague and a prominent lawyer with a reputation for dispassion. Rosenbacher's response was unqualifiedly negative. He told Teweles: "The play is impossible. The theatre would lose its Jewish subscribers. The women in the play are downright hatefully depicted." Teweles commented sarcastically: "Negotiating with a Jewish censor was useless." He passed Rosenbacher's comments on to Herzl.[54]

The play had evoked a similar reaction in Vienna. Adam Müller-Guttenbrunn, the director of the Raimundtheater, thought the play realistic, timely, and important, but he also considered it too controversial to be staged and doubted whether any major German-speaking company would be willing to perform it. He showed keen insight by commenting that if he were to stage the play: "we won't reap anybody's gratitude for it, neither the Jews, nor the antisemites." He wrote to Schnitzler that he was, nevertheless, going to pass the script on to some "wholly impartial" readers whose judgment he valued.[55]

Herzl told Teweles the Vienna readers' reactions. The play had been read by a Jew and a Gentile: "The Christian said: it's a dynamite bomb. The Jew said: it's an affront to Jewry." After that, Müller-Guttenbrunn had let the matter drop. Persevering, Herzl wrote Teweles that he would rewrite the character of Hermine in order to please the Prague reader Dr. Rosenbacher. The latter remained unmoved; indeed, he now informed Teweles that he had passed on the script to a prominent Jewish writer, Salomon Kohn, to be doubly sure, and that Kohn had confirmed his objections.[56]

Herzl had written a play that could not be staged, largely because of Jewish objections. Their outrage over its Jewish stereotypes was understandable: Rheinberg, Hermine, and Rabbi Friedheimer were an antisemite's dream. But none of his Jewish readers seem to have grasped Herzl's critique

of assimilation or his novel approach in conceiving of a new mode of Jewishness. Herzl's intent was more apparent once he founded political Zionism,
for nationalism gave fuller content to the concept of the new Jew. It was then
that the play found willing collaborators. One witty reviewer was later to
capture the play best in commenting that it "seemed too antisemitic for a
Jewish play and too Jewish for an antisemitic play."[57]

The initial Jewish response to the play has been a skeleton in the Zionist
closet. Bein does not even mention Jewish objections, only that Herzl's efforts to place "the Jewish question before the public, was rejected by the
leading German theatres." Elon, more candidly though rather gingerly, reports that Jews "were shocked by the play's impertinence." Only Stewart,
with some antipathy to Herzl and to Zionism, records the Jewish response
to the play.[58] But Jewish objections only highlight Herzl's daring in dealing
so candidly with a sensitive issue, in a manner that left him exposed to attack
by other Jews for giving aid and comfort to antisemites.

The New Ghetto on the Stage

In November 1897, Herzl tried once more to have his play produced, this
time successfully, for he was now a political figure of note. By then he had
eliminated some of the set speeches and tempered the stereotypes. This led
his brother-in-law Paul Naschauer to comment shrewdly that Herzl "had removed more that was Zionistic from the original version than he was later
to add." The play was performed in the Carl-Theater in Vienna, where it ran
from 5 January to 15 February 1898; it had its Berlin premier in the Thalia-
Theater on 5 February and was performed in Prague in June at the Deutsches
Theater.[59]

By then, both because of Herzl's political profile and antisemitism in
Vienna, Berlin, and Prague, the play became something of a cause célèbre.
The office of the chief of police in Vienna had recommended against a per-
mit for the play, fearing that its frank discussion of the Jewish question in
an era of "national and confessional antagonisms" would spark antisemitic
demonstrations. The prohibition was overruled by the provincial governor's
office. Herzl had read the play to Count Kielmannsegg, the provincial governor, at a private sitting, and he had approved. Comments sent back to the
police noted that the play's message was positive: "to break down the walls
of the 'new ghetto,' " Jews had to shun "dubious and dishonest speculation."
One passage, considered overly provocative, was to be excised; in addition,
Rabbi Friedheimer was not to appear in clerical costume.[60]

Curiously, this official exchange makes no mention of the one provocative incident in the play most likely to anger Gentiles: the scene in which
Jacob strikes von Schramm. Word of this scene preceded the play's opening

and evoked outraged comments in the antisemitic press. The Viennese *Figaro*, an antisemitic satirical weekly, asserted with an undertone of menace that "letting an officer be struck on a public platform showed a tactlessness and tastelessness that calls for a resolute response." As a result, the premières in Berlin and Prague gave rise to fears of antisemitic demonstrations.[61]

The play had come to be seen largely as a Zionist call for Jewish militancy. By then Herzl had tempered his Jewish stereotypes, which were probably understated in the staging, treated with humor and pathos rather than harshly caricatured. Jews flocked to the play to demonstrate their solidarity, as well as moral and even political support for Herzl. Some of the early performances in Berlin are described as virtual political demonstrations, with largely Jewish audiences applauding, even whistling and stamping their feet at certain watchwords such as: "You stand where history has placed you. But we must go forward if we wish to become men." or "What was the Jew doing there [at the coal mine]? His Christian duty!" The Viennese and Prague audiences were equally enthusiastic, though less demonstrative. The Viennese press noted the visible enthusiasm shown by the audience when von Schramm was struck; one reviewer pointed out that he was struck more than once, that once would have been enough.[62]

In the light of the initial hostile Jewish response to Herzl's play, it is noteworthy that the antisemitic press uniformly condemned it. The scornful tone of the *Deutsch Zeitung* was typical: "To see the suffering of a highly honest Jew glorified, and the repulsive failings of his compatriots excused with a historical explanation, for this we possess insufficient artistic enlightenment." For those who believed Jews were inherently base, the play's contention that Jewish faults were the outcome of gentile persecution was presumptuous. Herzl's portrait of Jacob as a model of courage and idealism was considered equally a travesty. The *Kikeriki-Anzeiger* caricatured Jacob, depicting him with a Yiddish whine, terrified of dueling von Schramm and requiring the help of others to eject him from the household.[63]

Among the reviews of the *The New Ghetto*, some stand out for their insight and, as such, add to our understanding of the play and Herzl's intent in writing it. The review by Felix Salten, the noted Viennese-Jewish writer, was one of these. He was well aware of the literary shortcomings of the play, but he valued Herzl's probing discussion of Jewish-gentile relations and admired his daring in confronting both Jews and antisemites from the stage. Salten maintained that Herzl's outlook on the Jewish condition reflected the "drawing-room anguish" of the Viennese-Jewish middle class. Because they had tasted freedom, the rise of antisemitism had left them "bewildered." "They try to flee from their Jewishness; they attempt to stop up their ears when 'Hepp Hepp' is shouted at them; as Jacob for Rachel's sake, they are ready to serve for decades in return for a bit of love; or they seek solace in themselves, loyally clinging together."[64] The dread of being outsiders once again, the craving to belong, immobilized their response to antisemitism.

Herzl's play foreshadowed his version of Zionism. It is therefore no surprise that one of the most penetrating reviews of the play was to come from the Russian Zionist Ahad Ha-Am, the leading opponent of Herzl within the Zionist movement. For Ahad Ha-Am, Zionism was a response not to antisemitism, but to the crisis of assimilation, the threatened loss of the Jewish national heritage through Jewry's absorption in Europe. Only Jewish nationalism, he believed, could bring Jews to modernity, while guaranteeing Jewish continuity and distinctiveness. He charged that Herzl's ideal of physical heroism introduced an alien element into Jewish life. It was in this light that he disparagingly described Jacob Samuel's enraged response to von Schramm's insults: "The real Jew . . . recognizes and senses inwardly that a centuries-old culture raises him high above such acts of barbarism, a relic of the brutality and cruelty of bygone days. His sense of honour remains unperturbed, undiminished . . . by the insults of some roughneck. He responds with a contemptuous glance and moves on."[65]

In addition, Ahad Ha-Am criticized the play's lack of political direction and its unsatisfying conclusion. He commented: "We do not know,—he [Jacob] himself apparently does not know—what he actually wants and where he wants to go, when he cries out before his death, 'Out. Out of the Ghetto.' " Ahad Ha-Am was right, but there is no reason for us to be surprised by this, if we remember that the essential drama of the play was an inward one. The play was no less—and no more than—the expression of an inner breakthrough on Herzl's part, from assimilationist ambivalence to a new mode of Jewishness. Herzl recalled that after finishing the play: "I had thought that . . . I had written myself free of the matter." After the play had been turned down by several theaters, he wrote to Schnitzler that he was undaunted: "I will continue on my path. My new path! Something blessed lies in it."[66] He was now free to go much further. What he thought was an ending he soon realized was only a beginning.

7

The Jewish State

We shall depart as respected friends.[1]

Statehood: The Resolution of Herzl's Ambivalence

HERZL'S PROGRAM OF Jewish self-transformation came to be fully realized in his idea of a Jewish state. Zionism was the final phase in Herzl's long-time search for a new autonomous mode of Jewish assimilation. In this chapter, I will show how this interpretation illuminates the nature of Herzl's Zionism.

As closely as we can determine, Herzl conceived the idea of a Jewish state in early May, perhaps even late April, of 1895. That was when he drafted a letter to the Jewish philanthropist Baron Maurice de Hirsch, seeking his support. In his diary begun in early June, Herzl mentioned no immediate cause for his conversion to Zionism, certainly not the Dreyfus trial. Possibly, Second Curia election results in Vienna on April 2 took him over the brink.[2]

In those elections, Christian Social gains gave them a potentially narrow majority on the city council. John Boyer calls the elections "nothing less than a catastrophe" for the Liberals. The *Neue Freie Presse* lamented: "Just another small step and Lueger is master of the city council, and Vienna the only metropolis in the world with the stigma of an antisemitic administration." Herzl witnessed the electoral campaign, for he was in Vienna in late March. What is certain from Herzl's Zionist diary is that he was preoccupied with the crisis in Vienna from May 1895, when Lueger was first elected mayor and resigned in a tactical move, to the September elections, when the Christian Socials captured the city council by a wide majority.[3]

Herzl had considered Jewish statehood several times before, once in early 1893 and again in October 1894, some days before the illumination that led him to write *The New Ghetto*. Both times he rejected the idea, for he believed that Jews were acclimatized to a variety of homelands and national cultures and had little but their oppression in common.[4] But then came the crucial internal change we have documented in *The New Ghetto*. Having made that leap, nationalism must have loomed again as a possibility. Lueger's electoral victory may have been the spur, driving him to take this radical step.

During the month of May, Herzl remained tentative about the idea of a state, for it strained credulity; he treated it as one of several proposals to transform the Jews and end antisemitism. Indeed, the preparatory notes for his first meeting with Baron Hirsch, composed toward the end of May, are evidence that Herzl's conception of statehood was an outgrowth of—and continuous with—his earlier solutions to the Jewish question, for other less drastic means were still considered by him. Herzl suggested to Hirsch that he first try to perform a surrogate-state function, improving Jews by offering rewards for deeds of physical courage and virtue. If they could be reared to manliness in this way and become "respected and feared," there would be no need for Jews to depart from Europe. One could wait and see then if emigration "was still necessary." So intent was Herzl on still assimilating Jews and ending their despised status that he even revived his old project of intermarriage (with the children brought up in "the majority faith"), proposing that Hirsch offer rewards for this. He himself would negotiate with the pope, the Czar's mentor Pobedonostsev, and the kaiser, to get them to combat antisemitism in return.[5]

By early June, the state idea had taken hold of him with even more force than *The New Ghetto* once had. He felt possessed; elaborations of the idea raced through his mind out of control while at work, walking, when in conversation. Gripped by an obsession, he feared he was losing his sanity. His only relief lay in putting the rush of ideas down on paper, filling two hundred pages of his diary in June alone. Nevertheless, his mood was euphoric: "It would be torture if it were not such bliss," he exclaimed.[6]

Herzl's euphoria was induced by resolving the problem he had been wrestling with for several years, finding a new independent mode of assimilation that would bring Jews self-respect and honor in the eyes of Gentiles. State-making replaced mass baptism, socialism, and dueling as the most fully realized version of such an act. The latter now seemed to Herzl "petty solutions."[7] Everything came together for him in the notion of the Jewish state, all those aims that before had seemed so irresolvable: eliminating Jewish defects through emancipation and assimilation, thus remaking Jews on the gentile model; the attainment of Jewish pride and self-respect; making Jews independent, masters of their fate; finally, gaining honor in the eyes of Gentiles. Through Zionism, Herzl resolved his ambivalence both about his Jewishness and about Austro-German assimilation, a conflict which had entangled his aims in contradictions. Herzl had thus sought a proud mass Jewish conversion to Christianity, Jewish adherence to revolutionary socialism, and duels against antisemites. That is, he sought both Jewish honor and the submergence of Jewry into European culture and society. In *The New Ghetto* Herzl moved to a resolution of these conflicts by redefining Jewishness in terms of assimilationist models. Henceforth there was to be no conflict at all between assimilation and Jewishness, for they had become one and the same.

Finally, through statehood, Jews could realize the goals of emancipation and assimilation by themselves, overcome their defects, hence rid themselves of the stigma of Jewishness, gain in Jewish pride, become their own masters, and at the same time win gentile acceptance and respect by their new dignified, self-assertive stance. Relieved of his shame about Jewishness and finding a route to Jewish pride unburdened Herzl, gave him clarity and direction, a sense of mission, the source of his charisma as a Jewish leader.

The Jewish State as the Realization of Emancipation and Assimilation (I)

Herzl's preferred agency for Jewish self-transformation became the Jewish state, not only because he believed Jews should rule themselves, but because his view of Jewry was influenced by European emancipationist ideology. The notion that Jewish faults stemmed from their exclusion from the political sphere and could be cured by full citizenship was a keystone of this ideology. As we saw earlier, Christian Dohm had attributed Jewish vices to the loss "of the possibility of obtaining civil honors and of serving the common fatherland." In this sense, Jewish decline was blamed on their statelessness. Cut off from the prospect of the state's bestowal of status, honor, and glory, Jews had no incentive to develop civic and soldierly virtues such as self-sacrifice for the common good and physical courage. Neither did the state foster a range of occupations among Jews by providing educational opportunities and economic inducements. Thus Jews found their sole satisfaction in commerce, an occupation where private egotism was rampant. Dohm's solution was to grant Jews access to civil honors and army service, and for the state to award prizes for superior works of Jewish craftsmanship and industry, to instil a love of honest labor. A century after Dohm, the assimilated Theodor Gomperz, a Viennese contemporary of Herzl, took this analysis for granted: "Greed for gain became . . . a national defect [among Jews], just as, it seems, vanity (the natural consequence of an atomistic existence shunted away from a concern with national and public interests)."[8]

For Herzl as well, statehood was to transform a people pressed by historical circumstance into the highly individuated pursuit of money as its sole source of power and security. Repeating to Baron Hirsch the very same wording he had used thirteen years earlier in the Dühring review, Herzl insisted that the state had up to now educated Jews to be "leeches," while spurring Gentiles to courage and manliness with medals and patents of nobility. Patents of nobility were irresistible inducements, because benefits were extended beyond those rewarded to their progeny. By the same token, Jews were bad soldiers because the path of honors—promotions, medals, public glory—was closed to them.[9] Herzl now concluded that if antisemitism barred

Jews from improvement through the state, only a state of their own would make Jewish improvement possible.

Emancipationist prescriptions were intended to cure Jewish defects. Sharing in these prescriptions, Herzlean Zionism abounded in stereotypes of the Jewish character, which was now to find its ideal cure in Jewish statehood. Herzl's diagnosis of Jewish defects had not changed and even was highlighted by him to dramatize the efficacy of the cure.

Typical are his remarks in drafts for an appeal to the Rothschilds, whose fortune, he was convinced, could pry a Jewish state out of the Ottoman Sultan. Herzl called the banking family "an international menace," whose "accursed wealth" increased "only at the expense of the national prosperity." This may have been Herzl's way of warning the Rothschilds their position was shaky, and that underwriting a Jewish state was in their interest, but he could have done this without summoning forth images of parasitical and destructive Jewish wealth. On another occasion he referred to the "frightful financial power" of the Jews.[10]

Abandoned to statelessness, Jews had become materialists, bereft of higher ideals: "money-worshipping people," Herzl called them, "incapable of understanding that a man can act out of other motives than money." He feared that Jews were too far gone to be attracted to Zionism. Herzl even described the Jewish evacuation from Europe as an act liberating both Jews and Gentiles: "liberating them from us," he declared. Behind such statements lay the notion, and Herzl said as much, of Jews as an unsettling force in Europe, domineering in both finance capitalism and revolutionary socialism. History wreaked its own brand of justice, he observed: "Europe is being punished for the ghettoes now."[11]

Another defect of Jewry to be cured through statehood was its "over-production of mediocre intellects." Jacob Talmon has rightly seen this term as mirroring the view that Jews had become clever imitators and masters in "facile improvisation," but were too opportunistically minded to be genuinely creative.[12]

Sometimes Herzl expressed passionate sympathy when uttering these comments, for such traits—the outcome of centuries of oppression—made Jews vulnerable and invited victimization. But sometimes his tone was scornful, carrying the traces of his Jewish self-contempt. In one passage Herzl suggested that European states nationalize their stock exchanges and credit systems with Jewish help just prior to their departure from Europe. With his usual imaginativeness, he thought Jews could make a new start by aiding Gentiles to rid the world of the uncontrolled power of money. Otherwise, he remarked, "the civilized peoples will Judaize [*verjuden*] themselves after we are gone." Herzl was employing a German neologism—*verjuden*—which first appeared in an antisemitic essay by Richard Wagner in 1850 and soon

Herzl around 1895, about the time he was writing *The Jewish State*. Alex Bein, *Theodor Herzl: Biographie* (Vienna, 1934).

became widely employed in anti-Jewish discourse. Steven Ashheim has recently analyzed the term's pejorative uses. The background to the term was a conception of the "Jewish spirit" as the "antitype" to everything spiritual and ideal. The verb *verjuden* conjured up an image of contamination, caused by the "Jewish spirit" as it penetrated the nation.[13]

If the European view of Jewish defects had fostered Herzl's Jewish self-contempt, Zionism was Herzl's way of resolving this self-contempt, for it would create a new Jew. But there were many Jews who stubbornly resisted self-transformation through Zionism, and Herzl's Jewish self-contempt was now concentrated exclusively on them. Accordingly, he once referred to Albert Rothschild, the head of the Austrian branch of the family, as a "Jew-boy." He called anti-Zionist opponents "Jewish vermin," employing the German word *Schädlinge*, which also means parasite, a common anti-Jewish epithet.[14]

In his article "*Mauschel*," Herzl's fury at anti-Zionist opponents took him even further. *Mauschel* was, of course, a German anti-Jewish epithet; Herzl's portrait was an antisemite's dream. *Mauschel* was "unspeakably low and repugnant," "crafty profit seekers," pursuing "dirty deals." Self-preservation and money were all that moved *Mauschel*. His emotions were crude and base. Ordinary pain became in him "miserable fright"; he "cringes . . . ignominiously" in adversity. He was a stranger to beauty and to higher loyalties, pursuing art and knowledge and displaying patriotism only for profit. Toward *Mauschel* Herzl offered not kinship but distance, not pity but contempt, not a situational explanation of Jewish deficiencies, but surprisingly, a quasi-racial one. *Mauschel's* traits were not just the survivalist stratagems of the oppressed, rather "at some dark moment in our history some inferior human material got into our unfortunate people and blended with it."[15]

Herzl insisted there had always been two sorts of Jews in the world, the *Jew*, and *Mauschel*. His distinction was modeled on the emancipationist novel, of which Freytag's *Debit and Credit* was an example. Herzl's version of the *Jew* was a replica of the honorable Bernhard Ehrenthal; the base Veitel Itzig was the model for *Mauschel*. Herzl's version of the *Jew* was later embodied in Jacob Samuel, *Mauschel* in Fritz Rheinberg. Now, the *Jew* was the Zionist, *Mauschel* the anti-Zionist. Through statehood, Herzl believed, *Mauschel* would become merely a sorry left-over of an earlier epoch and no longer the embodiment of the Jewish essence.

The Jewish State as the Realization of Emancipation and Assimilation (II)

Gaining political sovereignty is the ultimate goal of every nationalist movement, but first a movement has to be created and gain strength. What distinguished Herzl was that he made sovereignty the immediate, rather than the eventual goal of Zionism. Aiming for statehood was to precede the formation of a broadly-based Jewish nationalist movement. Gaining a state was to precede the creation of its nucleus: a Jewish society and culture organically tied to a territory. Herzl envisaged a Society of Jews made up of English-Jewish notables, appointing itself the keeper of Jewish sovereignty, negotiating with the Great Powers and creating institutions for the new state. The pioneer immigrants would not create the germ of the new society by themselves, but would compliantly accept the constitution drawn up by this Society of Jews. Jews were to accept a predetermined state, whose enlightened officialdom would transform them.[16]

Herzl's emphasis on the state as an immediate goal led, later on, to conflicts with Russian Zionists. Jews from the Czarist empire were influenced by Russian populism and considered the renewed tie to the land and the creation of a Jewish peasantry their priority. Moreover, they distrusted the state, considering it oppressive and parasitical. For them, the state was to be Zionism's last offshoot, not its first, the outgrowth of a pre-existent national society and culture, not the creator of that society and culture.[17]

Herzl's call for immediate statehood has often been attributed to his audacious political approach, his stunningly bold, uncompromising assertion of maximum aims. Doubtlessly, a variety of conceptions and goals drove Herzl. He addressed himself to a genuine problem, Jewish political dependence and isolation. Statehood would mean freedom and power for Jews. Jews would no longer be ruled by Gentiles; they would rule themselves and depend only on themselves.

Nation-states had power; they were active forces in history, dealing with other states on the basis of realpolitik. In the nineteenth century, Europe's unified nation-states assured her dominion over the rest of the world, often handicapped by less unified and weaker political systems. With statehood Jews would no longer simply endure their history with its cycles of toleration and persecution, but enter the ranks of nations that controlled and shaped events. Herzl's single-minded focus on statehood or political sovereignty to be gained through diplomatic negotiations with the Great Powers provided Jews with a breathtakingly bold political posture, in marked contrast to their negligible political weight in the world.

Herzl's novel call for immediate—rather than eventual—statehood can be explained on other grounds as well. In keeping with the historical experience of Habsburg Jewry, Herzl saw Jewish improvement as initiated from above, by an enlightened officialdom. Side by side with his belief that Jews would have to transform themselves through an act of will, Herzl also saw the transformation of the Jews as the task of a beneficent paternalist state.

The Habsburg model of Jewish emancipation shaped Herzl's thinking about how Jewish improvement was to come about. Habsburg policy had been initiated by Joseph II's Patent of Toleration in 1781, which created a modern German school system for Jews, made them subject to military conscription, abolished Jewish juridical autonomy, insisted Jews drop the use of Hebrew in public documents and adopt German names, encouraged them to abandon their distinctive dress, and opened trades and handicrafts to them. In some ways Joseph adopted half-measures, for he did not abolish Jewish residence restrictions. But his overall purpose was to end Jewish separatism and make Jews "useful" subjects of the state. As an eighteenth-century enlightened despot, Joseph's policy was driven by utilitarianism and by realpolitik. This model of Jewish emancipation *from above*, out of state interest, loomed large in the nineteenth century, just as large as the French revolutionary model in which the ineluctable implications of the "Rights of Man" had led to Jewish emancipation.

In accord with this model, Herzl believed a Jewish state would transform Jews because states, out of utilitarian self-interest, required subjects who were productive and who possessed civic virtue and soldierly courage. The state's need to secure and even enhance its power led it to confer status on those who served it, honor physical courage, and bestow glory on its fallen. Jews had been deprived of the benefits of the state as educator: We "have inwardly gone to rack and ruin for there has been no one to train us to become real men, even if only out of imperial selfishness."[18] Such training could only come if the tutelary state was the first creation of Zionism, bestowed on Jews, rather than created by them.

Herzl drew his model of the Jewish state from Austrian statist traditions. He criticized Jean-Jacques Rousseau's theory that the state originated in a social contract. Herzl took this to mean that the state was an outgrowth of the popular will. Instead, he saw the state as "a mixture of human and superhuman elements."[19] The state was in part a creation of civil society. This was its "human" element: a state based on consent, expressed through a suffrage weighted toward property and education. But the state was also a power above civil society. This was its "superhuman" element: the state's efficacy required that it be experienced as a power above human artifice and will, evoking obedience and reverence.

Reflecting his own brand of Austrian statist liberalism and his admiration for imperial Germany as well, Herzl saw the state not so much as an emanation and agent of society, merely regulating competing social-economic interests, but as a creative force, shaping both society and the individual. This view of the state was strengthened by his years in France, which confirmed—and even intensified—his distrust of parliamentary democracy and popular sovereignty. Hence Jewish statehood was to come first; it was not to evolve out of a preexistent Jewish society or nation, but rather it was to create and shape them both. In keeping with these activist statist views, Herzl appealed to a provision in Roman civil law, the *negotiorum gestio*. This allowed a person who had no legal obligation or contractual engagement to do so, to act in someone else's interest without his/her consent in cases of his/her absence or incapacity. Such acts included carrying on litigation, paying debts due, or repairing a house. Roman law laid out the conditions under which *Gestors* could act and their accountability as well.[20] Herzl was acquainted with this provision from his law studies and year of legal internship, for it was part of the Austrian civil code. He extended this provision to the political realm. In the absence of a state, a people lacked representative institutions. Hence they required leaders whose "warrant derives from a higher necessity."[21] Such leaders would be accountable after the fact, when the state came into being. The doctrine of *negotiorum gestio* thus incorporated principles of both political guardianship and accountability, both the "superhuman" and "human" aspects of the state.

The *Gestor* of the Jews was to be the Society of Jews, made up of West European Jewish notables. Herzl thought the British Jews he had met on his voyage to London in November 1895 would be prime candidates, for they were both assimilated and committed Jews at the same time. In its role as *Gestor*, the society was to seek recognition as a "state-forming power." It was to enter into diplomatic negotiations on behalf of Jewry, and also appoint a council of jurists to devise a constitution which would be "gratefully" received by the Jews. Herzl ended with a warning: "But wherever resistance may appear, the Society will break it."[22]

Herzl saw Bismarck as his model nation-builder, for he knew how to break resistance. Bismarck had by-passed the German liberal and nationalist middle class and made Prussia, with its strong dynastic and statist institutions, the chief instrument of German unity. Bismarck too had acted as a *Gestor* for Germany. Herzl hardly shared all of Bismarck's views, and he had no monarch and army behind him, but he, in his own way, wanted to bestow—or if necessary impose—on Jews a "predetermined Constitution."[23]

Herzl extended the doctrine of the *negotiorum gestio* to the stage of statehood itself. In an article summing up his thoughts on French parliamentary democracy, he called French governments impotent, since they were appointed by Parliament, a body highly vulnerable to political intrigue and party maneuvers and buffeted by the parochial interests of its deputies. Herzl favored constitutional monarchy, where the monarch appointed cabinets made up of government officials. Government was still accountable, for government bills could be defeated and ministers were subject to parliamentary scrutiny and could be impeached. But the monarch could also dissolve parliament and rule by decree, though he was obligated to set new elections within a specific period of time. Such a system incorporated both guardianship and accountability. Herzl concluded: "Since the state historically has by no means arisen from a social contract, another legal principle must be operative. This is the *negotiorum gestio*. The people are and will always be incapable of directing their own affairs, whose scope and magnitude is beyond their comprehension."[24] Hence, Herzl emphasized the need for "strict centralization" in the Jewish state, even declaring that the "administrative maxims" not be published, for the "people must be guided to the good according to principles unknown to them."[25]

To his regret, Herzl believed a Jewish monarchy no longer possible, since no ruling house had survived the centuries of Jewish statelessness. Instead, he envisaged an ersatz monarch in the person of a prince elected through an indirect and privileged system of voting. Governments were to be appointed by the prince and could not be overturned by parliament. Ministers were then the servants of the prince, not of parliament, though parliament could exercise budgetary sanctions.[26]

Finally, Herzl believed such a state, established and led by West European Jews, would be specially suited to transform East European Jews, who were to constitute the bulk of its citizenry. By now, Herzl affirmed the solidarity and common nationality of all Jews. Nevertheless, his attitude to East European Jews was still patronizing, combining both sympathy and distaste. He viewed them as culturally backward, obscurantist, and stubbornly separatist, an outcome of centuries of victimization. He believed them to be economically parasitic, shunning productive labor, physically feeble and timid, and wholly given over to an overly-cerebral Talmudism.[27] Herzl's concern that East European Jews might stamp their own character on the Jewish state was expressed in an early declaration: "We shall remain part of civilization. . . . After all, we don't want a Boer state, but a Venice." The Boer state of South Africa was religiously fanatic and xenophobic. When Herzl first heard that Russian Zionists proposed the revival of Hebrew, he feared the Jewish state would become a "New Greece," for modern Greece was in the grip of a parochial religious nationalism drawing inspiration from Greece's Christian Orthodox Byzantine heritage.[28]

East European Jews were to be transformed through enlightened statism. State officials would press economic and educational modernization on them, out of the state's need for disciplined, energetic, and productive citizens. The Jewish state was to run labor exchanges, organize labor battalions, provide workers' pension (the best workers would receive licenses to open tobacco shops when they retired), in short erect a paternalistic system of benefits, inducements, and sanctions, in order to instill in Jews "the moral blessings of work." Usury and stock-market speculation were to be outlawed and their practitioners urged to enter state service, where they would learn "a sound code of discipline." The currency exchange was to be nationalized; the purpose of this was "to educate the people in our State." Equally, outstanding devotion to the common good, bravery in warfare, exceptional artistic talent, were to be rewarded with state medals, titles, patents of nobility.[29] Thus Jews would become "strong as for war, eager to work and virtuous." To counteract tendencies to religious fanaticism, religion would merely serve the state by emphasizing a common heritage uniting Jews and by teaching moral virtue. Beyond that, "We shall know how to restrict them [rabbis] to their temples." Civic peace and good relations with other states demanded state control over religion.[30]

Herzl's Political Maximalism

For Herzl the idea of Jewish statehood seemed so incredible that he doubted his own sanity for having conceived it. One may well ask, Why? The nineteenth century was the era of European nationalism, and the Habsburg Empire one of its seed-beds. What was so unusual about Jews joining the nationalist bandwagon? It was the prospect of Jews as state-makers that was so incredible to Herzl, far more even than the likelihood of prying a state out of the weakened, debt-burdened Ottoman Empire. East European Jews, aware of the key role of Jewish self-government and political authority in Diaspora Jewish history, were far less incredulous about the state-making capacity of Jews. For Herzl, such a goal required a radical transformation of the Jewish character: "Nor are we doing violence to anyone," he exclaimed, "except to ourselves, our habits, our evil inclinations, and our faults."[31]

How far Herzl considered state-making a self-transcending act for Jews can be illustrated by an incident that stung him deeply. The Viennese-Jewish journalist Julius Bauer once poured mockery on him in a verse, which went: "He sees a goal, a distant goal / While dreaming or awake: / He contemplates, in our time / To parade with Jews in state!" The mockery lies in a pun: *Mit Juden Staat zu machen* implies making a state with Jews, but really means to parade or show off with Jews.[32]

Bauer had cut Herzl to the bone, for he was reminding him how deep the sense of Jewish inferiority ran. Herzl wanted to found a Jewish state, but even the thought of Jews parading around together was embarrassingly comical. Herzl may have remembered how he had once recoiled from the cluster of Jewish vacationers in Ostende, or his observation in Nice in 1891 that Jews deliberately avoided one another—"turned up their noses at each other"— when out among the fashionable public.[33] Being seen together in public stirred Jewish insecurities, for each felt judged by how other Jews behaved, saw in their fellows a mirror image of traits they disliked in themselves, and read contempt in gentile glances. Jews did not even want to be seen in a

group in public, Bauer was saying, and Herzl expected to gather them together in a state.

It was not so much the substance of Bauer's criticism but the mockery
of Jewish problems that outraged Herzl. Such mockery was typically Jewish,
a recourse of those who "felt themselves ridiculous," "the feeble attempt of
prisoners to look like free men." Such mockery channeled aggressiveness into
wit, a habit feebly cerebral, and even worse, turned aggressiveness inward.
Mockery was a way of reviling oneself in other Jews and identifying with
gentile aggressors. Thus it crossed the thin line between self-criticism and
self-deprecation. Herzl was to pay Bauer back in kind with a sharp-edged
caricature in his novel *Old-New Land* of the wits and punsters Gruen and
Blau, favorites of Viennese-Jewish high society. He has someone say of Gruen
and Blau: "They are the last people to whom one could speak of something
big."[34]

Herzl was extremely sensitive to such mockery. To Stefan Zweig, he confessed that he could never have arrived at the idea of the Jewish state if he
had been living in Vienna instead of Paris, and subject to Jewish ridicule.
Mockery was only one symptom of the malady Herzl wished to cure through
Zionism, that of Jewish self-deprecation. Zionism had to be lofty and intoxicating, equal to the disease, able to compensate for deprecation with self-ex-
altation. Hence his extravagant political aims and short-range timetable;
aiming for a sovereign state in Palestine right away, before a Jewish socioeconomic infrastructure existed, seeking Great Power recognition even before
the national movement came into being, promising a social-reformist utopia
overnight, in defiance of the harsh realities of settlement and pioneering.

Zionism, in Herzl's extravagant claim, was no "long-drawn out project,"
but rather an "immediate solution." Ahad Ha-Am, who became Herzl's chief
opponent among Zionists, was to argue against Herzl that only a substantial
Zionist presence in Palestine rooted in the soil, constituted by Hebrew-speaking Jews, could bestow moral legitimacy on the Jewish claim to sovereignty.
The state had to be a long-term goal, emanating organically from a viable
Jewish society and Jewish majority. Herzl's vision was far more grandiose.
He criticized Hibbat Zion (Love of Zion), the Russian Zionist movement,
for its program of "slow sporadic settlement," commenting: "That means
expecting the people there to live in mud huts. We don't need that; we'll
build ourselves houses up to the sky." Palestine, he continued, would not be
built up "in bits and snatches, but on a grand scale." In a hyperbolic comparison, he insisted that the modern Jewish exodus would put the biblical one
in the shade: "The Exodus under Moses bears the same relation to this project as a Shrovetide play by Hans Sachs does to a Wagner opera.[35] Herzl's
concern with overcoming Jewish self-deprecation and restoring Jewish pride
also lay behind his preoccupation with ceremonial splendor and awe-inspiring

symbols, which later spurred his orchestration of the First Zionist Congress, held in an imposing edifice, its opening session attended by Jews in formal dress.

Herzl's sense of urgency had nothing to do with apprehensions of immediate physical dangers to Jews, but rather with his notion of Jewish self-transformation. Such self-transformation could not come about through plodding effort and incremental achievement. Herzl thought intuitively of Jewish psychological need. Gentile contempt had engendered self-contempt in Jews, which could only be erased by adapting over-compensating political goals. He was engaged in a frontal assault against what he saw as Jewish weaknesses and faults: minority fearfulness and caution, feelings of inferiority arising from the view of Jewishness as a stigma. The cure had to be adequate to the malady. In Herzl's view, it was precisely the utopian contrast between these Jewish faults and, on the other hand, the intrepid call for political sovereignty, that made the latter such a powerful cure.

One of Herzl's models for Jewish transformation was the Prussian one as he conceived it in his earlier German nationalist phase: manliness, boldness, bluntness, and openness, the politics of the fait accompli, uncompromising and rash, impelled by the sense of a great historical destiny. He was modeling his political strategy on the Prussian example, "the forthright grand old style, Open and above-board!" which left others no alternative: "the world would then have to come to terms with it." There could be no greater contrast to the Prussian model than Herzl's image of Jewish prudence, timidity, and anxious apprehension. From mass baptism, to socialism, to Jacob Samuel's transformation into a Jewish Siegfried, Herzl had thought of bold, heroic and assertive acts, which he viewed in virtually religious terms as redemptive, as creating a new ideal Jew. He now saw in state-making "an idea of such power," about to call forth these acts, and exalted enough to evoke passionate enthusiasm.[36]

If one of his models for such acts derived from his earlier German nationalist enthusiasms, another model seems closer to the revolutionary notions he first adopted in 1893. Employing a Marxist parallel, Adolf Böhm described Herzl's view as a "Zionist pauperization theory." Like Marx's proletariat, Jews would assert their humanity only when they had reached the depths of dehumanization. In Herzl's words; "Still, I know where that land lies; within ourselves! . . . But we shall have to sink still lower, we shall have to be even more insulted, spat upon, mocked, whipped, plundered, and slain before we are ripe for this idea." Just as Marx called upon the proletariat to affirm, "I am nothing and I should be everything," so Herzl contrasted present Jewish abasement to the dazzling prospects of future greatness and splendor.[37]

Herzl was no sober political strategist and pragmatist carefully weighing risks, pursuing prudent aims. His conception of the Jewish state and of the political strategy necessary to realize it was shaped by his preoccupation with erasing the stigma of Jewishness through a redemptive and self-transformative act. For this reason, his political goal and practice was romantic, even utopian. To borrow Yehoshafat Harkabi's ingenious distinction: Herzl's political approach was guided by "expressivity" rather than "instrumentalism," by conceptions of self-assertion, voluntarism, of a spectacular and redemptive act, rather than of gradual achievement, a sober weighing of consequences, prudence and compromise. The politics of "expressivity" aims at overcoming a sense of subservience, timidity, and powerlessness, at lifting one's morale. Hence, to quote Harkabi, it is oriented to "audacity," "heroism," "risk taking." Such an approach elevates the notion that "great results can be achieved at a single stroke" into a strategic dogma and disdains "the constraints of reality."[38]

Such was Herzl's political approach, solidified and fully displayed in *The Jewish State*, published in February 1896. There he articulated the maximum goal of Jewish sovereignty either in Palestine or Argentina, to be gained right away through negotiations with the Great Powers. For this he was accused of being precipitous. A sovereign territory without a national infrastructure would have been a helpless plaything in the hands of other states. That Jews for the most part lacked even a consciousness of political nationhood did not concern him. Indeed, he first formulated his ideas before he was aware of the existence of Hovevei Zion, the Russian Zionist movement. When at last, in July 1896, he was granted an interview with Baron Edmond de Rothschild, whose financial sponsorship he was seeking, the baron voiced the obvious practical objections to Herzl's scheme: the Turks had recently prohibited land sales to Jews; a public call for Jewish sovereignty risked further measures against Jewish settlers. Since Herzl envisaged a mass immigration, how would a flood of impoverished Jews be provided for in Palestine? Rothschild later summed up his objections: "I felt . . . that there was no point in hoisting the flag when there was still no edifice."[39]

Ahad Ha-Am was to shrewdly seize upon the intoxicating quality of Herzl's political maximalism. Herzl was an assimilated Jew rejected by his society, hence plagued by a "consciousness of inferiority." To restore his sense of self-worth, he sought immediate statehood for Jews because "the higher and more distant the ideal, the greater its power of exaltation."[40] All Ahad Ha-Am saw were the dangers of Herzl's approach: the prospect that such messianism would engender extravagant hopes and eventually lead to an equally massive demoralization. Hovevei Zion's prudent and cautious political practice, its modest objectives—the incremental creation of a Jewish national presence in Palestine unaccompanied by political proclamations—was far more in keeping with traditional Jewish political caution, ever attuned to the constraints of an inhospitable reality.

On the other hand, David Vital has argued, quite rightly, that Herzl's blunt and open proclamation of maximum aims raised Zionism's political sights to heights unimaginable to his cautious and prudent predecessors in the Russian Zionism movement. As one Zionist contrasted the two positions: "The new, unprecedented manner, the candid, proud language was a striking contrast to our hitherto inconspicuous conspiratorial method of operation.[41]

Similarly, Arthur Ruppin, who went on to play a leading role in settlement planning in Palestine, credited Herzl's "charter idea," the notion of an immediate grant of Jewish sovereignty by the European powers, with attracting the Jewish masses to Zionism. Like the Marxist concept of proletarian revolution, Herzl posited a visionary, maximum goal as an immediately realizable possibility. Jacob Talmon, comparing the charter idea to revolutionary theory, pointed out that both involved "a sudden break-through . . . a clean sweep," enabling humans "to start all over from scratch."[42] The charter idea had a mythical and symbolic ring, luring the popular imagination.

When Herzl died, none of his declared aims had been achieved. Diplomatic negotiations had not yielded a state. His promises of quick success were increasingly criticized as leading to the dead end of demoralization. Herzl was under fire for treating the Zionist movement as a base for his diplomatic efforts in the capitals of Europe, to the neglect of settlement activity and the national cultural revival. What Herzl had achieved was no less significant. At the time of the publication of *The Jewish State* in 1896, the pre-Herzlean Zionist movement, Hovevei Zion, was in an advanced state of enfeeblement. Mindful of repercussions from the czarist authorities and from the Ottoman rulers of Palestine, the movement had muted its nationalist political aims. Concentrating on settlement activity with modest means, it had become dependent on Rothschild largess and subject to Rothschild control. In the words of a Hovevei Zion adherent: Zionism was ensnared by "petty, stagnant projects and exceedingly small, downright microscopic resources."[43] Hovevei Zion's cautious policies and modest achievements had failed to mobilize Jews around Zionism and had even demoralized its own followers. With the Zionist will floundering, Herzl's political maximalism captured the imagination of Jews, raised Zionism's standing in the Jewish world, and implanted Zionism in the European political arena.

Zionism as a New Jewish Identity

Herzl once memorialized his conversion to Zionism through a story, "The Inn of Aniline." The narrative is contrived and didactic, of little literary interest but of considerable biographical significance. A professor driven to thoughts of suicide because of marital problems meets an innkeeper who tells him that he too was once on the verge of suicide. What saved him from complete despair was an encounter with a worker in need, on whom he pressed some money. The worker told the innkeeper that where he worked, worthless refuse was rendered valuable, for in his factory aniline dyes, which yielded "beautiful, radiant colors," were manufactured out of coal tar. (The worker was referring to the manufacture of synthetic dyes, a great nineteenth-century German technological achievement.) The innkeeper took these words as an omen. His life too was like a "residue" from which something useful could be made. As a result, his former "ironical, craven, and melancholy worldview" gave way, and out of his despair a new outlook awakened in him of "courage, self-denial, steadfastness, and devotion." Herzl had described his own inner transformation in strikingly similar terms to Schnitzler: "I have never been in such a happy mood of exaltation. I am not thinking of dying, but of a life full of manly deeds, which will expunge and eliminate everything base, wanton, and confused that has ever been in me."[44]

Herzl meant this allegory to have a twofold application, both to himself and to the Jewish people. Through his own transformation he had become "the man who makes aniline dyes out of refuse," for he would remake Jews, the "refuse of human society," into "new men."[45] Herzl saw his personal transformation as a model for the collective transformation of the Jews.

With his conversion to Zionism, depths of passion, enthusiasm, and zeal were unleashed in Herzl that he had never known before. Certainly there had been no evidence of such qualities in his writings. His plays had shown him to be clever and witty, with a streak of melancholy and cynicism. Light comedies, "good for an evening's entertainment," Arnold Zweig called them. Leon Kellner, an early Zionist associate and a professor of literature, once described Herzl's stage characters as having "spirit, temperament, intelligence, but little soul, almost never heart, and foibles instead of passions."[46]

Herzl had achieved his greatest success as a writer of *feuilletons*, impressionistic essays close to the style of today's *New Yorker* magazine, ranging from travel descriptions and stories to discussions of plays, books, or noted personalities. Carl Schorske has called the *feuilleton* the product of a bourgeois culture turned "inward to the cultivation of the self." Characteristic of the *feuilletonist*'s style was "passive receptivity toward outer reality and, above all, sensitivity to psychic states." As a reflection of his inner states, Herzl's essays have been described as "now faintly tinged with melancholy, now brilliantly sparkling, full of profound pathos and yet as lucid as crystal." These qualities found expression in the "elegance of his aphorisms, as well as his ironic skepticism."[47] There could be no greater contrast between this de-

tached lucidity, melancholy, and irony, characteristic of Herzl's Viennese aestheticism, and his new-found political enthusiasm and zeal.

If Herzl's *feuilletons* betrayed the melancholy aesthete, and his plays clever
invention without depth, it was because, as Kellner put it so well: "He denied
the existence of great passions, for he had not yet experienced them himself."[48] Embracing the Jewish cause, Herzl was transformed from an observer
of life to an enthusiast, from a skeptic to a prophet.

It was Herzl's identification with an idealized, transfigured Jewry that
allowed him to embrace the Jewish cause, unleashing his passion and zeal.
We saw that this change had actually begun earlier and led to the writing of
The New Ghetto. But Zionism provided Herzl with a critical ingredient absent
when he wrote the play. This aspect of Zionism has been defined by Stephen
Poppel as "a coherent, integrated, and compelling world view; in short, as
the source of a viable and supportive identity."[49] *The New Ghetto* marked
Herzl's conversion to a new Jewish ideal, but Zionism provided him with a
comprehensive ideology in which this new ideal could be grounded.

Herzl's Zionism certainly had the elements of a coherent worldview. He
redefined Jewry as a nation and proceeded to scan the symbols and rituals
of Judaism for nationalist associations. Religious objects like the *menorah*, the
seven-branched candelabrum used in the ancient temple, now symbolized and
celebrated "justice, truth, liberty"—secular and nationalist values.[50] Herzl
summoned Jews to return to Judaism, "the faith of our fathers," for the
religious heritage was the sole common element linking Jews. But Judaism's
value for Herzl was instrumental, not intrinsic; it promoted national cohesion
and served as a bridge to the Jewish masses. Hence rabbis in the Jewish state,
with their hold over the masses, were to foster civic virtues: morality, discipline, work, sacrifice for the state.[51]

Similarly, Herzl offered a new understanding of the course of Jewish
history. Centuries of Diaspora life were now viewed as an aberration, and a
merely interrupted Jewish political sovereignty as the norm. Jews were now
to regard themselves as a nation that had endured a two thousand-year period
of captivity. During these centuries, Jewish culture had become isolated and
stagnant, while Jews became pariahs, stigmatized and scorned. As such, Herzl
believed—and this reflected his own experience—Jews had come to scorn
themselves, to consider being Jewish a taint. A modern state would bridge
twenty centuries of passivity, isolation, and self-contempt and link Jews once
more with their heroic past, the ancient era of Jewish kingdoms. Of course,
Herzl highlighted the political—not the religious—virtues of the ancient He-
brews.

Herzl reinvented the Jewish past and used Judaic traditions to legitimate
modern political nationalism. He linked modern political goals to a recon-

ceived Jewish heritage, a futuristic program to the notion of a revived archaic community. Such linkages between past, present, and future gave his nationalist worldview its pedigree, its authority, and its ability to reshape personal identity.

Calling Herzl's Zionism a new worldview suggests that it represented a total break with his past view. This is correct, but only in the sense that Herzl's Zionism blended old and new views, continuities and discontinuities, into a new synthesis. For one, he still carried into Zionism his liberal and assimilationist conceptions. Accordingly, the nationalist reinterpretation of Jewish history and Judaism did not lead Herzl to an intense reengagement with Jewish cultural or ethical or religious sources. Nor did he show any interest in the revival of the Hebrew language. Herzl's Zionism involved no attempt to restore a comprehensive Hebrew culture to the modern world. In addition, he was too rooted in Europe for Palestine to evoke any resonances in him. In what way then was Zionism a transformative ideology?

We find a clue in Stephen Poppel's analysis of the first generation of German Zionists. He has argued that Zionism provided this generation, fully as assimilated as Herzl, a basis for renewed pride in their Jewish origins. For them, Jewish self-affirmation was by itself a major achievement, which found its chief outlet and expression in working for a Jewish state. In Poppel's account these Zionists experienced a "fundamental and sweeping reorientation of personality and identity" akin to a religious conversion. Typically, one young German Jew described himself as having been rescued from "anomie, rootlessness, and pallid aestheticism" through Zionism.[52]

In Poppel's account, Zionists such as Richard Lichtheim, Max Bodenheimer, Adolf Friedemann, described themselves moving suddenly from inner slavery to freedom. Hannah Arendt has characterized this feeling of inner liberation as a restored sense of personal honor and a break with "hollow pretenses." Some seem to have endured the same conflicts as Herzl in an age of rising antisemitism, torn between assimilation, Jewish self-disdain, and the pull of Jewish loyalty and solidarity. Lacking an attachment to Judaism, unsteeped in Jewish culture, they found in political Zionism a basis for Jewish self-affirmation. The change was most succinctly put by Adolf Friedemann, a colleague and biographer of Herzl: "Zionism reconciles us with ourselves." Equally significant was Richard Lichtheim's declaration: "[Zionism] created a new problem—the question of the content of a Judaism that . . . had to enter into the family of nations anew. But that was not so important to begin with as the consciousness of belonging to the Jewish people, and the manly bearing that was a consequence. *It was a matter of affirming myself and thereby becoming free* . . . "[53]

Friedemann's and Lichtheim's declarations help us pinpoint exactly how Zionism functioned as a transformative ideology for Herzl. We need only recall Herzl's conception of Judaism and Jewry before he became a Zionist. Nothing was more characteristic of this than the copy of Heinrich Heine's poem "The New Israelite Hospital in Hamburg," found among Herzl's notes of the early 1890s. Agitated over rising antisemitism, he had copied it down. Heine described the hospital in the poem as treating three maladies: "poverty, physical pain, and Jewishness / The last named is the worst of all the three: / That thousand-year-old family complaint." In S. S. Prawer's recent sensitive analysis of the poem, the malady of Jewishness had a two-fold meaning for Heine: both that Jews had endured profound suffering at the hands of Gentiles, and that Jewishness itself was a defect, a sickness. It is no wonder the poem appealed to Herzl, for Heine was expressing ambivalent feelings familiar to him: both intense loyalty to a history of victimization and martyrdom—notwithstanding Heine's view of Judaism as—"the unhealthy faith from ancient Egypt"—and Jewish self-disdain. Not only did Herzl copy the poem down, but he later entitled a Zionist article after a key phrase "The Family Affliction." He had found in Zionism the cure for both afflictions: Jewish victimization and the defect of Jewishness.[54]

Martin Buber once said of Herzl that "He joined the ranks of active Jewishness not out of Jewishness, but out of a manly solidarity.[55] Herzl had devised a new definition of Jewishness, purely national and political, providing him with a basis for Jewish pride and self-respect, and confirming a new solidarity with the Jewish nation. What he offered assimilated Jews like himself was nothing more, but nothing less than inner liberation from feelings of Jewish inferiority and ambivalence, and thereby a new direction in their lives.

Zionism as the Reconciliation of Jews and Gentiles

Herzl's ideology combined a nationalist conception of Jewry with liberal and assimilationist ideals. Charting new territory, his image of the national Jew was eclectic. He could speak of restoring a unified, native Jewish character, untarnished by assimilationist mimicry: "Our own character, not a Marrano-like, borrowed untruthful character, but our own." He also observed that in a Jewish state the faults of Jews would not be ascribed to the Jewish essence. Jews would no longer be a minority, subject to invidious stereotyping by host peoples, but a sovereign majority, able to define themselves: "The Promised Land, where it is all right for us to have hooked noses, black or red beards, and bandy legs without being despised for these things alone."[56] One could add, where hooked noses will be renamed equiline noses, a mark of distinction. But at the same time, Herzl envisaged the Jewish state as a multinational federation on the Swiss model, where Jews would perpetuate their European host cultures and languages and German would be the *lingua franca*: "The language in every confederated province to accord with the local majority. No Hebrew state—a state of Jews, where it is no disgrace to be a Jew."[57] In this light, the commonly used English title *The Jewish State* for *Der Judenstaat* is a misnomer. The correct translation of *Judenstaat* is a state of Jews, or a Jews' state, not a Jewish state. The goal of the state was to continue the project of assimilation, but under Jewish self-rule, as peers of Gentiles.

Herzl depicted a Jewish state in Palestine as a Europeanist outpost, part of "the wall of defense against Asia," a transmitter of Europe's culture to the East; a state serving pan-European interests and protected by the European powers. An anecdote recalled by Olga Schnitzler shows how much Herzl regarded the Jewish state as a European transplant. He once told his friend Richard Beer-Hofmann, the Viennese-Jewish writer: "We will have a university and an opera [in the Jewish state] and you will attend the opera in your swallow-tailed coat with a white gardenia in your button-hole." Beer-Hofmann retorted: "Oh no, if it came to that I would dress in a silk burnoose, wear several necklaces, and a turban with a diamond brooch.[58] He was at least willing to acknowledge that Palestine would have Middle Eastern trappings.

The land of Israel evoked no stirring associations, no ancestral memories in Herzl. On his one visit in 1898, he was repelled by its filth and by its fanatical religious atmosphere. Typical of the way Europeans saw the non-European world, he considered Palestine a blank slate on which Jews could write at will. It was virgin soil, a laboratory for Europe's advanced technology and progressive social schemes, a land unencumbered by old infrastructures and inherited social privileges and grievances, a place where a new start was possible. Herzl agreed to concentrate diplomatic efforts on Palestine rather than some other territory, only after he came to see how much passion the land of Israel evoked in East European Jews. Palestine suited his own agenda as well because it was the nearest to Europe of any potential territory and linked to it by a railway network. He saw Jerusalem as a stop on the Berlin-Baghdad railroad.[59]

Rejected by Europe, Herzl wanted Jews to create a mini-Europe elsewhere. After the Christian Social sweep in the September 1895 Vienna election, Herzl declared: "In the election the majority of non-Jewish citizens—no, all of them—declare that they do not recognize us as Austro-Germans. . . . All right, we shall move away; but over there, too, we shall only be Austrians."[60] Not only would Jews perpetuate their host cultures, but they would, for the first time, be accepted by their European compatriots. Only by evacuating Europe would Herzl come to be recognized as an Austro-German. Concurrently, only by leaving would Jewish bitterness toward their European homelands dissipate and turn once more into love.

Though Herzl sought a state for Jews, he did not try to foster Jewish national cultural distinctiveness. Even the flag he envisaged for the Jewish state was social-reformist, evoking no nationalist symbolism: seven gold stars against a white background, to symbolize the seven-hour working day. He saw no value in the Hebrew language revival, only the danger of creating a "linguistic ghetto." The aim of Zionism was to end centuries of Jewish isolation, the misery of being scorned outsiders. Reviving Jewish cultural distinctiveness meant recreating a "monstrous ghetto" once more.[61] Still tied to his European matrix, Herzl was forging a new destiny for Jews as honored Europeans.

One of the chief ends of Herzl's Zionism was to bind former victims and oppressors together again, but in a new relationship of equality and mutual respect. In his utopian novel *Old-New Land*, a description of Jewish society twenty years after the acquisition of a charter, Herzl dwelt on the loving relationship between the Prussian Kingscourt and the infant son of a leading Jewish figure, David Littwak. Kingscourt was an aristocrat and cavalry officer like Jacob Samuel's nemesis, the antisemitic von Schramm. Even spit and polish "Aryans" now admired Jews.

The very first issue of *Die Welt*, the newspaper of the Zionist movement, described its program as seeking "the reconciliating solution to the Jewish question." Similarly, Herzl was to call Zionism "the redeeming reconciliation between Christians and Jews." This theme takes us back to *The New Ghetto* where the dying Jacob tells his gentile friend Franz Wurzlechner that his ultimate purpose was to seek their reconciliation. Though measuring history in centuries of unabated Christian persecution and Jewish victimization, Herzl was far from bearing Gentiles animosity. A comment by his friend Baron Arthur von Suttner was far off the mark when he called Zionism "an overly brusque and abrupt response to hatred in similar coin—warfare against warfare." On the contrary, the purpose of the Jewish departure from Europe and of statehood was to reconcile Jews and Gentiles, not to renounce Europe but to identify with it, not to emphasize differences between Jews and Gentiles, but to eliminate them.[62]

Such reconciliation was not possible in Europe. The continued treatment of European Jews as guests and second-class citizens only perpetuated Jewish faults. Denied social status, Jews chased after money; gentile disdain and Jewish insecurity promoted Jewish timidity, servility, and self-contempt. The existing psychological ghetto—though now without physical walls—still fostered clannishness and cut Jews off from participation in wider human struggles.

Seeking reconciliation, Herzl envisaged an extraordinarily amicable Jewish evacuation from Europe. Indeed, it is hard to think of a nationalist rupture taking place more benignly. Once Jews acquired a state, mass emigration would be organized with the approval of all the states in which they lived. The sale and lease of Jewish assets in Europe was to be controlled by the Jewish Company, a joint-stock company he charged with developing the economic infrastructure of the Jewish state. The Jewish Company would facilitate the sale or lease of Jewish property to Gentiles, by offering them highly favorable financial arrangements. Herzl called his plan an "amicable expropriation," bringing prosperity to Gentiles. To this end, he wanted the European staff of the Jewish Company to be composed of Gentiles, who are "in no way to become lackeys of the Jews." To ensure this, "respectable anti-Semites" would sit on the supervisory committee. Indeed, Herzl's plan resembled antisemitic proposals to bring general prosperity through a confiscation of Jewish wealth. Herzl seemed to share Christian Social fantasies that Jewish wealth was so abundant, its distribution could significantly ameliorate conditions for Gentiles. Herzl went on to propose that only those Jews would be accepted for settlement in Palestine who possessed a local certificate of honest dealing. It was essential, he insisted, that Jews "leave no dirty dealings behind."[63] This act of economic self-renunciation served several ends. It sealed the Jewish break with materalism, brought departing Jews respect, and initiated a new era of "forgiveness, peace, reconciliation" between Jews and Gentiles.[64]

In one of his drafts of an address to the Rothschilds, Herzl insisted that the departure of the Jews would alter the political, not only the economic face of Europe. He compared the transfer of Jewish property to Gentiles to the expropriation of aristocratic estates during the French Revolution. This violent divestment and the eventual sale of the land to peasants had changed French society, Herzl believed. With characteristic hyperbole, he called it minor compared to the "unprecedented" prosperity the transfer of Jewish property would bring the gentile masses: "Social discontent will be put at rest for some time, perhaps twenty years, possibly even longer."[65]

Such arguments—that the Jewish emigration would dampen European social discontent—were not merely ingenious appeals to Rothschild self-interest, linking Zionism to the protection of their fortune. Herzl's argument reflected his own experience of the economic roots of Austrian antisemitism. Antisemitism resulted from the rapid economic success of formerly despised outsiders. The correlate to this view was that emancipation had placed an intolerably heavy strain on Austrian Liberals, who had to defend an economic system that eased the way for recent outsiders into positions of prominence. Emancipation thus had the unintended effect of strengthening what Herzl called "the atavistic pressure of the Middle Ages."[66] Resentment at the rapid rise of former pariahs and at the Jewish role in revolutionary movements fed illiberalism by reviving dormant hatreds. Herzl was convinced that Zionism would aid the fortunes of liberalism in Austria and elsewhere by removing from it a major political liability, the Jewish presence in Europe and the pressure of Jewish immigration westward from eastern Europe.

Herzl's Zionism was, in this way, a response to the decline of European liberalism and the rise of mass movements of the left and right. He sometimes gave vent to fears about the danger to Jews from the explosive and destructive impulses of the primitive masses. But on other occasions, both before and after he became a Zionist, he felt confident that liberalism would renew itself and gain popular appeal once more. To cite one example: on 30 December 1894, one week after Dreyfus was convicted of treason, Herzl weighed the threat of an eventual Socialist majority in the French Chamber of Deputies, but concluded hopefully: "The energies of the Republic are by no means exhausted. . . . [France] is the land of experiments . . . the great vessel where political innovations simmer for the whole civilized world."[67] Herzl was referring to the adoption of the progressive income tax by the ruling republican parties in order to preempt the Socialists. Liberalism, he believed, could renew itself and regain popular appeal by becoming social reformist, combining free market policies with the nationalization of key economic sectors, backing producers' cooperatives, and social welfare policies.

Zionism, in Herzl's view, could further this liberal renewal. His notion of a transfer of Jewish property favoring Gentiles, enhancing general prosperity, and temporarily relieving European social distress was a way of buying time for liberalism. Even after he became a Zionist, Herzl continued to see the world according to the rationalist premises of liberalism. Mass distress, he was convinced, would eventually be eliminated by technological progress. His belief that progress was inexorable was put forth in terms identical to that of the French Enlightenment *philosophe*, the Marquis de Condorcet. The key to European history, from primitive times to the modern era, was the persistent expansion of the empire of reason. Accordingly, scientific and technological discovery and invention were the overriding creative force in European history, the key to its progressive course. Factories that herded laborers together, and mass production which led to cycles of oversupply and economic crises, he called a product of the age of steam power. New technologies—Herzl was thinking of electricity, a flexible medium which could supply power on either a large or small scale in a great variety of locations— would make factory labor and large-scale production obsolete and create new possibilities of small-scale, dispersed production. "Inventions will disperse those crowded and pressed together [in factories and urban slums] to happier surroundings."[68] Scientific and technological geniuses, who were the key benefactors of humanity, would by their inventions eliminate social distress. In the end, reason would retain its sway over human affairs.

Herzl's notion that the Jewish evacuation from Europe would buy liberalism time to regain influence seems far-fetched, but it was an outgrowth of his view of Zionism as the realization of emancipation and assimilation. The goal of Zionism was to make Jews equal partners in European civilization. From this he concluded that the Jewish State could only be linked to Europe on the basis of a shared liberalism. In addition, Herzl hoped that renewed liberalism would ease the assimilation—in a nonsubservient mode—of those Jews who chose to remain in Europe. Zionism was not so much a mass evacuation from Europe as the channeling of Jews out of Europe, at a pace controlled by the waxing and waning of antisemitism. Privately, Herzl claimed he sought, "*a self-regulating* outflow of Jews. If antisemitism diminishes in a country, the outflow will subside." The Jewish population in Europe had to exceed a certain threshold to evoke antisemitism. Zionism, by providing a homeland for the East European Jewish masses, would keep Jewish numbers in Europe within bounds. In *Old-New Land*, his futuristic novel, Herzl foresaw Zionism's contribution to the consummation of European emancipation. As Jews had attained equality and respect by gaining a state, and antisemitism had been eliminated, European assimilation was no longer an act of subservience, disloyalty, or cowardice. As Jewish competition with Gentiles abated, Jews were welcomed and appreciated for their abilities. With a Jewish state in existence, "the well-meant measures of emancipation became effective everywhere."[69]

Herzl's goal of reconciliation, his view of the Europeanist character of the Jewish state and of Zionism as the fulfillment of emancipation and assimilation determined his remarkably optimistic view about the elimination of antisemitism. Herzl concluded *The Jewish State* by declaring that once his plan was under way, "anti-Semitism will immediately grind to a halt everywhere."[70]

At each stage in Herzl's engagement with the Jewish question, from his initial solutions to Zionism, he had been convinced that once Jews transformed themselves antisemitism would disappear. His analysis of antisemitism reinforced this conviction, for he saw it as partly a relic of the intolerant medieval past and partly as an understandable reaction to an acute social irritant. Former pariahs had emerged from the ghetto as a "bourgeois people," "fearful" rivals to the native middle class. Concurrently, discrimination had pushed the too-numerous Jewish intelligentsia into the camp of revolution. Jews were caught in the middle, reaping the enmity of both the classes that prospered under capitalism and those victimized by it, natural targets for both bourgeois antisocialism and proletarian anticapitalism.

Herzl sometimes went so far as to see antisemitism as a natural response to this Jewish social irritant, though he criticized the unforgiving gentile refusal to make allowances for conduct that was the outcome of gentile persecution. "Europe is being punished for the ghettoes now. To be sure, we are suffering under the sufferings that we are causing." Antisemitism was as much a reflection of what Jews had become as it was of what Europe had become.[71]

Herzl's rationalistic explanation of antisemitism lay stress on the entry of the commercially gifted Jewish bourgeoisie into civil society, coinciding with the ascent of capitalism and industrialization. As such, antisemitism was situationally determined and natural. A gentile colleague was later to record Herzl's insistence to him that "antisemitism arose not from religious intolerance or racial antipathy, but from the mercantile superiority of the Jews." As former outsiders, Herzl concluded in *The Jewish State*, Jews had climbed too high. No majority would grant to "a minority that was but recently despised" the social legitimacy and access to political authority commensurate with the economic standing of the Jews. Herzl judged this entirely reasonable. In his diary he insisted that one could not expect a majority to "let themselves be subjugated" by formerly scorned outsiders whom they had just released from the ghetto. Herzl could go so far as to state: "I find that the anti-Semites are fully within their rights." This rational explanation of antisemitism was central to Herzl's conception of Zionism, which was premised on the ultimate gentile acceptance of Jews, once they ceased being an irritant in Europe.[72]

Surprisingly, at other times, Herzl insisted on the dark irrational side of antisemitism, emphasizing that Jews had always gratuitously served as convenient scapegoats and objects of murderous urges. Antisemitism was a dogged, virtually incurable survival of preemancipation anti-Jewish attitudes.[73] Thus, implied in some of Herzl's explanations of antisemitism was its irrationality and incurability.

Accordingly, Herzl could utter chilling prophecies about the fate that awaited Jews in Europe. One such was addressed to the Rothschilds: "Will it be a revolutionary expropriation from below or a reactionary confiscation from above? Will they chase us away? Will they kill us? I have a fair idea it will take all these forms, and others."[74] Such prophecies stemmed from Herzl's apprehensions about mass parties and demagogic politicians, the outcome of universal manhood suffrage. One impulse behind his Zionism was an ominous sense of the fanatic dimensions hatred of Jews could take, and hence the special dangers imperiling Jews in an age of potential political instability and disorder. On the other hand, Herzl's belief in Jewish-Gentile reconciliation with the emergence of Zionism led him to virtually domesticate antisemitism, to see it as nothing more than a natural response to the claims and success of formerly scorned outsiders. Accordingly, Herzl could posit the elimination of antisemitism and the wholesale acceptance of Jews, once they transformed themselves into state-makers.

Assessing Herzl's views on antisemitism, Amos Elon has concluded that he did not understand the phenomenon in that "he grossly overrated its rational component at the expense of the psychotic." While Elon overlooks statements by Herzl about the irrational nature of antisemitism, he is correct in concluding that Herzl predicted antisemitism would simply disappear once Jews had a state. The Israeli historian Shulamit Volkov was the first to shed light on Herzl's ambiguous view of antisemitism, by linking it to his conception of Zionism as the fulfillment of European emancipation and assimilation. Herzl submerged his view of antisemitism as irrational, because he would not let go of his belief in the viability of European humanism and universalism and in Europe's capacity to accept Jews. Thus Herzl could not view antisemitism as endemic to Europe and incurable, a constant in its history, nor could he view antisemitism as a sign of Europe's moral failure. Probing more deeply would have called into question Herzl's exalted view of European civilization and his optimism about Europe's ultimate acceptance of Jews.[75]

Herzl's Zionist Diplomacy

At the heart of Herzl's obsession with the Jewish question was a quest both for Jewish pride and for respect and status in Europe. Hence Zionism was to "lay the foundations of [Jewish] respect in the eyes of the world." When the Rothschilds refused him their aid, Herzl impulsively speculated that an attack on their wealth by a Jewish leader like himself would aid in the "rehabilitation of our despised name." Herzl elsewhere called the word Jew a "*Geusennamen*," to be transformed into a "term of honor." *Geusennamen* comes from the French *gueux*, or beggar, a term of contempt the ruling Spanish gave rebellious Flemish nobles in the sixteenth century. The rebel nobles then adopted this name, transforming it into a mark of pride. By the same token, Jews as state-makers would transform the pejorative Jew into a synonym for honor. Zionism would make "the derisive cry 'Jew!' . . . an honourable appellation, like 'German,' 'Englishman,' 'Frenchman.' "[76]

Once Jews changed, Herzl believed, gentile attitudes to them would also change. In the meantime, Jews needed the elixer of gentile esteem to see themselves in a new way. Almost as soon as he conceived of the Jewish state, Herzl pursued gentile esteem by casting himself in the role of a Jewish diplomat. Early on, he declared: " Today I say: I shall associate with the mighty of this earth as their equal." Adolf Böhm rightly noted in such remarks by Herzl "a touch of ghetto-like feelings." Herzl was still overcoming the stigma of Jewishness, reconstituting Jewish pride, and again measuring Jewish dignity in spoonfuls of gentile acceptance. Meeting with Count Badeni, the Austrian minister-president, and later Count Eulenberg, the German ambassador to Vienna, Herzl recorded the social nuances of these encounters. That Badeni lit Herzl's cigar was a triumph, sure to impress Jews when he told them. Eulenberg received him at his country estate outside of Berlin, and though Herzl observed that the count was aloof and condescending, he also reflected that only Zionism had made it possible for a Eulenberg to "associate with the Jew Herzl."[77]

Herzl's nationalism was born out of the ordeal of gentile rejection and carried the stamp of this experience. As a Zionist his need to be confirmed by Gentiles remained unabated. In this sense Herzlean Zionism was never a complete act of Jewish self-emancipation. That it was not complete influenced his political priorities, which were fixed, singlemindedly, on gaining political recognition for Zionism in the capitals of Europe. Herzl's deepest obsession was with Jewish honor. Honor was a social category. It was not conferred by one's own conscience, but by social standing, which included self-awareness of status and confirmation of that status by others. For Herzl both were essential.

It was in part because Herzl sought Jewish honor that the goal of his Zionist politics was diplomatic recognition for Jewish sovereignty in the capitals of Europe. From the beginning, he directed his appeal to Gentiles as much as to Jews. Almost immediately, Herzl sought interviews with the sultan, the German kaiser, the foreign ministers of the major European powers, to gain their public endorsement for a Jewish state.

It can be said that Herzl's approach resulted from a shrewd assessment of where world power lay at the turn of the twentieth century and that the door to a Jewish state had to be opened in Constantinople, or Berlin, or London, or Moscow. Herzl was certainly not the first nationalist statesman to seek a client-sponsor relationship with a major power. It is not, however, Herzl's search for diplomatic recognition that requires explanation, but its exclusiveness, at the cost of other nationalist strategies. After all, a national politician can cultivate sources of power in a variety of ways: by developing a foothold in the homeland—a population base and social and economic infrastructure—as the foundation for a state; by creating national consciousness through fostering a national cultural revival and national language; by creating a grass-roots movement to take over already existing communal institutions; by demanding national rights wherever a portion of the nation resides; by military preparations; finally, by seeking political and diplomatic recognition from other states for national sovereignty. Though the need to make concessions to other Zionists was to lead him in several of these directions, Herzl himself wished to pursue just the last of these strategies.

Bein noted that, after publishing *The Jewish State*, Herzl had just three goals in mind: organizing the Society of Jews, to be made up of prominent Jews who would negotiate for a state; seeking influential contacts to gain him an entrance to the sultan and the kaiser; and founding a newspaper as a publicity organ for the movement. Accordingly, Herzl opposed Zionist de-

mands for national representation, national rights, and national cultural institutions in the lands where Jews resided, for it was necessary to "everywhere
gain and keep the sympathies of governments." Herzl's priorities led the Austrian Zionist Robert Stricker to observe that "Herzlean Zionism was, in the
first instance, an appeal not to the Jewish world, but to the Gentiles."[78]

Herzl envisaged the acquisition of statehood as a smooth process; the
grant of statehood would be endorsed by all the powers as in the pan-European interest. The Israeli historian Jacob Talmon has observed about this
facile scheme: "The Jewish predicament revealed to Herzl something of the
abyss, of the ultimate intractable unreasonableness and horrible beastliness of
man, yet in his vision of the solution of the Jewish question there is nothing
apocalyptic or catastrophic, no war, no clash of rights, no human sacrifices,
no gnashing of teeth, no dreadful break-through."[79] A state would not be
gained by Jews through the spilling of blood, harsh military struggles, a clash
with Arabs holding competing claims. Preoccupied with issues of Jewish
honor, with terminating the condition of Jews as scorned outsiders and pariahs, Herzl envisaged statehood as virtually a joint Jewish-Gentile project,
one that bound Jews to Europe in a new relationship.

To realize his goal Herzl had to assume a far-fetched scenario: That states
such as imperial Germany and czarist Russia would consider it in their self-
interest to allow mass immigration to a Jewish state, to rid their nations of
Jewish competition and political radicalism; that fervently Christian rulers
would have no objection to Jewish sovereignty over the Holy Land; that the
Ottoman Empire, already weakened by emergent nationalisms, would consider it in its self-interest both to create a beachhead within its borders for
yet another nationalist movement, and to receive massive Jewish financial aid
to ease its foreign debt. As the Austrian-Jewish sociologist Ludwig Gumplowicz chided Herzl: "And now your *political naiveté!* . . . do you count on
gondola Willy [the German emperor, Wilhelm II] and Abdul-Hamed [the
Turkish sultan]? You believe that these two fat meat-clumps are capable of
creating a state for Jews—even if they are not the *'achbroishim'* (rats) that
they are!"[80]

It was Ahad Ha-Am, Russian Zionism's foremost ideologist, who took
the measure of some of the deepest impulses behind Herzl's adherence to
Zionism. A reluctant attendant at the First Zionist Congress, Ahad Ha-Am
noted that those he disdainfully called "the Western 'Zionists' always have
their eyes fixed on the non-Jewish world." Ahad Ha-Am was not wrong, for
one of Herzl's chief purposes in organizing the congress was to publicize the
solution to the Jewish question to the gentile world and win over gentile
opinion to Zionism. Ahad Ha-Am noted this in the regular practice of *Die
Welt*, the Zionist weekly, of publishing statements favorable to Zionism by
Gentiles, and in Herzl's effusive public expression of thanks to gentile guests

at the First Congress. Ahad Ha-Am saw these practices as more than canny strategy, and he described what lay behind them through an allegory about a woman abandoned by her lover: "There is an old lady who, despairing utterly of regaining her lover by entreaties, submission and humility, suddenly decks herself out in splendour and begins to treat him with hatred and contempt. Her object is still to influence him. She wants him at least to respect her in his heart of hearts, if he can no longer love her." In "aiming simply at finding favour in the eyes of nations," Ahad Ha-Am concluded that such Zionists did not differ much from assimilated Jews. The only difference was that assimilated Jews sought "love," while these Zionists sought "respect."[81]

For Ahad Ha-Am, Herzl's avid search for gentile respect led to a flawed political strategy, an exclusive concern with gentile political recognition. Arthur Ruppin as well voiced a widespread criticism when he pointed out that a state handed to the Jews on a silver platter carried no political or moral legitimacy. The Jewish claim to the land of Israel had to be earned by reestablishing a Jewish presence there closely tied to the land and by fostering a new Hebrew-speaking Jew. Without such an organic presence, and in the absence of a Jewish society with incipient national institutions, not only would the state be merely a colonialist offshoot, but a charter would be an ephemeral creation, easily withdrawn if the granting powers so wished.[82]

But if Herzl's Zionism was symbiotic on Europe, his radical redefinition of the Jewish relationship to Europe must also be underlined. Herzl was declaring that Jews no longer wished to live in a state with a gentile majority or be ruled by Gentiles, that they wanted to rule themselves. Jews would no longer address appeals to the better nature of Gentiles, to their sense of justice and humanity. Jews and Gentiles were to be independent parties, negotiating their relations on the basis of cool self-interest, a quid pro quo. Hence Herzl was resourceful in conjuring up real and exaggerated, actual and potential benefits to governments from the creation of a Jewish state: these included loans to ease the Ottoman foreign debt, a millstone that gave European governments political leverage over the Ottomans; the defense of European interests in the Middle East; ridding Europe of Jewish revolutionaries and of politically destabilizing antisemitism; finally, easing pressure on Europe to provide an asylum for the East European Jewish masses. By convening annual Zionism congresses, Herzl sought to magnify Jewish power by projecting to the world the image of a tightly unified and worldwide Jewish political movement. Evoking sources of Jewish power wherever he could, Herzl even played on fearsome antisemitic stereotypes of Jewish wealth and international solidarity. In this sense, he raised the Jewish political posture to new levels of boldness and independence. Though Herzl failed to gain the sought-after charter, his campaign for political recognition culminated in the admittedly highly tentative offers by the British of a grant of land in the Sinai Peninsula, and later in East Africa. These offers enhanced Zionism's political credibility and legitimacy as the keeper of Jewish sovereignty and placed Zionism on the European political agenda.

The First Zionist Congress

The publication of *The Jewish State* in February 1896 recorded Herzl's pristine vision of his political goals. Afterward, he had to adjust to new realities and modify his goals. Initially, Herzl pursued his agenda of diplomatic activity through meetings with Ottoman officials in Constantinople, efforts to cultivate the kaiser through the mediation of his uncle, the grand duke of Baden, and other such initiatives. For his diplomacy he needed and sought the financial sponsorship of wealthy Jews and the support of Jewish notables. David Vital has pointed out that by late 1896 and early 1897 Herzl's efforts had failed. He became demoralized, fearing his cause had lost its momentum.[83]

In these discouraging circumstances, Herzl decided to call a public congress of Jews to regain impetus for his campaign. The congress was to be a display of Jewish boldness and candor, in Herzl's words: "A glorious demonstration to the world of what Zionism is and of what it wants."[84] No less important, Herzl hoped to establish a unified and centralized Zionist political movement, with an appointed executive committee to direct its affairs until the next congress. The congress was to be a kind of parliament—Herzl called it a "Jewish National Assembly"—with elected delegates to whom the executive was accountable. Herzl's conception—still vague—was of a polity-in-being. This accorded with his initial view that Jews needed a state which, out of its imperious necessities, would train them to become "real men."[85] He wished to instil Jews with political virtues, get them used to political authority and discipline, as a prelude to statehood.

Herzl's preferred course of action was to enlist Western and Central European Jewish notables to his cause, men of wealth and influence in the gentile world, who would lend his efforts credibility and aid him in his diplomatic negotiations. He concentrated his efforts on recruiting such notables to the congress. Turned down almost universally, he then shifted his efforts to Eastern European Jewry, to the followers of Hibbat Zion in czarist Russia. With the publication of *The Jewish State*, Herzl had received some enthusiastic declarations of support from Zionist societies in the Habsburg Empire. However on the whole, Hibbat Zion, particularly in czarist Russia where it was strongest, had kept its distance from Herzl, troubled by his political maximalism, his call for quick solutions, the exclusive priority he set on diplomacy, and the passive role he assigned to the Jews of Eastern Europe in the campaign for a state. Now, in calling for a congress, he met with greater success, in part because of Hibbat Zion's despair over its own fortunes, in part because it hoped to act as a counterweight to Herzl. As a result, East European Hibbat Zion predominated at the First Zionist Congress.[86]

Vital describes the first congress as a watershed event. Most of those in attendance were deeply moved by the gathering and felt that its reverberations would not soon fade away. Herzl's charismatic gifts as a leader first emerged at the congress. But the congress went so well because both Herzl and the followers of Hibbat Zion showed themselves willing to accommodate each other's priorities by compromising on the wording of the Zionist platform. Thus the demand for a sovereign state was put somewhat ambiguously and Hibbat Zion's agenda of incremental settlement and Hebraic cultural revival were recognized in equally ambiguous formulas. The alliance between Herzl and Hibbat Zion, based on mutual need, necessarily attenuated his initial goals, but this story of compromise and conflict over Zionist priorities would take us beyond the limits of our study.

8

The Dreyfus Legend

How I proceeded . . . to a practical program is already a mystery to me, although it happened within the last few weeks. It is in the realm of the unconscious.

(May or June 1895)

What made me a Zionist was the Dreyfus trial . . . which I witnessed in 1894.[1]

(September 1899)

I HAVE ARGUED THAT Herzl's transformation into a Zionist was a lengthy process, abounding in inner conflict and contradiction as he struggled with his ambivalence over both Jewishness and assimilation. I have insisted that this process can even be divided into distinct phases. I have also maintained that Herzl was chiefly reacting against Austrian antisemitism. This interpretation flies in the face of Herzl's subsequent explanation of his conversion, as an abrupt transition spurred by one dramatic event in France, the Dreyfus trial. In order to refute Herzl's own explanation of his transformation, I shall have to make a broad excursion in time and place, to 1898–1899, when Herzl made this claim, then to the France of the Dreyfus trial and the later Dreyfus Affair.

In 1899 Herzl created the remarkable legend that the earth-shattering impact upon him of the trial of Captain Alfred Dreyfus in Paris turned him to Zionism. The legend had begun to take shape earlier. In an 1898 letter, Herzl maintained that his play *The New Ghetto* was written "after the first Dreyfus trial and under its impact." On the contrary, we know from his correspondence at the time he wrote the play that Herzl was preoccupied with antisemitism in Austria. Even more damning, the handwritten copy of the play records its start and completion dates, 21 October and 8 November, but the espionage trial of the French-Jewish army officer began on 19 December, and the guilty verdict was handed down on 22 December. Such unreliability on Herzl's part does not promote confidence in his next and more celebrated claim.[2]

In an article in 1899 Herzl insisted: "What made me a Zionist was the Dreyfus trial . . . which I witnessed in 1894." Herzl had covered the trial for his newspaper, but his reports of the event do not confirm his assertion. None of his dispatches suggest the trial led to a new realization on his part, to some great awakening. What is more, at the time of his conversion to Zionism in May 1895, he made no mention of the Dreyfus case.[3]

Nevertheless, scholars have generally given credence to Herzl's version, perhaps out of deference to the founder of political Zionism, perhaps in the light of Herzl's usual candor and forthrightness, a quality that stands out in his Zionist diary. Both Alex Bein and Amos Elon accept Herzl's assertion— well after the fact—that he knew from the start Dreyfus was falsely accused, even though Herzl did not so say at the time of the trial. Neither insist, as unequivocally as Herzl did, that the Dreyfus trial by itself triggered his conversion to Zionism. Elon calls it "merely the last straw." But even granting as much as they do to Herzl's account requires a leap of faith. Bein knew full well that Herzl was preoccupied with the Jewish question—and had been alarmed about antisemitism—for years prior to the Dreyfus trial. He also acknowledged that Herzl did not mention the trial in his Zionist diary, his first account of his conversion to Zionism, nor in his "Autobiography," written three years later, just when the Dreyfus Affair—the issue of reopening the trial—had begun to tear France apart. Still and all, Bein managed to accommodate Herzl's claim. Fancifully, he reconstructed Herzl's experience: "The ground was pulled out from under his feet. A deep abyss opened up before him, a boundless solitude engulfed him. He despaired of humanity." Bein concluded: He saw " how deeply Jew-hatred was rooted in the instincts of the masses." Thus for Bein, the trial remained the decisive if culminating experience in Herzl's conversion to Zionism.[4]

Among Herzl scholars, David Vital is more circumspect, arguing that the trial, at most, "contributed to tipping the balance between the opposing drives within him." Others have rejected Herzl's claim altogether. In a carefully documented article, Henry Cohn has demonstrated its implausibility, arguing instead that Herzl's conversion was a response to events in Austria. Desmond Stewart has called Herzl's claim a "legend." However those who reject Herzl's assertion offer no convincing explanation for it, nor do they account for Herzl's conversion to Zionism.[5]

Another version of the Dreyfus legend takes a somewhat broader view. Carl Schorske has judged the cumulative impact of French antisemitism during Herzl's four years in Paris, rather than the Dreyfus trial, as central to his conversion to Zionism. Since I have argued that French antisemitism had less impact on Herzl than the antisemitism of his Austrian homeland, I must deal with the Schorske thesis at length. He insists on "Herzl's deepening concern with the Jewish question in France to its climax in the condemnation of Captain Dreyfus. Through one episode after another—an anti-Semitic play, an officer's death in a duel in defense of his honor as a Jew, anti-Semitic demonstrations, libel trials, the Panama scandal—Herzl reported, reflected, and became ever more deeply engaged." Schorske claims that Herzl's experience in France was uniquely shattering, since he considered that country "the font of liberty and civilization, the motherland of the rights of man." Because he "expected more" from France, the home of Jewish emancipation, his disillusion was all the more devastating. Five years after the Dreyfus trial, Herzl did indeed claim to have been especially shocked by antisemitism in France: "Republican, modern, civilized France, a hundred years after the Declaration of Human Rights." Nevertheless, we must ask if this was a retrospective view. Did it accord with his experience during the crucial years 1891–1895?[6]

We can retrace Herzl's thoughts during these years through his newspaper reports on French antisemitism. During that time he covered a number of antisemitic outrages. On 23 June 1892, the Jewish army officer Captain Armand Mayer was killed in a duel, fought in response to a campaign launched by the antisemitic newspaper *La Libre Parole* to impugn the loyalty of Jews in the military. Herzl sent his newspaper an account of this tragedy. Earlier in June he had covered the Drumont-Burdeau trial, a libel action initiated by Burdeau against Edouard Drumont, France's most prominent antisemite and the editor of *La Libre Parole*. Drumont had charged that Burdeau, the vice-president of the Chamber of Deputies, had been bribed by Baron Alphonse Rothschild to renew the privileges of the Bank of France. Later that year Herzl reported on the Panama scandal, after the collapse of the French effort to build the Panama Canal. The Panama Company had gone into bankruptcy in 1889, wiping out the savings of thousands of small investors. In September 1892, *La Libre Parole* exposed the endemic corruption in the company's operations: newspapers had been paid to report favorably on the company, parliamentary deputies had been bribed to approve government loans. *La Libre Parole* wildly exaggerated the role of several Jews in the affair, seeing the hand of a Jewish conspiracy behind the scenes. The Panama affair was a major political scandal dominating the news for several months, shaking the credibility of Parliament and ruining political careers.[7]

Before we turn to Herzl's assessment, it must be said that most of these incidents were setbacks to the antisemitic cause. After Captain Mayer's death, the Grand Rabbi of France, Zadoc Kahn, issued a ringing denunciation of *La Libre Parole* for its press campaign against Jewish army officers. Almost the whole of the Paris press acclaimed Rabbi Kahn's initiative. As we saw in chapter 5, Mayer's military funeral, proceeding through the streets of Paris, attracted tens of thousands of sympathetic onlookers. The minister of war, Charles de Freycinet, rose in the Chamber of Deputies to condemn antisemitism for sowing divisions in France and proclaimed that "The army does not distinguish between Jews, Protestants and Catholics." Similarly, the Burdeau-Drumont libel trial was a blow to the antisemitic movement. Drumont was unable to support his allegations. His fabrications were exposed, and he was sentenced to three months in prison, fined, and ordered to publish a recantation of his charges in eighty newspapers. Burdeau's lawyer, the distinguished moderate Republican politician René Waldeck-Rousseau, a former cabinet minister and future premier, denounced antisemitism during the trial. Evidently, Drumont's campaign of provoking libel suits and duels in order to gain publicity for the antisemitic cause had backfired.[8]

Drumont's one great success in 1892 was his exposure of the Panama scandal. This time he had seized upon a genuine issue. The scandal seemed to vindicate antisemitic charges that Parliament, the press, and high finance were working hand in glove to rob ordinary French people. The Panama scandal shook the authority of Parliament and fueled antisemitism. It dominated the news from September 1892 to the end of that year and marked a high point in Drumont's celebrity.[9]

Contrary to Schorske's claim, the tone of Herzl's commentary on these events was hardly one of despair at France's rejection of Jewish emancipation and equality. Indeed, the Viennese reporter spoke admiringly of the French to his Austrian readers. In September 1892, Herzl published a broad assessment of French antisemitism for the *Neue Freie Presse*. His comments about Captain Mayer's posthumous honors were bitterly ironic: "A Jew really cannot ask for more without being presumptuous." But he judged the prospects of French antisemitism to be dim. His analysis deserves to be quoted at length:

> It [antisemitism] is wholly and completely dissimilar here from other lands. One should not let oneself be misled by an identical term. It is not the Asiatic [czarist Russian] kind. Here Jews are not thrown to the mob, as the fearful sleigh driver in the steppe does who has just heard a wolf howl and hastily unhitches and shoots a horse to distract him momentarily. Here antisemitism is neither a wedge slyly driven from above into the national parties. [Herzl was probably referring to the tactical use of antisemitism by Bismarck.] In France, antisemitism is an informal gathering-place, as was Boulangism, where few introductions are required and one can shine with humbler means than elsewhere; a rendezvous for the discontented, a sort of salon for the castoffs.
>
> In France it is surely difficult to ignore that this century of Jewish equality is the same one in which the masses have become prosperous in larger numbers than was ever anticipated. Thus, for the time being, antisemitism is alien to the French people, and they are unable to comprehend it.

There is a core of common sense and a love of justice in the French people. . . . Here the movement will pass, if probably not without excesses and individual catastrophes.

By contrast, several months later, in letters to Moriz Benedikt and Baron Leitenberger, Herzl was to offer a far different assessment of antisemitism in Austria, as a powerful and mainline movement on an upward course. Moreover, his fury over Austrian antisemitism had no parallel in his reaction to French antisemitism.[10]

None of Herzl's opinion pieces about the subsequent Panama scandal singled out antisemitism as an area of particular concern to him. Herzl seemed not to have been shattered nor deeply disillusioned by the power of antisemitism in progressive France.

Herzl's relatively optimistic judgment on French antisemitism is not hard to account for. Robert Byrnes concluded that from early 1893 up to the trial and degradation of Dreyfus in December 1894/January 1895, political antisemitism in France was on the decline. As the leading spokesman of organized antisemitism, Drumont's defense of anarchist bomb-throwing and political assassinations placed him on the extremist margin of French politics. When Sadi Carnot, the president of France, was assassinated by anarchists in June 1894, Drumont fled to Belgium, fearing arrest. He was, at the time, endeavoring to sell *La Libre Parole*, which was in financial difficulty because of a steep drop in its readership.[11]

The antisemitic movement in France, in contrast to its success in Austria, was never able to translate its popular support into political gains. Drumont was no Karl Lueger; moreover, the republican parties in France were successful in mobilizing those with social grievances under their banner. Drumont's attempt to forge a political alliance of anti-republican clerical-conservatives and socialist workers foundered. The former were frightened off by his radicalism, the latter by his clericalism. As early as 1892, the socialists had largely ceased flirting with antisemitism, and its main supporters were to be found in the clerical and monarchist camp, an ebbing force in French politics. Byrnes speaks of the "collapse" of organized antisemitism by the summer of 1894. Marrus calls it "a relatively minor movement until the Dreyfus Affair." Herzl was correct in viewing political antisemitism in France as marginal, a refuge for the most extremist and die-hard of the Boulangists, desperately seeking a new rallying cry after their antiparliamentary alliance collapsed in 1889.[12] As the events surrounding the death of Captain Mayer had shown, the French government was clear and decisive in its opposition to antisemitism. No Liberal abandonment of the Jews had occurred as in Austria, and French Jews did not feel politically isolated as did Jews in Vienna.

The decline of antisemitism and, by contrast, the viability of French liberalism, shows the French political constellation to be far different from Austria's. By 1890, the last serious threat to republican institutions had passed with the disintegration of the Boulangist movement. Its collapse had demonstrated the impossibility of mobilizing a multiclass alliance against the liberal order. By then, a solid middle class had seized the reins of national and local power from the former elite of landowning notables. Republican control of the machinery of state had democratized patronage, creating an army of state and local officials beholden to the new regime. France's unusually wide stratum of contented middling peasants strongly supported the Republic. Most of the French lower middle class enjoyed relative well-being and backed the left-of-center Radical party. France's individualistic democracy, supported, socially and ideologically, by the rugged individualism of small proprietors, had established solid roots. Even those with social and economic grievances chose either the Radicals or the Socialists as their advocates. Thus the parties of the left were able to steer social and economic discontent into democratic channels. Accordingly, the parliamentary elections of August 1893 resulted in an overwhelming victory for the republican parties.[13]

Repeatedly during his stay in Paris, Herzl had reported upon the stability of the French body politic. Assessing developments in 1891, Herzl had explained to his Austrian readers why the vast majority of the French supported the republican parties. As he insisted, the belief that a recent socialist upsurge threatened to duplicate the revolutionary era a century earlier "misses the point," since far too many of the French had a stake in the status quo. He concluded: "The number of these is far greater than the politically privileged in the century preceding. Precisely in France social strata enjoy a middling level of well-being, that in other lands still present a picture of misery. The same new industries that created a proletarian army of the discontented, have also raised an army of defenders." Herzl's subsequent assessment of the Moderate Republican sweep in the elections of 1893 reiterated this theme. Though the French had become cynical and contemptuous of Parliament as a result of the Panama scandal, they desired stability above all. Widespread well-being promoted a defensive posture on the part of the vast majority, not least because of socialist gains. The French desired "peace and the maintenance of the status quo."[14]

It must be said that Herzl was not uniformly optimistic about the solidity of the French republic, nor unconcerned over French antisemitism. The judgment of historians that antisemitism was in decline on the eve of the Dreyfus trial is a retrospective view, not unambiguously apparent to those living in the France of the 1890s. Marrus has observed that the fear of revolution pervaded French society from 1892 to 1898, aroused by strikes, demonstrations, and anarchist bombings. Herzl, too, expressed such fears, most anxiously in late 1892, after the Panama scandal had tainted the republic. Speaking of the masses drawn to revolutionary upheaval, Herzl wondered: "What convulsions will once again shake Europe and particularly France, before a liberal order of things will once more appeal to the people." The "frenzy" during the last session of Parliament ominously recalled the "seething passions of the Convention," just a century before. Would the nemesis of revolution return on its hundredth anniversary? Two years later, Herzl observed that the French Socialists now concentrated on the electoral route to power, rather than on revolutionary agitation. This made them an even greater rallying point for the discontented and a greater threat to the existing order. In expressing these fears about social upheaval, Herzl made no mention of its special danger for Jews, but we can be sure this was on his mind, for he had in the past conjured up images of the "primitive" and "savage" masses, bent on "destruction."[15] As formerly despised outsiders, prominent in both the socialist movement and in finance capitalism, Jews were the natural targets for both bourgeois antisocialism and proletarian anticapitalism and prime scapegoats in times of upheaval. Herzl was well aware that French socialists had identified Jewry with capitalism. He wrote Schnitzler in January 1893 that if revolution came to France, he would probably be shot "as a bourgeois, or a German spy, or a Jew, or a financier."[16]

Nevertheless, there is no indication that Herzl's experience in France was as crucial for him as Schorske contends. He argues that Herzl experienced the "shattering of confidence in the viability of political liberalism" in the very country where it was born. If anything, Herzl judged liberalism to be stronger in France than elsewhere. Nor is there any evidence for Schorske's contention that Herzl was particularly affected by antisemitism in France because it was the home of the Rights of Man, the cradle of republicanism, the first European power to have emancipated the Jews. In December 1894, one week after Dreyfus was convicted of treason, Herzl praised France: "The strength of the Republic is by no means exhausted. The world can still look with anticipation to this land, where the concerns of humanity are always taken up . . . France is the great vessel in which political innovations bubble for the whole civilized world."[17]

In December 1894, Herzl covered the Dreyfus trial for his Austrian readers, the seeming climax of his experience of French antisemitism. But nothing in his dispatches suggests that Herzl viewed the trial, or the public response, as a high point in French antisemitism. Indeed, there is no evidence that Herzl was convinced of Dreyfus's innocence, nor that he believed him deliberately framed, let alone accused, because he was a Jew. But neither, it must be said, did Herzl unreservedly accept the guilty verdict passed by the military tribunal.

As a reporter Herzl navigated through a mass of sometimes contradictory rumors, official statements, press reports, soundings of public opinion, assessing them as best he could for his readers. He calmly reported that Captain Dreyfus had access to defense secrets, that he was believed to be a gambler, and that it was said he had become infatuated with a woman who was an Italian espionage agent. The case reminded him of those of other French officers convicted of treason. Present at the preliminary hearing, he reported that questions had been raised about the authenticity of the evidence that only a public trial could answer. He strongly approved those opposed to the decision to hold the trial *in camera*, for reasons of military security. But when the guilty verdict was announced, he told his readers that "everything led" to confidence in the decision. Seven judges had voted unanimously, and the foreign power Dreyfus allegedly spied for—the German government—had issued no protest or denial. Still, he reported that Dreyfus acted with the composure and dignity of someone convinced of his innocence and quoted a guard who said he was told by Dreyfus that he was being persecuted because he was a Jew. In another dispatch that same day, Herzl reported that Dreyfus had apparently told another guard that he had indeed delivered documents to a foreign power, but as a ruse, to gain vital secrets from them in exchange. Even Dreyfus's protestations seemed contradictory. The most that could be said is that Herzl may have had some lingering reservations about Dreyfus's guilt. Even this is conjecture. Nothing indicates he considered the trial of historical significance or read into it an object lesson about the fate of French Jewry.[18]

One might respond that Herzl suppressed his personal opinion in these dispatches. But surely he could have made more of the few expressions of doubt about Dreyfus's guilt, of the uneasiness some had voiced over the secret proceedings, or of the antisemitic rallying cries unleashed by the trial. In his *Journal de l'Affaire Dreyfus*, Maurice Paléologue recorded shouts from the crowd of "Death to the Jews!" and "Death to the traitor!" during Dreyfus's public ordeal of military dishonor. Émile Durkheim was later to recall the public expressions of joy and triumph over the conviction of a Jew, when public mourning over an act of high treason would have been more appropriate. No mention is made by Herzl of these antisemitic utterances at the degradation ceremony. Alex Bein, to sustain his thesis that Herzl was already convinced Dreyfus was being victimized because he was a Jew, informs us that Herzl's report of the ceremony of degradation is "incomplete," because no mention is made of the antisemitic cries. All he offers in support is sheer conjecture: "We cannot avoid the impression that Herzl's telegrams were edited before they were printed, and it was fear that motivated the excisions." Quite the contrary, the *Neue Freie Presse* frequently carried extensive reports on antisemitism, as well as strong editorials denouncing it.[19] Herzl had every opportunity of taking up the Dreyfus trial again in the *feuilletons* he wrote for the *Neue Freie Presse* in late 1894 and early 1895, as well as in his end-of-year survey, "Frankreich im Jahre 1894." In these pieces Herzl could roam at will, yet in none of them does he discuss the case. The only mention of Dreyfus in his political pieces on France is a reference to the socialist leader Jaurès's argument, that if Dreyfus's treason merited only life imprisonment, then the death penalty for military insubordination should be repealed. Even more telling, in describing his conversion to Zionism in diary entries begun in June 1895, no mention is made of the Dreyfus trial. The first six months of Herzl's diary entries, from June to November 1895, show him to be preoccupied with the electoral success of political antisemitism in Vienna. The Dreyfus trial is mentioned just once. Similarly, in *The Jewish State*, published in January 1896, Herzl's reference to French antisemitism was mild, compared to what he said of its Austrian incarnation: "In Austria the anti-Semites terrorize all of public life. . . . In Paris the so-called higher society walls itself off and excludes the Jews from its clubs."[20]

Like other Jews, Herzl was desolated by the trial, which strengthened French antisemitism. However, throughout 1895 Herzl did not endow the case with special significance. As Bredin explains the Jewish response in his magisterial study of the trial: "It was not fear that predominated, but the strength of the evidence."[21] Jewish indignation was directed against Dreyfus, who had betrayed his fellow Jews, as well as France. Seven officers had unanimously voted him guilty. No one knew at the time that Dreyfus's lawyer had been denied access to an incriminating secret file seen by the judges. The entire press welcomed the court's decision. In January the newspapers were full of rumors that Dreyfus had finally confessed. After that the matter died down. Dreyfus was deported to Devil's Island; he became a forgotten man.

Indeed, all of Herzl's assertions about the impact of the Dreyfus trial upon him came after 1897 when the Dreyfus Affair first began to simmer. In late 1897 evidence pointing to another suspect surfaced, Major Esterhazy. In January 1898, after Esterhazy's acquittal, Émile Zola launched his historic broadside "J'accuse," accusing the army of a cover-up. From that moment, France began to divide into warring camps. Anti-Dreyfusards viewed efforts to reopen the case as a Jewish conspiracy to undermine patriotism and defame the French army. In January and February 1898, and from June to September 1899, France experienced waves of antisemitic riots, wider in scope than those in 1789, 1830, and 1848. The parliamentary elections in the spring of 1898, resulting in a clear victory for the anti-Dreyfusards, showed that popular opinion was against reopening the case. Only a significant but numerically limited corps of intellectuals hammered away on Dreyfus's behalf. Politicians who doubted Dreyfus's guilt prudently remained silent. Only gradually did the circle of Dreyfusards widen. In 1899 popular sentiment swung against the anti-Dreyfusards, now seen as a source of civil unrest and a threat to republican stability. By then the anti-Dreyfusard cause had become a rallying point for Royalists and Clericals, opposed to the republic. Moderates now believed that only a new trial would lay the matter to rest and end divisions in France. In June 1899, the Waldeck-Rousseau government was formed with a mandate to settle the affair. In September, Dreyfus was retried and then pardoned, an outcome widely welcomed.[22]

In the light of these developments, Herzl, in his article of September 1899, assumed the mantle of a prophet after the fact. Implicit was his contrast between the far-seeing discernment of Zionism and the ostrich-like complacency of assimilated French Jews. He now conferred historic significance on the Dreyfus Affair, comparing it to the revocation of the Edict of Nantes in 1685, which initiated the persecution and repression of the Huguenots, and their mass exodus from France. The affair had unfolded in the home of the Rights of Man, where Jews had been emancipated for over a century. The impact of the affair for Zionism was clear: "But if a nation which in other matters certainly is highly civilized and progressive has come to such a pass, what can be expected from peoples who to this day have not yet reached the level which the French had attained a hundred years ago?" The Dreyfus Affair was an object lesson for Europe's Jews, for whom "there is no other help and salvation than a return to their own nation and settlement on their own soil."[23]

Herzl's article contains inaccuracies. There is no truth to his claim that French Jews presumed Dreyfus innocent from the start "because they had had countless victims of false accusations to mourn over the centuries." A year earlier, he himself had stated the reverse, that French Jews had accepted Dreyfus's guilt. In addition, Herzl claimed that just after the verdict he had discussed the trial with a military attaché, probably the Italian major Panizzardi, and argued to no avail that Dreyfus was innocent. His version of this conversation seems doubtful. Both Major Panizzardi and his colleague in the German embassy, Colonel von Schwarzkoppen, were engaged in espionage and were the recipients of the documents that had incriminated Dreyfus. They knew he was not the informant. What is more, the Italians were suspected of being implicated in the case. It is difficult to believe that Panizzardi, of all people, would have argued for Dreyfus's guilt to one of Europe's star journalists.[24]

What drove him to this web of fabrications? One possibility is that Herzl, like so many who experience momentous events, imparted to himself a degree of prescience, even prophecy, nonexistent at the time. He may even have been inflating a half-truth. Though Herzl did not see great meaning in Dreyfus's condemnation when it occurred, he seems to have been convinced of Dreyfus's innocence earlier than most. In November 1896, when Dreyfus's supporters were only a tiny handful, he wrote a letter to Paul Goldman, a

German-Jewish colleague, who had just published several pieces on Dreyfus in the *Frankfurter Zeitung*. Herzl commended him for his courage in calling for the case to be reopened, and declared: "The man is probably innocent, and his unparalleled martyrdom as well as the magnificent staunchness of his defenders will always interest all righteous men." Evidently Herzl privately expressed doubts about Dreyfus's guilt at a relatively early date, though long after he became a Zionist. Probably the pamphlet of the French-Jewish anarchist Bernard Lazare, challenging the verdict, which appeared in Paris about the same time as Herzl's letter to Goldman, persuaded him of Dreyfus's innocence. Herzl had first met Lazare in July 1896. At the time he was a virtually lone voice, and such assertions met a blank wall of hostility. It may be that Herzl's relatively early belief in Dreyfus's innocence provided him with the rationale for his later claims to prophetic foresight. By then, Herzl had become the leader of a political movement. His position depended upon maintaining the spell of his charisma. By establishing his reputation for prophecy he may have sought to enhance confidence in his leadership.[25]

For an alternate and reliable description of Herzl's path to Zionism, we need only turn to the account he gave on the heels of his conversion. In his diary he spoke of a gradual process, enacted "in the realm of the Unconscious." How he had arrived at the idea of the Jewish state was a "mystery" to him. To Teweles he characterized his Paris years differently than he would in connection with his later claims: as a time when "I gained a freer and more detached relationship to the antisemitism of my far off homeland."[26] Living in Paris had sheltered him from the personal agonies of antisemitism, afforded him distance, allowed him space for cool reflection.

The discrepancy between Herzl's earlier and later versions of his conversion to Zionism is clear. The earlier one is the polar opposite of his later retrospective account, which was a kind of parable, demonstrating how assimilationist smugness was abruptly jolted and replaced by Zionist prescience. References to a lengthy inward struggle, punctuated by thoughts of mass baptism and spectacular duels, did not suit the leader of a movement wishing to accent canny Zionist foresight. Herzl's claim quickly entered the popular canon of Zionism. What could be more engaging than to see Zionism arise out of Herzl's oracular realization that the progressive nation that had emancipated Jews first, was fully capable of framing one of her most devoted Jewish sons?

Abbreviations

AHY	*Austrian History Yearbook*
BuT	*Briefe und Tagebücher*
CD	*The Complete Diaries of Theodor Herzl*
CZA	Central Zionist Archives
DG	*Das Ghetto* (Handwritten draft)
DnG	*Das neue Ghetto*
HYB	*Herzl Year Book*
JS	*The Jewish State*
JSS	*Jewish Social Studies*
LBIYB	*Leo Baeck Institute Year Book*
NFP	*Neue Freie Presse*
NZ	*Die Neuzeit*
O-NL	*Old-New Land*
OW	*Oesterreichische Wochenschrift*
PB	*Das Palais Bourbon*
SJA	*Studia Judaica Austriaca*
TNG	*The New Ghetto*
ZW	*Zionist Writings*

Notes

Introduction

1. CD 1: 105.
2. Alex Bein, *Theodore Herzl*, pp. 114–16.
3. David Vital, *The Origins of Zionism*, p. 244; for a clinical discussion of ambivalence, Alfred Freedman, Harold Kaplan, and Benjamin Sadock, eds., *Comprehensive Textbook of Psychiatry*, 2d ed., 2 vols. (Baltimore: Williams & Wilkins, 1975), 1: 814.
4. For a Freudian analysis, Peter Loewenberg, "A Psychoanalytic Study in Charismatic Political Leadership," in *The Psychoanalytic Interpretation of History*, ed. Benjamin B. Wolman (New York: Basic Books, 1971), pp. 150–91.
5. DnG, p. 30.
6. Max Nordau, "Speech to the First Zionist Congress," in *The Zionist Idea: A Historical Analysis and Reader*, ed. Arthur Hertzberg (New York: Atheneum, 1971), pp. 235–41.
7. On Herzl's German nationalism and his Jewish problem, Amos Elon, *Herzl*, pp. 52–54, 68–71.
8. O-NL, p. 252.
9. CD 1: 9–10.

1. Herzl as Assimilationist

1. BuT 1: 612.
2. For Herzl's avowal of Vienna's great appeal, Amos Elon, *Herzl*, p. 30; BuT 1: 67; for the pace of Magyarization in Budapest, Andrew Handler, *Dori*, pp. 101–102.
3. For Herzl's parents, Elon, pp. 17–19; for Jacob Herzl's preference for German, Handler, p. 31.
4. "Einladung zur 'Konfirmation' " 3.5.1873, H I A 2, CZA. Herzl was born on 2 May; for the history of nineteenth-century confirmations, Michael A. Meyer, *Response to Modernity*, pp. 39–40, 102, 132, 150, 154, 160, 194–96; for the Dohány Street synagogue ritual, Raphael Patai, *Apprentice in Budapest: Memories of a World That Is No More* (Salt Lake City: University of Utah Press, 1988), pp. 180, 291, 370.
5. The youthful writings are preserved in the Herzl archives.
6. The encyclical was *Quanta cura*, with the appended *Syllabus errorum* (Gordon Craig, *Germany: 1866–1945*, pp. 69, 73).
7. The essay on Savonarola for which Herzl made numerous drafts is quoted at length in Joseph Patai, "Herzl's School Years," in HYB 3: 62; Herzl had probably read the epic poem *Savonarola*, composed in 1837 by the Hungarian Nikolaus Lenau, a German writer. Lenau was a liberal and anticlerical and portrayed Savonarola as a fighter against political and intellectual tyranny. The historical Savonarola, a charismatic preacher, fought the misuse of papal power in the name of an older conciliar conception of the church. For the Lenau reference, Desmond Stewart, *Theodor Herzl*, p. 42. Herzl's statement on religious frauds is quoted in Leon Kellner, *Theodor Herzls Lehrjahre, 1860–1895*, pp. 125–26. The Count of Saint-Germain was an eighteenth-century adventurer who wielded enormous

influence in the royal courts of Europe because of his reputed miraculous scientific discoveries, which included a liquid that could prolong life.

8. The full poem appears in Kellner, pp. 17–18.

9. An excerpt of Bismarck's speech appears in Ernst C. Helmreich, ed., *A Free Church in a Free State? The Catholic Church, Italy, Germany, France, 1864–1914*, Problems in European Civilization (Boston: D. C. Heath, 1964), pp. 65–66.

10. For this view of the German heritage by a leading Austro-German left liberal, see Harry Ritter, "Progressive Historians and the Historical Imagination in Austria: Heinrich Friedjung and Richard Charmatz," AHY, vols. 19–20, pt. 1 (1983–1984): 49–60.

11. BuT 1: 608–16.

12. Christian Wilhelm Dohm, *Concerning the Amelioration of the Civil Status of the Jews*, pp. 65–67, 75–76, 81.

13. Dohm, pp. 18, 20–21, 27, 51–52, 58.

14. Dohm, pp. 34, 66, 79–80.

15. David Landes, "The Jewish Merchant: Typology and Stereotypology in Germany," LBIYB 19 (1974), p. 12.

16. George L. Mosse, *Germans and Jews*, p. 70.

17. Quoted in Ernest K. Bramsted, *Aristocracy and the Middle Class in Germany*, p. 134.

18. Bernhard's wish that he had been born a Christian is quoted in Mark H. Gelber, "An Alternate Reading of the Role of the Jewish Scholar in Gustav Freytag's *Soll und Haben*," *The Germanic Review* 58 (1983): p. 85; Bernhard's admonition to his father is quoted in Jacob Katz, *From Prejudice to Destruction*, p. 205; Bensen is quoted in Gelber, p. 85.

19. Freytag's condemnation of medieval German antisemitism quoted in Mosse, p. 70; his comments on Jewish merchants and on German-Jewish achievements are quoted in Bramsted, p. 135; his condemnation of modern antisemitism is cited in Katz, *From Prejudice to Destruction*, p. 207.

20. For evidence that Jews read and approved of Freytag, Mosse, pp. 74, 235–36.

21. For the full Dühring review, BuT, 1: 611–16.

22. ZW 2: 111

23. BuT 1: 647–48.

24. For Herzl's gymnasium courses and his youthful essays, Handler, pp. 80–82, 91–93.

25. For the full Jensen review, BuT 1: 608–10.

26. For this widely held view of Judaism, Salo Baron, "Ghetto and Emancipation," *The Menorah Journal* 14 (1928): pp. 515–16, 525, and Ismar Schorsch, "Introduction," in Heinrich Graetz, *The Structure of Jewish History and Other Essays*, pp. 17–19; David Sorkin has argued that this "lachrymose" view of Jewish history was central to the ideology of the German-Jewish *Haskala* (Enlightenment) (*The Transformation of German Jewry, 1780–1840*, pp. 93–94).

27. *Wilhelm Meister* is quoted in Isaac Eisenstein Barzilay, "The Jew in the Literature of the Enlightenment," JSS 4 (1956), pp. 245–46, 254; Goethe on the ghetto is quoted in Mosse, p. 46; for Herzl's many references to Goethe's prose and poetry, BuT 1: 506, 699, 701, 718, 727, 794, 822, 829.

28. Ismar Schorsch, "Moritz Güdemann: Rabbi, Historian and Apologist," LBIYB 11 (1966), pp. 53–66; Jellinek quoted in Wolfgang Häusler, " 'Orthodoxie' und 'Reform' im Wiener Judentum in der Epoche des Hochliberalismus," Kurt Schubert, ed., *Der Wiener Stadttempel, 1826–1876*, SJA, vol. 6, p. 44.

29. Gneist is quoted by Uriel Tal, *Christians and Jews in Germany*, p. 64; [Ludwig John Oppenheimer] *Austriaca*, pp. 221–22, 244. Oppenheimer was of Jewish origin, a parliamentarian and owner of a large landed estate. In 1878, he was made a baron and in 1895 he entered the House of Lords.

30. John W. Boyer, *Political Radicalism in Late Imperial Vienna*, p. 125. Boyer's discussion of Austro-Liberals and religion is unrivaled; for the liberal belief in a unitary culture, Tal, pp. 50–51.

31. Theodor Gomperz, *Ein Gelehrtenleben im Bürgertum der Franz-Josef-Zeit*, pp. 173–75; for Jewish advocacy of conversion, Sanford Ragins, *Jewish Responses to Anti-Semitism in Germany, 1870–1914*, pp. 73–77.

32. BuT 1: 611; Dohm, pp. 32, 49.

33. Quoted in Arthur J. May, *The Hapsburg Monarchy, 1867–1914*, p. 49.

34. Gustav Kolmer, *Parlament und Verfassung in Österreich*, 1: 16, 27, 157.

35. Quoted in Richard Charmatz, *Österreichs innere Geschichte von 1848 bis 1895* 1: 86.

36. Marsha L. Rozenblit, *The Jews of Vienna, 1867–1914*, pp. 21, 33–36.

37. For Jewish Reichsrat deputies, Kurt Schubert, ed., *Zur Geschichte der Juden in den östlichen Ländern der Habsburgermonarchie*, SJA, vol. 8, p. 67; for Jewish city councillors, Sigmund Mayer, *Die Wiener Juden*, pp. 374–77.

38. Mayer, *Die Wiener Juden*, p. 462. For university enrollments, Anna Drabek et al., *Das österreichische Judentum*, p. 112; Arthur Schnitzler, *My Youth in Vienna*, p. 129; for this comparison between Jewish and Gentile students, Rozenblit, pp. 108–14.

39. Wilhelm Goldbaum, "Schlussbetrachtung," in Gerson Wolf, *Die Juden*, pp. 171–72; BuT 1: 613.

40. Freud quoted in Carl Schorske, *Fin-de-Siècle Vienna*, pp. 188–89; Arthur Schnitzler, *The Road to the Open*, pp. 248–49, 269–70; Mayer, *Die Wiener Juden*, p. 373.

41. Mayer, *Die Wiener Juden*, p. 478.

42. Joseph S. Bloch, *My Reminiscences*, p. 137. An incident recalled by the Liberal Jewish deputy Ignaz Kuranda, who served in Parliament from 1867 to 1884, illustrates the strained relationship between Christian and Jewish members. According to Kuranda, a Liberal party associate approached him during a session of Parliament and said: "My dear colleague, I am really sorry to be unable to keep the appointment we made yesterday," and then he quickly remembered that he had not settled anything with [me] . . . and said: "Oh, I beg your pardon, I have made a mistake, it was the other . . . " He halted before the obvious finish, "the other Jew" (Bloch, p. 137).

43. Rozenblit, pp. 2–9.

44. Stefan Zweig, *The World of Yesterday*, pp. 111, 116; Martin Freud cited in Josef Fraenkel, ed., *The Jews of Austria*, p. 204; for similar testimony, Schnitzler, *My Youth in Vienna*, p. 131.

45. Mayer, *Die Wiener Juden*, pp. 461, 470.

46. Schnitzler, *My Youth in Vienna*, p. 131.

47. Gomperz, p. 104. In 1882 the Jewish journalist Isador Singer described Austrian antisemites as transmitters of the "poison weed" of German antisemitism (quoted in Dennis Klein, "Assimilation and the Demise of the Liberal Political Tradition in Vienna: 1860–1914," in *Jews and Germans from 1860 to 1933*, ed. David Bronsen, p. 250).

48. On the economic effects of the crash, Herbert Matis, *Österreichs Wirtschaft 1848–1913*, pp. 278–91. On antisemitism, Matis, pp. 410–11. On stock-exchange regulations, Kolmer 2: 476–77. On the newly expanded Jewish bourgeoisie, Mayer, *Die Wiener Juden*, pp. 405–406, 458–62.

49. Schnitzler, *My Youth in Vienna*, pp. 7, 63.

50. Boyer, pp. 90–98.

51. Wolf, p. 166.
52. On Clerical-Conservative antisemitism, Drabek et al., pp. 109–10; on the muting of Clerical-Conservative radicalism, Richard Charmatz, *Deutsch-österreichische Politik*, p. 95.
53. Kolmer 3: 128–29, 216–17.
54. For the newspaper's circulation figures, Peter Pulzer, *The Rise of Political Anti-Semitism in Germany and Austria*, p. 154; for government harassment, Andrew G. Whiteside, *The Socialism of Fools*, pp. 98–99, and Boyer, p. 93.
55. Charmatz, *Deutsch-österreichische Politik*, pp. 93–94.
56. Sigmund Mayer, *Ein jüdischer Kaufmann, 1831 bis 1911*, p. 281; for the emperor and antisemitism, Drabek et al., p. 118.
57. For Joseph II, Paul P. Bernard, "Joseph II and the Jews: The Origins of the Toleration Patent of 1782," AHY 4–5 (1968–69), pp. 111–17; for the period of reaction, Drabek et al., pp. 93–94; for the period of neoabsolutism, Kolmer 1: 27; for the modernizing bureaucracy, Boyer, pp. 17–20, 55–56.

2. Herzl as German Nationalist

1. ZW 1: 18.
2. Alex Bein, *Theodore Herzl*, pp. 30, 40.
3. William T. McGrath, "Student Radicalism in Vienna," *Journal of Contemporary History* 2 (1967): pp. 193, 195–97, 199–200.
4. The official name Austria was only adopted in 1917. I shall use it though to refer to the non-Hungarian part of the empire, all the lands and provinces represented in the Reichsrat.
5. For a full account in English, William A. Jenks, *Austria under the Iron Ring, 1879–1893*, pp. 59–61, 71–74, 120–21.
6. For a classic portrayal of the different Austro-German political camps, Adam Wandruszka, "Österreichs Politische Struktur," in *Geschichte der Republik Österreich*, ed. Heinrich Benedikt, pp. 370–74.
7. *Jahresbericht der Akademischen Lesehalle in Wien über das zehnte Vereinsjahr, 1879–80*, pp. 16–21, 26, 32.
8. *Die Lesevereine der deutschen Hochschüler an der Wiener Universität*, p. 33.
9. Tulo Nussenblatt, "Aus Theodor Herzls Schul—und Universitätszeit," *Die Neue Welt*, 26 February 1932. Herzl's declaration is also in BuT 1: 73–74.
10. For detailed accounts, *Jahresbericht*, pp. 6–7, *Die Lesevereine*, pp. 34–36, and Alfred von Terzi, "Aus der Geschichte der Deutschnationalen Studentenbewegung in Österreich und ihre Bedeutung für das Deutsche Reich," *Akademische Rundschau*, 5 (1917/18): 389.
11. For *Albia*'s affiliation to the *Lesehalle*, Terzi, p. 389; for Schönerer's first speech to the *Lesehalle*, Paul Molisch, *Politische Geschichte der deutschen Hochschulen in Österreich von 1848 bis 1918*, p. 103; Schönerer is quoted in Robert Hein, *Studentischer Antisemitismus in Österreich*, p. 30; for the election of the nationalist slate, the Lessing banquet, and the dissolution of the *Lesehalle*, *Die Lesevereine*, pp. 37–39.
12. Leon Kellner, *Theodor Herzls Lehrjahre, 1860–1895*, pp. 26–27. Kellner is our source of information that Herzl chaired the *Lesehalle* social club after the November election of a German nationalist executive. The final annual report of the *Lesehalle* only goes up to September; for Schnitzler's memory of Herzl's speech, *Briefe, 1875–1912*, p. 124; for his description of Herzl, *My Youth in Vienna*, p. 129.
13. For valuable details on Herzl's *Albia* days, Josef Fränkel, "Theodor Herzl in der akademischen Burschenschaft 'Albia,'" *Die Neue Welt*, nos. 235, 236, 238 (1932); and Karl Becke, *Wiener akademische Burschenschaft "Albia," 1870–1930*. Fränkel published a similar

account in *Theodor Herzl*, pp. 117–31. Both Fränkel and Becke used data from the *Albia* archives, destroyed during World War II. For Herzl as fencer, Fränkel, *Die Neue Welt* no. 235 (1932), and Becke, p. 38; Hermann Bahr, "The Fateful Moment: The Birth of Herzl's Zionism," in *Theodor Herzl: A Memorial*, ed. Meyer Weisgal, p. 67.

14. For Herzl's activities in *Albia*, Fränkel, *Theodor Herzl*, pp. 121–22; Schnitzler, *My Youth in Vienna*, p. 129; the cornflower in Herzl's lapel has been identified recently by Dietrich Herzog, "Theodor Herzl als Burschenschafter—und die Folgen," *Beiträge zur Österreichischen Studentengeschichte* 2 (1974): 76.

15. Becke, pp. 7–23.

16. For *Albia* and the *Lesehalle* takeover, Kurt Knoll, *Die Geschichte der schlesischen akademischen Landsmannschaft "Oppavia" in Wien* 1: 149; for *Albia's* protest demonstration, Becke, p. 37; for the Schönerer invitation, Spulak von Bahnwehr, *Geschichte der aus den Jahren 1859–1994 stammenden Wiener Couleurs*, p. 199; Schönerer quoted in O[skar] F. Scheuer, *Burschenschaft und Judenfrage*, p. 47. Most of the histories of the nationalist fraternities were written by enthusiastic alumni. I have used them cautiously.

17. For the *Korps*, Herzog, p. 75; Andrew Whiteside estimates that a small minority of students belonged to German nationalist fraternities (*The Socialism of Fools*, p. 47).

18. Typical of its small scale, in 1875 *Albia* consisted of six "old boys" (Alten Herren), one honorary member (Ehrenbursch), three inactive members, fourteen active members, and three "foxes" or initiates (Füchse). In 1884 there were fourteen "old boys," four honorary members, fifteen inactive members, four active members, seven "foxes," one Ehrenkonkneipant, and five Konkneipanten (nonmembers allowed to participate in *Albia* drinking sessions) (Becke, pp. 14–15, 51). On fraternity practices, Whiteside, *Socialism of Fools*, pp. 46–47.

19. Andrew G. Whiteside, "The Germans as an Integrative Force in Imperial Austria: The Dilemma of Dominance," AHY, vol. 3, pt. 1, pp. 163–69.

20. *Jahresbericht*, p. 7.

21. Molisch, *Politische Geschichte*, pp. 91–92, 107–108.

22. For the *Schulverein*, P. G. T. Pulzer, "The Austrian Liberals and the Jewish Question, 1867–1914," *Journal of Central European Affairs* 23 (1963): 137–38; Knoll, pp. 205–206.

23. Whiteside, *Socialism of Fools*, p. 62.

24. ZW 1: 170.

25. Whiteside, *Socialism of Fools*, p. 23.

26. BuT 1: 614; the poem appears in Bein, *Theodor Herzl*, pp. 53–54.

27. McGrath, pp. 183–84, 189, 196; for the *Deutscher Klub's* close ties to Schönerer, Eduard Pichl [Herwig], *Georg Schönerer und die Entwicklung des Alldeutschtumes in der Ostmark* 2: 57; Alfred Aschner, of Jewish origin, was perhaps the leading pan-German student politician in the late 1870s.

28. Whiteside, *Socialism of Fools*, pp. 84–85.

29. Pernersdorfer quoted in Robert Wistrich, *Socialism and the Jews*, pp. 238–39; Schnitzler, *My Youth in Vienna*, p. 130.

30. Pernersdorfer and Adler quoted in Wistrich, pp. 235, 239; Heinrich Friedjung, "Die 'Democratie' in Nöthen," *Deutsche Wochenschrift*, 4 January 1885, pp. 3–4. In response to Friedjung's admonition to Jews, the *Oesterreichische Wochenschrift*, organ of militant Viennese Jews, sarcastically labeled him an "oriental German" ("Semitischer Antisemitismus," OW, 30 January 1885).

31. Pernersdorfer quoted in Whiteside, *Socialism of Fools*, pp. 101–102.

32. Becke, p. 50; on *Albia's* wreath-laying, Knoll, p. 242.

33. Becke, pp. 31, 34–35, 38, 52; Herzog, p. 78.

34. Theodor Billroth, *The Medical Sciences in the German Universities*, trans. William

Welch (New York: Macmillan, 1924), pp. 105–108; Schnitzler, *My Youth in Vienna*, pp. 7, 115, 129; for Jewish student support for Billroth, Hein, pp. 17–19. Jewish members of the *Leseverein* included Sigmund Freud, Emil Franzos, Heinrich Friedjung, and Viktor Adler.

35. BuT 1: 100.

36. Knoll, p. 207.

37. For the *Turnverein*, Whiteside, *Socialism of Fools*, p. 131; Becke, p. 41.

38. Becke, pp. 38, 52; as late as 1884, fully seven of *Albia's* fourteen "old-boys" were Jews, an indication of their high proportion in *Albia* in the past (Becke, p. 51).

39. Becke, p. 38.

40. For a full and vivid account, Whiteside, *Socialism of Fools*, pp. 94–96; NFP, 6 March 1883; BuT 1: 126.

41. Bein, *Theodor Herzl*, p. 66, and Amos Elon, *Herzl*, pp. 59–60.

42. Hein has reviewed the press reports (p. 35). The two liberal newspapers I consulted confirm this finding. See NFP and *Neues Wiener Tagblatt* for 6 March 1883.

43. From the late 1870s, demands for an "Aryan paragraph" had been voiced in some nationalist fraternities. The first to adopt this measure was *Libertas* in 1878, excluding even baptized Jews from membership. *Teutonia* followed suit in 1883, after a debate of three years' duration. By 1883, three *Burschenschaften* had joined together in the first formal association excluding Jews. See Scheuer, p. 48, and Molisch, *Politische Geschichte*, pp. 120–21. By Becke's count, there were eleven "important" German nationalist fraternities in the late 1870s (p. 232). For the antisemitic trend in *Albia*, Becke, p. 46, and Fränkel, *Theodor Herzl*, p. 129; BuT 1: 126. The term "Semite" for Jew had long been used. What was new was the term "antisemite," coined by Wilhelm Marr in Germany in 1879, which quickly came into widespread use. For Marr, as for Schönerer, antisemitism was a total ideology, explaining the cause of all the world's evil. See Jacob Katz, *From Prejudice to Destruction*, p. 261.

44. For *Albia's* motto, BuT 2: 770, and Herzog, p. 87; for the German nationalist song, ZW 1: 59–61, and Herzog, p. 87; "Fiducit," CD 3: 1,090; Wagner, ZW 1: 18.

45. McGrath, pp. 192–94, 197, 199–200.

46. Carl Schorske, *Fin-de-Siècle Vienna*, pp. 164–66.

47. CD 1: 43, 165–66, 200.

48. JS, p. 101.

49. CD 1: 19, 27.

50. "Lesehallias," H IV B 79, CZA; for the play, Bein, *Theodor Herzl*, pp. 48–49.

51. Knoll, p. 194.

52. Terzi, pp. 424–25. My assessment of Schönerer's appeal is based upon Paul Molisch, *Geschichte der deutschnationalen Bewegung in Oesterreich von ihren Anfängen bis zum Zerfall der Monarchie*, pp. 151–53, and Wandruszka, Österreichs politische Struktur, pp. 378–79.

53. Terzi, p. 389.

54. On government harassment, Molisch, *Politische Geschichte der deutschen Hochschulen*, pp. 108–10, and Knoll, p. 57; on the student response, Whiteside, *Socialism of Fools*, pp. 48–50; on Bahr's expulsion and celebrity, Hermann Bahr, *Selbstbildnis*, pp. 143–47.

55. Bahr, pp. 125–26; for radical nationalism as youthful rebellion, Whiteside, *Socialism of Fools*, pp. 308–309, and Wandruszka, Österreichs politische Struktur, pp. 376–77.

56. Bahr, p. 127; Jenks, p. 237.

57. For Austro-German identification with the Second Reich, Wandruszka, Österreichs politische Struktur, pp. 379–80, and Molisch, *Geschichte der deutschnationalen Bewegung*, p. 112.

58. Wandruszka, Österreichs politische Struktur, p. 375; Bahr, pp. 134–35.

59. Bahr, p. 135; Steed, *The Hapsburg Monarchy*, pp. 202–204; the image of the elder

and younger brother comes from Wandruszka, Österreichs politische Struktur, p. 375; Schönerer quoted in Molisch, *Geschichte der deutschnationalen Bewegung*, p. 155.

60. Becke, p. 33.

61. CD 2: 693; 1: 23, 194–96.

62. For the German model, CD 2: 693. For Herzl's adulation of Bismarck, CD 1: 117–27, 236; for Herzl's maximalism, David Vital, *The Origins of Zionism*, pp. 272–73, 277, 280–82, 332–35, 338, 345.

3. Herzl, an Ambivalent Jew

1. Herzl, "Fürst Aurec," NFP, 14 June 1892.

2. BuT 1: 219–20, 635, 639–40.

3. BuT 1: 649–50; Carl E. Schorske, *Fin-de-Siècle Vienna*, p. 9; letter to Kana and diary entries, BuT 1: 107, 649–57.

4. Schorske, p. 298; for aristocratic pursuit of the arts, A. S. Levetus, *Imperial Vienna: An Account of Its History, Tradition and Arts* (London: John Lane, The Bodley Head, 1905), pp. 366–67; for middle-class emulation of the aristocracy, Schorske, pp. 7–8, and Henry Wickham Steed, *The Hapsburg Monarchy*, pp. 133–34.

5. Stefan Zweig, *The World of Yesterday*, pp. 14–20. Actors and actresses received a royal pension after six years' service and were granted the title of "Imperial-Royal Hofburg Actor or Actress," Levetus, pp. 325–26.

6. Schorske, p. 148; Zweig, p. 95.

7. "Aus dem Abgeordnetenhause," NZ, 21 December 1894; CD 1: 28.

8. Schorske, pp. 148–49; Arthur Schnitzler, *Briefe, 1875–1912*, p. 125; Zweig, pp. 21–22, 54.

9. See note 2, this chapter. For a despairing letter to Schnitzler, BuT 1: 498–502.

10. Schorske, pp. 9, 152; for glowing praise of Herzl's literary art by two noted writers, Stefan Zweig, "Herzl in Wien," in *Zeitgenossen über Herzl*, ed. T. Nussenblatt, p. 256, and Hermann Bahr, "Erinnerung," *Die Welt*, 3 July 1914; for Herzl's denigration of his journalistic literary pieces, Friedrich Fürst von Wrede, "Herzls Meisterwerk," in *Zeitgenossen über Herzl*, pp. 247–48.

11. For press corruption, Steed, pp. 184–201. Marred by antisemitism, Steed's account is nevertheless informative; for Herzl on corrupt Jewish journalists, O-NL, pp. 4–5. For Herzl's own fastidiousness, Herzl to Eugen Holzer, 22 March 1901 in *Theodor Herzl Jahrbuch*, ed. T. Nussenblatt, pp. 116–17.

12. For journalism and Jews, Sander L. Gilman, *Jewish Self-Hatred*, pp. 145–46, 230 (for *Schmock*); Wandruszka, "Die österreichische Presse in der franzisko-josephinischen Epoche," in Erich Zöllner, ed., *Öffentliche Meinung in der Geschichte Österreichs*, p. 93; BuT 1: 422. *Schmock* was slang for "fool" or "penis." The term came to be widely used after the success of Freytag's play, *The Journalists*, featuring a Jewish journalist of that name.

13. Steed, p. 193. Steed's view of Jewish literary facileness was a stereotype. Our subject is the power of such stereotypes; Herzl spoke of Jewry's "overproduction of mediocre intellects," in BuT 2: 199, 201. Hannah Arendt, *The Jew as Pariah*, p. 119; for the observation that in the arts Jewish origins were overlooked, [Ludwig John Oppenheimer] *Austriaca*, p. 199.

14. Isaiah Berlin, "Benjamin Disraeli, Karl Marx and the Search for Identity," *Against the Current*, p. 258.

15. Alex Bein, *Theodor Herzl*, p. 28; though our conclusions differ, my argument owes a great deal to Carl Schorske's classic *Fin-de-Siècle Vienna*. He first pointed out the importance of Herzl's idealization of aristocrats (pp. 149–51).

16. *Hagenau* was published years later as *Die Heimkehr (The Homecoming)* under the pseudonym H. Jungmann. See CD 3: 920. It ran in the *Neue Freie Presse* in twenty installments from 23 March to 15 April 1900. All my quotes are from installments no. 5 (29 March) and no. 8 (1 April).

17. Quoted in Bein, *Theodor Herzl*, pp. 48–50.

18. Richard Charmatz, *Deutsch-österreichische Politik*, pp. 45–47.

19. For the deputy's complaint, Charmatz, *Deutsch-österreichische Politik*, pp. 46–47; for aristocratic involvement in capitalism, Renate Wagner-Rieger, ed., *Die Wiener Ringstrasse* 5: 275–78, and Oscar Jászi, *The Dissolution of the Habsburg Monarchy*, pp. 172–73.

20. Arthur J. May, *The Hapsburg Monarchy, 1867–1914*, pp. 163–64.

21. Jellinek quoted in Werner J. Cahnman, "Adolf Fischhof and his Jewish Followers," LBIYB 4 (1959), p. 116; CD 2: 687.

22. [Ludwig John Oppenheimer] *Austriaca*, p. 194.

23. Quoted in Charlene A. Lea, *Emancipation, Assimilation and Stereotype*, p. 100. The play was written in 1849.

24. George L. Mosse, *Germans and Jews*, pp. 38, 63–65. The quote is from Dahn.

25. BuT 1: 644: *"Lesehallias,"* H IV B 79, CZA.

26. For the duel he wanted to fight as Zionist leader, Erwin Rosenberger, *Herzl as I Remember Him*, pp. 135–39; CD 1: 58.

27. Zweig, p. 94; Schnitzler recalled a Jewish colleague from his student years who announced that dueling was not for him because he was a coward. He remembered being astonished at the courage it took for a Jew to say this (*My Youth in Vienna*, pp. 127–28); for Lueger and dueling, John W. Boyer, *Political Radicalism in Late Imperial Vienna*, p. 413.

28. *Albia* sought to outshine the liberal *Korps* and become the leading German nationalist fraternity. What counted was the number of duels fought and the prestige of those defeated. In 1881–1882, *Albia* engaged in 59 duels, considerable for its six to twelve active members (Karl Becke, *Wiener akademische Burschenschaft "Albia," 1870–1930*, pp. 22, 24, 30, 37–38, 42); for the army physical, BuT 1: 99, 703.

29. V. G. Kiernan, *The Duel in European History*, pp. 14–18; quoted in Bein, *Theodor Herzl*, p. 54; for Guy de Montsoreau, BuT 1: 631.

30. For this low point in his life, BuT 1: 637–39.

31. Letter from Heinrich Kana and Julius von Ludassy, H I K 4, CZA.

32. Exchange of apologies with Videcky, H I K 4, CZA.

33. For the Herzl letter, Josef Fränkel, "Wie 'Das neue Ghetto' entstand," *Selbstwehr*, 15 July 1938.

34. TNG, p. 23.

35. Adolf Dessauer, *Grossstadtjuden*, pp. 140, 273.

36. Becke, pp. 28, 33, and Dietrich Herzog, "Theodor Herzl als Burschenschafter— und die Folgen," *Beiträge zur Österreichischen Studentengeschichte* 2 (1974): p. 75; Hermann Bahr, *Selbstbildnis*, pp. 136–37.

37. Dessauer, pp. 7, 104, 140, 273–76.

38. Kiernan, p. 15; for status honor, Friedrich Hertz, "Das Duell als soziale Erscheinung," *Österreichische Rundschau* 22 (1910), pp. 404–405; for dueling scars, Zweig, *The World of Yesterday*, p. 94.

39. For corporate honor, Kiernan, p. 15; for army officers, Dieter Prokowsky, "Die Geschichte der Duellbekämpfung" (Doctoral diss., Rheinischen-Friedrich-Wilhelms-Universität Bonn, 1965), pp. 161–62. The same principle prevailed in *Albia*. When one brother did not show up for a duel, not only was he branded "dishonorable," but *Albia* was placed under boycott "in disrepute for cowardice," till the fraternity erased the stain by fighting a series of duels (Becke, pp. 47–49).

40. *Was wird man sagen?* pp. 18–19, 37–38; for *His Highness* and *The Poachers*, Oskar K. Rabinowicz, "Herzl the Playwright," *Jewish Book Annual* 18 (1960–61): pp. 109–10.

41. BuT 2: 205, 212; the letter written from Nice is in Leon Kellner, *Theodor Herzls Lehrjahre, 1860–1895*, p. 139.

42. O-NL, pp. 10–16, 108, 171, 179.

43. Steed, pp. 133–34; Ilsa Barea, *Vienna*, pp. 282–92.

44. For the varieties of parvenu behavior, Dessauer, pp. 35–36, 67–68, 111–114, 160–62, 180, and Wagner-Rieger 5: 286–92.

45. Horace Rumbold, *Recollections of a Diplomatist*, 2 vols. (London: Edward Arnold, 1902), 1: 271.

46. The cafe in the Prater, Francis H. E. Palmer, *Austro-Hungarian Life in Town and Country* (New York: G. P. Putnam's Sons, 1903), pp. 187–88; Maria Horner Lansdale, *Vienna and the Viennese* (Philadelphia: Henry T. Coates, 1902), p. 117; "Moriz Feigelstock beim Morgenkaffee" was a regular feature of the satirical paper *Figaro*.

47. Hans Tietze, *Die Juden Wiens*, p. 267; S. S. Prawer, *Heine's Jewish Comedy*, pp. 132–55.

48. For the new high bourgeoisie, called the "second society," the first being the aristocracy, Wagner-Rieger 5: 281, and Boyer, pp. 80–84; for non-Jewish parvenu vulgarity in Germany, Jost Hermand, "Der gründerzeitliche Parvenu," in *Aspekte der Gründerzeit*, pp. 7–11. For the canard about Jewish banking houses, Lansdale, p. 20. For an illuminating discussion of the difference between overrepresentation and predominance, Simon Kuznets, "Economic Structure and Life of the Jews," in *The Jews*, ed. Louis Finkelstein, 2: 1, 623–34. This distinction has been made for Austrian Jewry. "Even in the area of money and credit dealing—the occupation on which the Jewish stereotype rested *par excellence*—they [Catholics] outnumbered the Jews by a ratio of four to one" (Ivar Oxaal and Walter R. Weitzmann, "The Jews of Pre-1914 Vienna," LBIYB 30 [1985], p. 423).

49. Boyer, p. 452. Boyer notes that in 1893, 15,000 of the 26,000 Jewish families in Vienna were exempt from even the minimum Jewish communal tax of 10 florins, and of the rest, 90 percent paid the minimum amount (pp. 79–80); Sigmund Mayer, *Die Wiener Juden*, p. 405; statistics on Jewish lawyers, Kurt Schubert, ed., *Zur Geschichte der Juden in den östlichen Ländern der Habsburgermonarchie*, SJA, vol. 8, p. 36.

50. For the view that Jewish immodesty and arrogance were causing antisemitism, see statements in Gordon A. Craig, *Germany, 1886–1945*, pp. 153–54; Geoffrey G. Field, *Evangelist of Race: The Germanic Vision of Houston Stewart Chamberlain* (New York: Columbia University Press, 1981), p. 263; and Friedrich Meinecke, *The German Catastrophe*, trans. Sidney B. Fay (Boston: Beacon Press, 1963), p. 15; "everything is for sale," is in [Ludwig John Oppenheimer] *Austriaca*, p. 193; O-NL, p. 171.

51. For this analysis of parvenus, Ernest K. Bramsted, *Aristocracy and the Middle Class in Germany*, pp. 165–66; quotes are in Wagner-Rieger 5: 286, 290.

52. Gilman, pp. 2–4.

53. Heinrich von Treitschke, *A Word about Our Jewry*, p. 2; for the genealogical claims of the Sephardic Jews of France, Arthur Hertzberg, *The French Enlightenment and the Jews*, p. 181.

54. Jacob de Haas, *Theodor Herzl* 1: 30–31; for the version told Brainin, Amos Elon, *Herzl*, pp. 14–15.

55. Paul J. Diamant, *Theodor Herzls väterliche und mütterliche Vorfahren*, pp. 6–9; for the origin of the family name *Herzl*, Oskar K. Rabinowicz, Review of Israel Cohen, "Theodor Herzl, Founder of Modern Zionism," JSS 22 (1960), p. 184.

56. BuT 1: 158–62; Gomperz quoted in Steven Beller, *Vienna and the Jews, 1867–1938*, pp. 131–32.

57. BuT 1: 143.

58. BuT 1: 75; "Lesehallias," H IV B 79, CZA. The *Lesehalle* membership register for 1879–1880 lists Heinrich Abeles, Leo Meissels [sic] and Heinrich Schmelkes. All three were enrolled in the Faculty of Law with Herzl (*Jahresbericht der Akademischen Lesehalle in Wien, 1879–80*, pp. 28–31); for Herzl's comment about "self-ridicule," ZW 1: 20.

59. N. H. Tur-Sinai, "Viennese Jewry," in *The Jews of Austria*, ed. Josef Fraenkel, p. 312.

60. Anton G. Rabinbach, "The Migration of Galician Jews to Vienna, 1857–1880," AHY 11 (1975), pp. 43, 48.

61. Marsha Rozenblit, *The Jews of Vienna, 1867–1914*, pp. 22–23, 40–44. In 1880, 13.7 percent of Jewish fathers were born in Galicia; for the highly exaggerated perception of a "flood" of Galician-Jewish migrants, Ivan Oxaal and Walter R. Weitzmann, "The Jews of Pre-1914 Vienna," pp. 397–403; Mayer, *Die Wiener Juden*, p. 463.

62. Wilhelm Goldbaum, "Schlussbetrachtung (1848–1883)," in Gerson Wolf, *Die Juden*, p. 168.

63. Steven E. Aschheim, *Brothers and Strangers*, pp. 27–31; Franzos lived in Vienna from 1877 to 1886. As publisher of the *Neuen Illustrierten Zeitung*, he ran several of Herzl's pieces (BuT 1: 719, 734).

64. CD 2: 671; for Herzl's spoken German, Rosenberger, p. 44.

65. Anna Drabek et al., *Das österreichische Judentum*, p. 127.

66. O-NL, p. 251.

67. CD 1: 4–5; Friedjung to Herzl, 17 June 1886, H VIII 253a, CZA; for the adoption of non-Jewish pen names, Dennis B. Klein, "Assimilation and the Demise of the Liberal Political Tradition in Vienna, 1860–1914," in *Jews and Germans from 1860 to 1933*, ed. David Bronsen, p. 257.

68. For the evidence that Herzl alienated his brothers, Josef Fränkel, *Theodor Herzl*, p. 122. Hermann Bahr's memory of Herzl's standing in *Albia* was far more favorable. But evidently Herzl antagonized some of his brothers and never became the "exceptional" Jew who passed. Hermann Bahr, "The Fateful Moment," in *Theodor Herzl: A Memorial*, ed. Meyer W. Weisgal, p. 67; Jacob Wassermann, *My Life as German and Jew*, pp. 65–66.

69. BuT 1: 125–27; for *Albia*'s response, Fränkel, *Theodor Herzl*, pp. 125–26, and Kellner, pp. 29–30.

70. Becke, pp. 29–30, 38; Staerk practiced as an architect in Graz. Pichl places him on the Graz executive of the *School Association for Germans (Schulverein für Deutsche)* in 1887 and the *German Peoples' Association (Deutscher Volksverein)* in 1889, both devoted to Schönerer's racist program. (Eduard Pichl [Herwig], *Georg Schönerer und die Entwicklung des Alldeutschtumes in der Ostmark* 2: 127–28, 288); Herzl also confessed enduring "friendly feelings" to Ernst Hörner, an influential *Albia* brother and another paragon of rugged Aryan good looks. Hörner chaired the committee that struck Herzl's name from *Albia*'s membership list (BuT, 1: 127). Becke confirms that Hörner's fraternity name was Dankwart, the person addressed in Herzl's letter. For Hörner and the Wagner memorial, Bahr, *Selbstbildnis*, pp. 140–41, Becke, p. 43, Fränkel, *Theodor Herzl*, p. 124.

71. For Jewish residential concentration, Rozenblit, pp. 76–77.

72. Quoted in Bein, *Theodor Herzl*, p. 99.

73. *Feuilletons* 2: 226.

74. BuT 1: 611, 614.

75. BuT 1: 612–13. The catastrophic pattern of extortion and expulsion and the status of personal unfreedom enforced by chamber serfdom was the Jewish experience in Europe in the high Middle Ages. It was unknown in Poland, the demographic heartland of Jewry from about the sixteenth century on, where Jews had the privileged status of freedmen,

and expulsions and confiscations were rare. Moreover, ghettos in the sense of a walled quarter where Jews were forced to live were a late phenomenon, first appearing during the Counter-Reformation. The usual pattern during the Middle Ages was for all corporate groups, including guilds and nationality groups, to practice residential self-segregation.

76. O-NL, pp. 26, 43, 187. For Herzl's other confessions of filial loyalty, BuT 1: 508, and CD 1: 4.

77. O-NL, p. 26, and BuT 1: 511.

78. Prawer, pp. 758–63; Wassermann, p. 92; Dreikurs quoted in Peter Loewenberg, "Antisemitismus und jüdischer Selbsthass," *Geschichte und Gesellschaft* 5 (1979), p. 468.

79. Berlin, p. 255.

4. Herzl and Vienna, the New Capital of Antisemitism

1. "Die Resorption der Juden," H IV C 1, CZA.

2. Not usually noted is that a relative of Herzl's, living in Paris, Josef Siklósy, for a time his private secretary, was the Paris correspondent for the *Freies Blatt*, the weekly of the Viennese Defense Association against Antisemitism (Tulo Nussenblatt, *Ein Volk unterwegs zum Frieden*, p. 70).

3. CD 1: 5–6; for a pioneering article on the impact of Austrian antisemitism on Herzl, Henry Cohn, "Theodor Herzl's Conversion to Zionism," JSS 32 (1970): 101–10.

4. On Austria, BuT 1: 517 and "Resorption," H IV C 1; on France, "Französische Antisemiten," NFP, 3 September 1892.

5. "Resorption," H IV C 1.

6. Liberal hegemony rested on an exceedingly narrow suffrage base: in the elections of 1879, 6 percent of the male population was eligible to vote. Voters were assigned to curias according to income and occupation. As a result, the urban Chambers of Commerce elected 21 deputies to the Reichsrat, large landowners elected 85, urban voters who paid at least ten gulden tax elected 118 deputies, and rural voters in the same tax bracket elected 129. This system translated into one deputy for every 27 voters in the curia of the Chambers of Commerce, one deputy for every 63 voters in the curia of large landowners, one deputy for every 1,600 voters in the urban curia, and one deputy for every 7,900 voters in the rural curia (Jenks, *Austria under the Iron Ring*, p. 18). The power of the new mass parties rested on an intense and sustained mobilization of supporters. Hence, broadening the franchise was accompanied by heightened political participation. During the 1870s, about 10 to 30 percent of eligible voters participated in municipal elections. By 1890 the figure had climbed to over 66 percent, and in 1891 to over 71 percent. The greatest jump in voter participation was in the Third Curia, where the newly enfranchised voters were concentrated (Maren Seliger and Karl Ucakar, *Wien: Politische Geschichte 1740–1934*, part 1, pp. 594, 597).

7. John Boyer, *Political Radicalism in Late Imperial Vienna*, pp. 215–16, 228. My account of the rise of the United Christians, later known as the Christian Social movement, owes a great deal to Boyer's superb book.

8. Boyer, p. 257.

9. Boyer, p. 287–88, 296. For detailed election results, Seliger and Ucakar, pp. 597–601.

10. Boyer, p. 118; Adam Wandruszka, "Österreichs politische Struktur," in *Geschichte der Republik Österreich*, ed. Heinrich Benedikt, p. 302; on the support of teachers, state officials, and owners of real estate, Boyer, pp. 118, 258–68, 278–87, 385–403.

11. Boyer, pp. 393–94, 401–402.

12. Seliger and Ucakar, p. 593; A. Kannengieser, *Juifs et Catholiques en Autriche-Hongrie* (Paris: P. Lethielleux, 1896), p. 176; Boyer, pp. 121, 149–54.

13. Platform cited in Peter G. J. Pulzer, *The Rise of Political Anti-Semitism in Germany and Austria*, p. 174. For the complaint that the University of Vienna was not Catholic enough and too Jewish, Gustav Kolmer, *Parlament und Verfassung in Österreich* 3: 303. Lueger quoted in Richard S. Geehr, ed. and trans., *"I Decide Who Is A Jew!"* pp. 325–35; for the brilliant and provocative thesis that Jews created Viennese modernist culture, Steven Beller, *Vienna and the Jews, 1867–1938*, pp. 1–8.

14. For this assessment that the Christian Socials fulfilled the Liberal ideal of the "unitary Bürgertum," Boyer, pp. 37–39, 402–403.

15. For Liberal electoral manipulation and the Christian Social response, Boyer, pp. 296–97; for antisemitic zealots, Boyer, pp. 72–73; Schneider quoted in "Von österreichische Regierung," NZ, 29 September 1893.

16. "Rede im Vereine zur Abwehr des Antisemitismus," NZ, 3 June 1892; on antisemitism in the schools, "Der Antisemitismus in der Schule," OW, 5 October 1894; "Bürgermeister Prix für die besoldeten Antisemiten," OW, 27 January 1890; and "Antisemitismus in der Schule," NZ, 19 October 1894. The term "Jüdeln" is not easily translated; it means acting like a Jew, bargaining like a Jew. In this case it refers to mocking mimicry of Yiddish speech and (so-called) Jewish gestures such as abrupt, excited arm movements; for a valuable account of a Jewish schoolboy's ordeal in turn-of-the-century Vienna, Walter Krauss, *Austria to Australia*, A Melbourne Politics Monograph, no. 7, n.p., n.d., pp. 17–18, 35–36.

17. On slanders of Jewish doctors, Kolmer 5: 318–19; Deckert quoted in Joseph S. Bloch, *My Reminiscences*, p. 384; Plener quoted in Pulzer, *The Rise of Political Anti-Semitism*, p. 181; for Jewish complaints of official inaction, "Lasset alle Hoffnung schwinden!" OW, 1 June 1894.

18. "Die Excesse in den westlichen Vororten," NFP, 8 and 9 April 1890, and "Politische Uebersicht," NFP, 9 April 1890.

19. For violence against peddlers, "Was man in Wien erleben kann," OW, 15 June 1894, and "Wien," OW, 22 June 1894; Arthur von Suttner is quoted in Bertha von Suttner, *Memoiren* (Bremen: Carl Schünemann Verlag, 1965), p. 176.

20. For prosecutions of anti-Jewish violence, Bloch, pp. 367–71; for a vivid description of Viennese theatricality, Hanns Sachs, *Freud: Master and Friend* (London: Imago, 1945), pp. 30–32. For official appeasement of the Christian Socials, Kolmer 5: 237, 315.

21. Seliger and Ucakar, p. 590.

22. For artisan distress, Boyer, pp. 42–53. Vienna in the later nineteenth century was a city of small retail shops and artisanal workshops. As late as 1902, 90,714 of its 105,507 business establishments were small shops or workshops employing one to five people (Ilsa Barea, *Vienna*, p. 333).

23. For Habsburg economic policies, N. T. Gross, "The Industrial Revolution in the Habsburg Monarchy," in *The Fontana Economic History of Europe*, vol. 4, pp. 252–61.

24. Hans Rosenberg, "Political and Social Consequences of the Great Depression of 1873–1896 in Central Europe," *Economic History Review* 12 (1942): 61. On economic policies in the 1880s, Herbert Matis, *Österreichs Wirtschaft 1848–1913*, pp. 353–56.

25. On these economic policies, Jenks, pp. 305, 307.

26. For "rapacious" and "productive" capital, John Bunzl and Bernd Marin, *Antisemitismus in Österreich*, pp. 29–30; capitalism as anarchy, quoted in Peter G. J. Pulzer, *The Rise of Political Anti-Semitism*, p. 164; Adolf Dessauer, *Grossstadtjuden*, pp. 133–35.

27. On Vogelsang, Seliger and Ucakar, pp. 588–89; on Liechtenstein, Boyer, p. 107.

28. On Liechtenstein, Kolmer 4: 164; Lueger quoted in Seliger and Ucakar, p. 589; party platform quoted in Bunzl and Marin, p. 21.

29. Liechtenstein quoted in Kolmer 5: 234; Vogelsang quoted in Jacob Katz, *From Prejudice to Destruction*, p. 283; Vogelsang quoted in Bunzl and Marin, p. 28. Jaques quoted in *Mitteilungen der Oesterreichisch-Israelitischen Union*, vol. 3, no. 10 (February 1891): 6.

30. Herzl's "Jewish Novel," CD 1: 5; "Fürst Aurec," NFP, 14 June 1892, and "Französische Antisemiten," NFP, 3 September 1892; to Leitenberger, BuT 1: 517–18; BuT 1: 506–507 refers to an even earlier concerned exchange with his publisher Bacher. Similarly, a letter from Bacher to Herzl of 23 December 1892 refers to Herzl's earlier suggestions for dealing with the "antisemitic question" (H VIII 34, CZA). Though Herzl's letter is lost, this suggests that his alarm over Austrian antisemitism dates from late 1892. "Hate-speeches" in "Resorption," H IV C 1. These unpublished notes contain ideas that reappear in his letters to Leitenberger and were therefore recorded before or soon after the letters.

31. BuT 1: 512, 518; "Resorption," H IV C 1; on his dread of insults, CD 1: 5; on Gittel Rubin, "Resorption." In the 1891 riots, violence was directed against Galician-Jewish brandy shops.

32. "Resorption," H IV C 1.

33. BuT 1: 513; BuT 1: 537. Herzl called them "dealers in orviétan," a "wonder" drug commonly called "charlatan's drug."

34. CD 1: 5; for the observation that developments in France foretold Austria's future, BuT 1: 536.

35. On universal manhood suffrage, CD 1: 7–8; PB, p. 237.

36. PB, p. 243.

37. PB, p. 40.

38. "Frankreich im Jahre 1892," NFP, 31 December 1892; on the seduction of the masses by demagogues, PB, pp. 23–27, 92.

39. BuT 1: 523, 533; "Resorption," H IV C 1; Lafargue, PB, p. 23.

40. Lueger quoted in Menachem Rosensaft, "Jews and Antisemites in Austria at the End of the Nineteenth Century," LBIYB 21 (1976): p. 72.

41. "Notizen zur Judenfrage," H IV C 2, CZA. These notes from 1893 are reproduced in Leon Kellner, *Theodor Herzls Lehrjahre, 1860–1895*, pp. 140–41.

42. BuT 1: 520; on electricity, PB, p. 104; "Frankreich im Jahre 1891," NFP, 31 December 1891.

43. To Bacher, CD 1: 7–8; to Chlumecky, BuT 1: 537–38; "Arbeitshilfe," NFP, 2 August 1893.

44. BuT 1: 507; "Resorption," H IV C 1. In reality, most Jews were not, in Herzl's meaning, "emancipated from . . . money." As Marsha Rozenblit has shown, the common pattern of upward mobility in Vienna was for the sons of small merchants and tradesmen to move into large industrial and commercial enterprises, including banks and insurance companies, as clerks, salesmen, and managers. Composite statistics for 1870 to 1910 show only 11 percent of Jewish grooms in the professions and 70 percent as industrialists, merchants, and business employees (Marsha L. Rozenblit, *The Jews of Vienna, 1867–1914*, pp. 48–50).

45. TNG, pp 38, 40–47; O-NL, pp. 4–5, 19.

46. Restrictions in the judiciary, Kolmer 5: 136; restrictions in the civil service and university, "Antisemitische Gönnerschaft," NZ, 17 April 1891. Restrictions in the university, "Professor Suess über die politische Lage," OW, 26 October 1894, and "Aus dem Abgeordnetenhause," NZ, 21 December 1894; on career restrictions, see also "Die Coalition und die Juden," OW, 28 September 1894.

47. BuT 1: 512; "Resorption," H IV C 1.

48. TNG, pp. 30–32, 35–38.

49. Sigmund Mayer, *Die Wiener Juden*, pp. 469–70. Mayer also observed that mixing among Jews and Gentiles in theaters, concerts, lectures, restaurants, had declined from its high point in the 1860s and 1870s.

50. P. G. J. Pulzer, "Liberals and the Jewish Question," *Journal of Central European Affairs* 23 (July 1963): pp. 137–38, and Robert Hein, *Studentischer Antisemitismus in Österreich*, pp. 51–52.

51. The Friedjung controversy, Andrew G. Whiteside, *The Socialism of Fools*, pp. 120–21; quote in Kolmer 4: 159.

52. BuT 1: 219; CD 2: 618–19.

53. Hein, pp. 24–25, 37, 42.

54. Hein, p. 53; for a Jewish student organization that adopted dueling in 1893, Julius Schoeps, "Modem Heirs of the Maccabees—The Beginnings of the Vienna Kadimah," LBIYB 27 (1982): 164–67.

55. Hein, pp. 55–56.

56. Hein, pp. 56–57.

57. To Chlumecky he spoke of "our Liberal Party," BuT 1: 537.

58. "Sharper key," a contemporary term for the new political stridency (Kolmer 4: 1), aptly adopted more recently by Carl E. Schorske (*Fin-de-Siecle Vienna*, pp. 116, 120); Ernst Plener, *Erinnerungen*, 2: 234; Liberal platforms on antisemitism, Pulzer, *The Rise of Political Anti-Semitism*, p. 157.

59. Kolmer 5: 235; Mayer, "Offener Brief an den Herrn Dr. Joh. Nepomuk Prix, Bürgermeister der Stadt Wien!" NZ, 24 January 1890.

60. Sigmund Mayer, *Ein jüdischer Kaufmann*, p. 316.

61. Plener 2: 234; "Epilog zur jüngsten Wiener Reichsrathswahl," OW, 6 April 1894.

62. "Professor Suess über die politische Lage," OW, 20 October 1894; "Ein Denker und Politiker gegen den Antisemitismus," NZ, 6 March 1891.

63. "Notizen zur Judenfrage," H IV C 2.

64. *Beyond Good and Evil*, trans. Walter Kaufmann (New York: Random House, Vintage Books, 1966), p. 187; Mauthner quoted in Hein, p. 21; Pernersdorfer quoted in Sigurd Scheichl, "The Contexts and Nuances of Anti-Jewish Language," in *Jews, Antisemitism and Culture in Vienna*, ed. Ivan Oxaal, Michael Pollak, and Gerhard Botz, p. 107.

65. CD 1: 12. Herzl seems to have conceived of this book in the summer.

66. Friedrich Nietzsche, p. 188; BuT 1: 611.

67. TNG, p. 36. Herzl first made the connection between Jewish marginality and feelings of inferiority in a theater review, "First Aurec," NFP, 14 June 1892; "Spring in Elend," Ludwig Lewisohn, ed., *Theodor Herzl: A Portrait for This Age*, pp. 103–109.

68. O-NL, p. 252. "Three Steps," in David Hardan, ed., *Sources of Contemporary Jewish Thought* (Jerusalem: World Zionist Organization, 1970) 1: 57.

5. The Reabsorption of the Jews

1. "Die Resorption der Juden," H IV C 1, CZA. Herzl's title for his notes on the Jewish question in early 1893 reveals his goal, "the reabsorption of the Jews" in Europe; CD 1: 7.

2. For the invitation to Herzl to write for the *Freies Blatt*, Tulo Nussenblatt, ed., *Ein Volk unterwegs zum Frieden*, pp. 54, 70. The request came from the actress Regina Friedländer, widow of the founder of the *Neue Freie Presse*, and a friend of both Herzl and the President of the Defense Association, Baron Arthur Gundaccar von Suttner, as well as its honorary president, Baron Friedrich Leitenberger. She was writing on behalf of Leitenber-

ger, whose personal fortune supported the weekly. Herzl responded with a sharp critique of the Defense Association, which she passed on to Leitenberger. Herzl's letter to her is not extant (Kurt Lorber, *Friedrich Freiherr von Leitenberger: Eine Biographie* [Vienna: Peter von Blaas, 1981], p. 145); for the conversion plan, BuT 1: 511–12, 516–17. Herzl made the same proposal to his editor (BuT 1: 507–508). The idea reappears in "Resorption," H IV C 1. Herzl recalled the idea in his Zionist diary (CD 1: 7–8).

3. For the Leitenberger letter, Nussenblatt, *Ein Volk unterwegs zum Frieden*, p. 55; Nothnagel is quoted in Chaim Bloch, "Herzl's First Years of Struggle," HYB, ed. Raphael Patai, 3: 85. Bloch cites no source for the quote, but other statements documented by him make Nothnagel's response highly probable.

4. Theodor Gomperz, *Ein Gelehrtenleben im Bürgertum der Franz-Josefs-Zeit*, pp. 173–74. Gomperz was one of the few Jews to rise to full professor at the University of Vienna. He recommended conversion only to those Jews who no longer believed in Judaism; some German liberals in the forefront of the struggle against antisemitism considered conversion the solution. In 1893 this view unleashed quarrels in the German Defense Association against Antisemitism. An article in the association's newspaper had counseled intermarriage for Jews and the abandonment of offensive beliefs and practices in Judaism. The writer had also complained about the rise of exclusively Jewish student organizations. The writer's conclusion that integration must entail the disappearance of Jewry offended most German Jews (Ismar Schorsch, *Jewish Reactions to German Anti-Semitism, 1870–1914*, pp. 96–97).

5. Amos Elon calls the idea "a happy stage effect" (*Herzl*, p. 113). Bein considers it no more than a reversion to Herzl's earlier assimilationism (*Theodore Herzl*, pp. 90, 94–95); Herzl to Benedikt, BuT 1: 506.

6. CD 1: 7; Herzl to Benedikt, BuT 1: 507.

7. BuT 1: 517.

8. BuT 1: 507; for Herzl's rage, "Resorption," H IV C 1.

9. "Die Protest-Versammlung des Vereines zur Abwehr des Antisemitismus," OW, 21 October 1892; for the public letter, "Gegen die Judenhetze im Abgeordnetenhaus," NFP, 9 December 1892; epithets like "Jewish stooge" were regularly aimed at the leaders of the association ("Abwehrvereine," [OW, 29 June 1894]). Professor Nothnagel faced demonstrations and disruptions of his lectures by antisemitic students at the University of Vienna (Gustav Kolmer, *Parlament und Verfassung in Österreich*, 5:239–40, and Brigitte Hamann, *Bertha von Suttner: Ein Leben für den Frieden* [Munich: Piper, 1986], p. 211).

10. BuT 1: 511, 517; for Herzl on antisemitism ten years before, "Resorption," H IV C 1; for the association's call for Jewish militancy, Hamann, p. 213.

11. Gomperz, p. 174; Max Grunwald, *Vienna*, pp. 416–17.

12. Gomperz, p. 173; Todd Endelman, "Conversion as a Response to Antisemitism in Modern Jewish History," *Living with Antisemitism*, ed. Jehuda Reinharz, pp. 63–79; so deep-seated were Gomperz's seemingly marginal Jewish attachments that he expressed the wish that on his death his sons say *Kaddish* (the Jewish prayer of mourning) for him annually. His resolve to baptize his sons was paralyzed by qualifications. His eldest son wished to convert to Catholicism rather than Protestantism, but Gomperz felt this would be a bad example for his two youngest, less resistant to Catholic religious enthusiasms (Gomperz, pp. 75, 101–102, 186); the conversion rate in pre-World War I Vienna was surprisingly low: 559 Jews converted in 1900, a high annual figure compared to other years, but still just .04 percent of Viennese Jewry (Marsha Rozenblit, *The Jews of Vienna, 1867–1914*, p. 132).

13. CD 1: 7.

14. BuT 1: 508, 516. By Jewish law, the children of Jewish *mothers* were considered

Jews. Thus total assimilation would have required the mass baptism of Jewish girls. But for Herzl, whether he knew of this Jewish law or not, conversion as a bold, self-assertive posture could only be a male act.

15. BuT 1: 508. Endelman (pp. 75–79) points to abundant evidence that Jewish converts were still considered Jews; "Die Panama-Kammer," NFP, 26 July 1893, for another statement by Herzl on the futility of mere conversion. Spanish Jews in the Middle Ages "had themselves baptized in vain. They were oppressed just as before, simply under a new name; they were called *new Christians.*"

16. CD 1: 7–9; for the reference to reciprocity, "Resorption," H IV C 1; BuT 1: 508. In January 1893 the rumored decision of the board of the Berlin Jewish Community to appeal to the kaiser for aid against antisemitism provoked an angry response in an anonymous article, which led to a flood of supportive letters from Jewish readers. The Berlin Board was criticized for reverting to the medieval status of "protected Jew." Jews were now citizens with rights and had to claim and assert their rights through the courts, the Reichstag, and the press. By doing anything less, Jews were demeaning themselves (Schorsch, *Jewish Reactions to German Anti-Semitism*, pp. 107–108).

17. BuT 1: 506–507, 512, 518.

18. For a comprehensive analysis of Austrian Socialist attitudes toward Jewry, Robert Wistrich, *Socialism and the Jews*, pp. 242–61, 332–48.

19. "With universal suffrage . . . a blockhead is not worth less than Alexander Dumas" (PB, p. 35). Herzl also condemned democracy's need "to destroy the superior individual for the good of the whole" (PB, pp. 237–38); DG, H V B 14, CZA, pp. 53–54.

20. "Resorption," H IV C 1.

21. BuT 1: 512; "Resorption," H IV C 1.

22. PB, p. 27.

23. "Der Kampf gegen die Gesellschaft," NFP, 29 April 1892.

24. "Ravachol!" *Feuilletons* 2: 55–65.

25. Carl Schorske, *Fin-de-Siècle Vienna*, p. 154; PB, pp. 19–25.

26. BuT 1: 512.

27. BuT 1: 516; CD 1: 83.

28. BuT 1: 516; for some assimilated Jews, dueling seems to have been a favored recourse against antisemitic slanders. In 1892 Lueger was challenged to duel by two prominent Viennese Jews. One was Michael Etienne, cofounder of the *Neue Freie Presse*; the other was the radical German nationalist Heinrich Friedjung, then a city councillor. Lueger had doubted whether a Jew like Friedjung could be a patriotic German. Dueling may have been Friedjung's way of claiming his German-ness. Lueger unabashedly refused both challenges, calling the duel "illegal, un-Christian and immoral" (Richard Kralik, *Karl Lueger und der christliche Sozialismus* (Vienna: Vogelsang Verlag, 1923), pp. 86–87, 90, 103–105).

29. "Französische Antisemiten," NFP, 3 September 1892; for Herzl's fantasized speech, CD 1: 83.

30. Michael Marrus, *The Politics of Assimilation*, pp. 196–201.

31. BuT 1: 506

32. BuT 1: 511; Herzl expressed the same thought to Benedikt (BuT 1: 507).

33. "Die Wahrheit über den Reichtum der Juden," NZ, 26 October 1894. For more articles in this vein see "Ein Jahr Coalition," 16 November 1894, "An Diejenigen, die es angeht," 23 November 1894, "Die Reichtum der Juden," OW, 11 July 1890.

34. "Fürst Aurec," NFP, 14 June 1892.

35. "Pariser Theater," NFP, 17 October 1894.

36. [Ludwig Oppenheimer] *Austriaca*, p. 193. Baron Oppenheimer, in 1895 the second

Jewish appointee to the Austrian House of Lords, seems to have shared the widespread public disdain for Jewish parvenus.

6. *The New Ghetto*

1. DG, p. 163; H IV B 14, CZA.
2. CD 1: 11; Herzl to Teweles in Heinrich Teweles, *Theater und Publikum*, p. 122. Herzl also recounted the incident to Arthur Schnitzler, BuT 1: 569; DG, p. 164.
3. Teweles, pp. 123–24.
4. CD 1: 9–10; for a discussion of the Zionist idealization of the distant Jewish past as a way of restoring Jewish self-esteem, Shmuel Almog, *Zionism and History*, pp. 23–29; Christian Wilhelm Dohm, *Concerning the Amelioration of the Civil Status of the Jews*, pp. 78–80.
5. Felix Salten, "Ein Judenstück." *Wiener Allgemeine Zeitung*, 8 January 1898.
6. CD 1: 11; letter to Schnitzler in BuT 1: 562; Teweles, p. 122.
7. CD 2: 612; letter to Agai in Tulo Nussenblatt, ed., *Theodor Herzl Jahrbuch*, p. 173; for interpretations of *The New Ghetto*, Alex Bein, *Theodore Herzl*, pp. 101–108, Amos Elon, *Herzl*, pp. 122–25; Desmond Stewart, *Theodor Herzl*, pp. 146–57.
8. DnG, p. 37.
9. DnG, p. 85.
10. DnG, pp. 30, 35–36, 41.
11. DnG, p. 72.
12. George Mosse, *Germans and Jews*, pp. 64–65, 69.
13. DnG, p. 29; for Kobi, DnG, p.39; for Jacob's remark about Hermine, DG, p. 22. In the published version, Herzl eliminated the remark about Hermine's Christian appearance. All that remained were references to Hermine's golden blond hair and Jacob's wish that their children resemble her (DnG pp. 8, 15).
14. TNG, pp. 37–38. As the English version will be accessible to readers, I have used the Norden translation as much as possible, and my own only in cases of disagreement.
15. TNG, p. 36.
16. TNG, p. 36.
17. TNG, p. 23.
18. TNG p. 32. For similar observations, Arthur Schnitzler, *The Road to the Open*, pp. 153–54. "We have been egged on from our youth to look upon Jewish peculiarities as particularly grotesque and repulsive." See also Fred B. Stern, "Ludwig Jacobowski, der Autor von 'Werther, der Jude,' " *Bulletin des Leo Baeck Institute* 7 (1964): pp. 123–24. "Petty moral failings were inflated into terrible vices"; Jewish defensiveness about so-called Jewish faults seems to have been widespread. Even the *Oesterreichische Wochenschrift*, at the forefront of Viennese-Jewish militancy, regularly carried stories about Jewish deeds of physical courage to refute charges that "Jews were cowards, lacked personal courage, ideals, and a penchant for lofty pleasures." "Wien. (Die Beschuldigung der Feigheit gegen die Juden)," OW, 5 January 1894 and 6 July 1894, p. 526.
19. TNG, p. 23; on Jewish family devotion, TNG, pp. 16, 26–27. This Jewish virtue had been underscored by Dohm, pp. 50–51.
20. Georg Brandes, "Ludwig Jacobowski" in *Gestalten und Gedanken*, p. 19; for Jacobowski and his novel, Stern, pp. 118–24. The novel went through seven printings by 1920 and was translated into six languages.
21. Adolf Dessauer, *Grossstadtjuden*, pp. 6, 250, 273–76.
22. CD 1: 11.
23. TNG, p. 41.

24. TNG, p. 8; BuT 1: 559.

25. Herzl's portrait of Rabbi Friedheimer accords with his later remarks about rabbis "who think of their wedding fees from the rich Jews" (CD 3: 1, 161). See also ZW 2: 85.

26. TNG, pp. 26, 59.

27. TNG, p. 60.

28. Michael Meyer, *Response to Modernity*, pp. 150–51; for Jellinek's liberal universalism, Wolfgang Häusler, " 'Orthodoxie' und 'Reform' im Wiener Judentum in der Epoche des Hochliberalismus," Kurt Schubert, ed., *Der Wiener Stadttempel, 1826–1976*, SJA, vol. 6, pp. 42–45. For a ringing appeal for militancy against antisemitism by a Rabbi L. Goldschmied, OW, 29 June 1895, pp. 512–13. The leading figure in the fight against Austrian antisemitism was the rabbi turned politician, Dr. Joseph Bloch.

29. CD 1: 9.

30. For *Schmock*, Joannes Stoffers, *Juden und Ghetto*, pp. 360–61. The term *Schmock* is colloquial German for "fool." It came to refer to hack journalists after Freytag's popular portrayal. See Harry Zohn's helpful etymology in CD 2: 475; Charlene Lea, *Emancipation, Assimilation and Stereotype*, pp. 87–89, 108–10.

31. DnG, p. 3, for Wasserstein's fractured German: "Wie heisst, was ich will?" Correct German would be "Was heisst das?" Herzl was not interested in mocking Wasserstein; he made his German awkward, but not outlandish. See p. 63 for another example; TNG, p. 72.

32. DnG, p. 85; these are among his last words in the handwritten draft of the play (DG, p. 163); Herzl removed the crucial words "learn how to die" in the final version (DnG, p. 200) in response to Schnitzler's objections, discussed below.

33. DnG, pp. 30, 36; DnG, p. 90. The reference to the Maccabees appears in the first draft only (DG, p. 141).

34. DnG, p. 36.

35. Sander Gilman, *Jewish Self-Hatred*, pp. 155–57; Steven Aschheim, *Brothers and Strangers*, p. 8; examples of distancing among assimilated Viennese Jews abound. George Clare has described how he resented "the Yiddish sing-song intonations" of his grandmother's German (*Last Waltz in Vienna*, p. 31). In Dessauer's Viennese novel whenever Lotti becomes excited and lapses into a Yiddish sing-song, her brother Leopold complains: "You are *Mauscheling*: it's pitiful." He himself tries to mimic the languid Viennese drawl spoken by aristocrats, bureaucrats, and soldiers (Dessauer, pp. 7, 67–68). The German *Mauscheln* was a pejorative for speaking garbled German with a Yiddish accent. The verb derived from *Mauschel*, a variant of Moses and a name for the haggling Jewish trader. For etymology, ZW 1: 163; Theodor Gomperz could only recall the foul body odor in the local prayer houses of immigrant Jews (*Ein Gelehrtenleben im Bürgertum der Franz-Josefs-Zeit*, pp. 104–106). Sigmund Mayer called upon his liberalism to remind himself of the need for tolerance toward immigrant Jews (*Die Wiener Juden*, p. 463).

36. DnG, p. 72; DG, pp. 141–42, 145.

37. DG, p. 142; Nordau to Herzl, 7 January 1898, H VIII 614–15, CZA.

38. DnG, p. 98. Norden's English term "fellowship" (TNG, p. 78) is far off the mark. The German is "Versöhnen," or reconciliation, a restoration of harmony.

39. Salten, "Ein Judenstück," *Wiener Allgemeine Zeitung*, 8 January 1898.

40. Erwin Rosenberger, *Herzl, as I Remember Him*, p. 61. For the servant's mockery, TNG, p. 4. For Herzl's reference to his Jewish nose, CD 1: 11.

41. DG, p. 25. In the published version Jacob's mother declares: "He is proud. He suffers, and has always suffered immensely from this—and I along with him" (DnG, p. 16).

42. Quoted in Leon Kellner, *Herzls Lehrjahre 1860–1895*, pp. 49–50.

43. Schnitzler, *Briefe, 1875–1912*, pp. 124–25; Bahr, "The Fateful Moment," in Meyer Weisgal, ed., *Theodor Herzl: A Memorial*, p. 67; BuT 1: 620.

44. CD 1: 5–6; BuT 2: 45–46. An unpublished note by Herzl in early 1893 seems to carry the bitter traces of the first incident: "The cowardice of Jews. Each of us has now and then repressed" ("Die Resorption der Juden," H IV C 1, CZA).

45. Schnitzler, *Briefe, 1875–1912*, p. 238.

46. For this account of Herzl's marriage, Elon, pp. 82, 90–94.

47. O-NL, pp. 14, 103, 171

48. BuT 1: 553.

49. BuT 1: 553–54, 560–61.

50. Schnitzler, *Briefe, 1875–1912*, pp. 235–36, 251–53; BuT 1: 575; Teweles, pp. 120–24, 126–27.

51. Schnitzler, *Briefe, 1875–1912*, pp. 237–39.

52. Schnitzler, *Briefe, 1875–1912*, pp. 238–39, 244.

53. Schnitzler, *Briefe, 1875–1912*, pp. 237–38; Schnitzler, *The Road to the Open*, p. 69.

54. Teweles, pp. 125–26.

55. Schnitzler, *Briefe, 1875–1912*, p. 802.

56. Teweles, pp. 123, 127. Salomon Kohn (1825–1904), an observant Jew, wrote German novels on Jewish themes.

57. *Das Neue Ghetto*, "Theaterkritiken," H N IV B 9, CZA. Whoever clipped this review of the 1898 production in Vienna cut off the newspaper's name.

58. Bein, *Theodore Herzl*, p. 117; Elon, p. 125; Stewart, pp. 154–55.

59. Quoted in Adolf Pollak, "Zionistische Chronologie," p. 2, CZA; for a while the play entered the Zionist repertory. *Die Welt* reported six productions of the play from 1899 to 1901 and several later in the decade. See *Die Welt*, nos. 7, 52 (1899), nos. 20, 39, 40 (1900), no. 26 (1901), no. 9 (1909), no. 13 (1910), no. 17 (1912). The play was serialized in *Die Welt* in nos. 9, 11, 12 (1898).

60. Josef Fränkel, *Theodor Herzl*, pp. 112–15. It is not clear what passage was excised. For Herzl's account, CD 2: 600–601.

61. *Figaro*. Dates are not identifiable on many of these press clippings from the CZA files. The play ran in Vienna from 5 January to 15 February 1898. Reviewers in the German nationalist *Deutsche Zeitung* and the *Ostdeutsche Rundschau* were similarly outraged by this scene; for apprehensions about demonstrations, *Prager Abendblatt*, June, and for Berlin, *Staatsbürger Zeitung*, 6 February 1898.

62. For the Vienna performance, *Arbeiter Zeitung*, 8 January 1898, and *Wiener Allgemeine Zeitung*, 7 January. For Berlin, *Hamburgischer Correspondent*, 7 February, and *Berliner Börsencourier*, 6 February. For Prague, *Prager Abendblatt*, June; on the blows to von Schramm, *Neues Wiener Tagblatt*, 6 January.

63. *Deutsche Zeitung*, February 1898; *Kikeriki-Anzeiger*, 10 January.

64. "Ein Judenstück."

65. Achad Haam, "Nationale Ethik," in *Am Scheidewege*, pp. 153–54.

66. Achad Haam, "Nationale Ethik," p. 153; CD 1: 11; BuT 1: 570–71.

7. The Jewish State

1. CD 1: 183.

2. CD 1: 13–17, "Around Pentecost," the date Herzl inscribed at the start of his Zionist diary, referred to the Christian Whitsunday, which fell on 2 June 1895.

3. John W. Boyer, *Political Radicalism in Late Imperial Vienna*, p. 349; NFP, 2 April 1895, quoted in Alex Bein, *Theodor Herzl*, p. 191; Herzl was in Vienna from 25 to 30 March

(BuT 1: 580); for Herzl's preoccupation with the crisis in Vienna, Henry J. Cohn, "Theodor Herzl's Conversion to Zionism," JSS 32 (1970), pp. 105–108.

4. In early 1893, "Die Resorption der Juden," H IV C 1, CZA. "To Jerusalem? This wouldn't be so bad. Unfortunately also not possible. We are natives of this land!" The second time in "Femme de Claude," NFP, 17 October 1894.

5. BuT 2: 760–70. Parts of these preparatory notes reappear in Herzl's account of his conversation with Hirsch (CD 1: 18–24).

6. CD 1: 93, 95–96, 104, 106, 111.

7. CD 1: 116.

8. Christian Wilhelm Dohm, *Concerning the Amelioration of the Civil Status of the Jews*, p. 27; Theodor Gomperz, *Ein Gelehrtenleben im Bürgertum der Franz-Josefs-Zeit*, p. 122.

9. BuT 2: 763, 769.

10. CD 1: 163–64, 180.

11. CD 1: 72, 182, 190, 194.

12. BuT 2: 199; J. L. Talmon, "Types of Jewish Self-Awareness," *Israel among the Nations*, p. 110.

13. For expressions of passionate sympathy, CD 1: 72, 190, CD 1: 179. The German "verjuden" is in BuT 2: 197; Steven Aschheim, " 'The Jew Within': The Myth of 'Judaization' in Germany," *The Jewish Response to German Culture*, ed. Jehuda Reinharz and Walter Schatzberg, pp. 212–14, 227.

14. CD 1: 238. The German *"Judenjunge"* is in BuT 2: 248; for *Schädling*, ZW 2: 88, 287. The epithet was used by antisemites in Vienna in connection with a cholera scare in 1892. Jews were accused of spreading epidemics. See the newspaper of the Viennese Defense Association against Antisemitism, "Die Cholera und die Antisemiten," *Freies Blatt*, 30 October 1892.

15. ZW 1: 163–65. For the etymology of *Mauschel*, see chap. 6, n.35, above.

16. JS, pp. 94, 99.

17. For these contrasting attitudes to the state, see my "Ahad Ha-Am and Herzl," *At the Crossroads*, ed. Jacques Kornberg, pp. 127–28.

18. CD 1: 19.

19. JS, p. 92.

20. Ernest Lorenzen, "The Negotiorum Gestio in Roman and Modern Civil Law," *Cornell Law Quarterly* 13 (1928): 190–210.

21. JS, pp. 92–94.

22. JS, pp. 95, 99; Herzl spoke elsewhere of the need for imposed "limits on public opinion, especially in the beginning" (CD 1: 170).

23. On Bismarck, CD 1: 120; CD 1: 211.

24. PB, p. 243.

25. JS, p. 83; CD 1: 55.

26. CD 1: 211.

27. CD 2: 713. For Herzl's acid comment on an East European rabbi: "This sort of Jew performs, inside the cage of his world outlook, the thousand-leagued journeys of a squirrel on its wheel" (CD 1: 240); for a valuable discussion of Herzl's attitude to Russian Jews, Steven Aschheim, *Brothers and Strangers*, pp. 84–87.

28. CD 1: 213; on "New Greece," CD 1: 306; it was not until the First Zionist Congress in 1897 that Herzl met Russian Jews formed by both modern European culture and their Jewish heritage. Herzl confessed rather patronizingly: "But we had always imagined them dependent on our intellectual help and guidance . . . they are not Caliban but Prospero" (ZW 1: 153). Caliban was the deformed, half-human slave in *The Tempest*, a symbol of humanity's primitive urges. Prospero was the wise ruler, just and philosophical.

29. CD 1: 64, 84–85, 162–63, 173.
30. JS, 100.
31. CD 1: 107.
32. Tulo Nussenblatt, ed., *Zeitgenossen über Herzl*, p. 280.
33. Quoted in Leon Kellner, *Herzls Lehrjahre (1860–1895)*, p. 139.
34. BuT 2: 626; CD 1: 106–07; O-NL, pp. 12–16, 173–75. Herzl never shook off his irritation over Bauer's verse. Further comments are in CD 2: 979, 3: 940 and ZW 2: 43.
35. Stefan Zweig, "König der Juden," *Theodor Herzl: A Memorial*, ed., Meyer Weisgal, p. 57; CD 1: 182; Herzl's critique of Hibbat Zion is quoted in Erwin Rosenberger, *Herzl as I Remember Him*, p. 17; "Wagner opera" in CD, 1: 38.
36. CD 2: 693; CD 1: 116.
37. Adolf Böhm, *Die Zionistische Bewegung* 1: 303; CD 1: 116; Marx, "Toward the Critique of Hegel's Philosophy of Law: Introduction," in *Writings of the Young Marx on Philosophy and Society*, ed. and trans. Lloyd D. Easton and Kurt H. Guddat (New York: Doubleday, Anchor Books, 1967), p. 261; for Herzl's vision of Jewish greatness, CD 1: 105.
38. Yehoshafat Harkabi, *Israel's Fateful Hour*, pp. 71–77.
39. Quoted in David Vital, *The Origins of Zionism*, p. 307; in the same vein, a Russian Zionist observed that Herzl wished "to bring forth a nation in a single generation" (quoted in Vital, p. 320).
40. Achad Ha-Am, *Ten Essays on Zionism and Judaism*, trans. Leon Simon, p. 41.
41. Vital, pp. 277, 334–38; Z. Bychowski, "Die Intuition Herzls," in Tulo Nussenblatt, ed., *Zeitgenossen über Herzl*, p. 46.
42. Arthur Ruppin, *Die Juden der Gegenwart*, p. 253; Talmon, pp. 121–22.
43. Osias Thon, "Wie ich ihn sah," in Nussenblatt, ed., *Zeitgenossen über Herzl*, p. 225.
44. "Das Wirtshaus zum Anilin," *Philosophische Erzählungen*, pp. 263–65. "Das Wirtshaus" first appeared in 1896; Arthur Schnitzler, *Briefe, 1872–1912*, pp. 808–809. I have used the Joel Carmichael translation of this letter, "Excerpts from the Correspondence between Theodor Herzl and Arthur Schnitzler (1892–1895)," *Midstream* 6 (Winter 1960), p. 64.
45. CD 1: 36, 157.
46. Stefan Zweig, "The Emergence of Theodor Herzl," in Meyer W. Weisgal, ed., *Theodor Herzl: A Memorial*, p. 297; Kellner, p. 67.
47. Carl Schorske, *Fin-de-Siècle Vienna*, p. 9; the description of Herzl's essays is by Stefan Zweig, "König der Juden," in Weisgal, ed., *Theodor Herzl: A Memorial*, p. 55.
48. Kellner, p. 67.
49. Stephen M. Poppel, *Zionism in Germany, 1897–1933*, p. 92. Though Poppel was describing the first generation of German Zionists, his conception adds greatly to our understanding of Herzl.
50. ZW 1: 203–206.
51. CD 1: 104, 151.
52. Poppel, p. 93. For some, reading Herzl's *The Jewish State* sparked their conversion.
53. Hannah Arendt, *The Jew as Pariah*, p. 144; both are quoted in Poppel, pp. 27, 89–90. For another account of Zionism as emancipation from Jewish self-contempt, Robert Weltsch, "Zionism in Central Europe," in Weisgal, ed., *Theodor Herzl: A Memorial*, p. 241.
54. For Herzl's copy of Heine's poem, "Notizen zur Judenfrage," H IV C 2, CZA; S. S. Prawer, *Heine's Jewish Comedy*, pp. 433–34. I use the Prawer translation; "The Family Affliction," ZW 2: 43–47. Prawer translates "Familienübel" as "family complaint."
55. Mattin Buber, "Herzl und die Historie," *Ost und West* 4 (August/September 1904), p. 590.
56. ZW 1: 58; CD 1: 101.
57. BuT 2: 767; for the Swiss model, CD 1: 171.

58. JS, p. 52; Olga Schnitzler, *Spiegelbild der Freundschaft*, p. 96.

59. For Herzl's visit to Palestine, CD 2: 742–47; for the reasons Herzl preferred Palestine, Alex Bein, "Some Early Herzl Letters," Raphael Patai ed., HYB 1: 308, 314.

60. CD 1: 246–47. For similar statements, CD 1: 171 and 2: 694–95.

61. CD 1: 306; ZW 1: 75; for the flag, JS, p. 101.

62. *Die Welt* quote in Adolf Friedemann, *Das Leben Theodor Herzls*, p. 121; CD 2: 451; Suttner in Nussenblatt, *Ein Volk unterwegs zum Frieden*, p. 84.

63. JS, pp. 56, 68–69; "dirty dealings" in CD 1: 32; for Drumont's scheme to confiscate Jewish property, Stephen Wilson, *Ideology and Experience*, p. 675.

64. CD 1: 183.

65. CD 1: 143. Herzl repeated this claim in *The Jewish State* with only slight modification (JS, p. 69).

66. CD 1: 182.

67. "Frankreich im Jahre 1894," NFP, 30 December 1894.

68. PB, p. 104. Herzl expressed this optimism in November 1894, the month he completed *The New Ghetto*. For similar statements in his Zionist diary, CD 1: 143–44.

69. Herzl to Harden, 24 February 1897, *Briefe: Von der Jugendzeit bis zum Tode.*; O-NL, p. 178.

70. JS, p. 109.

71. JS, pp. 44–45, 47; CD 1: 71.

72. Friedrich Fürst von Wrede, "Herzls Meisterwerk," in Nussenblatt, ed., *Zeitgenossen über Herzl*, p. 248; JS, p. 35; CD 1: 83, 182.

73. "There are still deep-seated prejudices against us . . . fairy tales and proverbs are anti-Semitic" (JS, p. 34).

74. CD 1: 131.

75. Amos Elon, *Herzl*, p. 407; Shulamit Volkov, "Antisemitismus in Deutschland als Problem jüdisch-nationalen Denkens und jüdischer Geschichtsschreibung," *Geschichte und Gesellschaft* 5 (1979): pp. 527–30.

76. CD 1: 31, 2: 622; "Geusenamen," in Herzl to Rathenau, 7 August 1901, *Briefe: Von der Jugendzeit bis zum Tode*; CD 1: 101.

77. CD 1: 42; Böhm, *Die Zionistische Bewegung* 1: 185; on Badeni, CD, 1: 254–56; on Eulenberg, CD, 2: 688.

78. Bein, *Theodor Herzl*, pp. 293, 322–26; Herzl to Belkowsky, 23 May 1897, *Theodor Herzl Jahrbuch*, Tulo Nussenblatt, ed., p. 91; Josef Fraenkel, ed., *Robert Stricker* (London: Ararat Publishing Society, 1950), p. 83.

79. Talmon, p. 117.

80. Cahnman, "Scholar and Visionary: The Correspondence between Herzl and Ludwig Gumplowicz," HYB 1: 177.

81. Achad Ha-Am, *Ten Essays on Zionism and Judaism*, pp. 50–51.

82. Arthur Ruppin, *Memoirs, Diaries, Letters*, pp. 207–208.

83. Vital, pp. 325–26.

84. Quoted in Vital, p. 332.

85. CD 2: 534, 1: 19.

86. For this account of the congress and the events leading up to it, Vital, pp. 333–34, 340–53, 366–72.

8. The Dreyfus Legend

1. CD 1: 13; ZW 2: 112.

2. Herzl to Adolf Agai, 6 May 1898, Tulo Nussenblatt, ed., *Theodor Herzl Jahrbuch*, p. 173; for Herzl's preoccupation with Austria, BuT 1: 569; for the dates he began and

completed the play, DG, H IV B 14, CZA, title page and final page. For the dates of the arrest and charges, Jean-Denis Bredin, *The Affair*, pp. 76–81; for Herzl's very first statement, 3 years after the fact, that writing his play coincided with the Dreyfus trial, CD 2: 601.

3. ZW 2: 112; Herzl's first reference to the trial in his Zionist diary is on 17 November 1895 (CD 1: 273).

4. Amos Elon, *Herzl*, pp. 127–28; Alex Bein, *Theodore Herzl*, pp. 114–16; the "Autobiography" was published in January 1898. See ZW 1: 15–19; for the Bein quote, "Herzl und der Dreyfus-Prozess," *Die Stimme*, 5 October 1934.

5. David Vital, *The Origins of Zionism*, p. 244; Henry J. Cohn, "Theodor Herzl's Conversion to Zionism" JSS 32 (1970), pp. 105–10; Desmond Stewart, *Theodor Herzl*, p. 163; some have offered shrewd insights into Herzl's conversion: Vital argues that "the roots of his obsession lay deeper [than the Dreyfus experience]" (Vital, p. 244). Josef Fränkel observed: "Herzl's ideas were not suddenly conceived and formulated; they took years to evolve and ripen like fruit on a tree" (Josef Fränkel, "Simon Dubnow and the History of Political Zionism," in Aaron Steinberg, ed., *Simon Dubnov: L'Homme et Son Oeuvre* [Paris: French Section, World Jewish Congress, 1963], p. 154). Stewart comes closest to explaining Herzl's claim: "The [Dreyfus] legend has its roots in the Herzl of a few years later, a man then battling as a politician and modifying his past in the interests of a cause" (Stewart, p. 163).

6. Carl E. Schorske, *Fin-de-Siècle Vienna*, pp. 153, 157; ZW 2: 114.

7. "Französische Antisemiten," NFP, 3 September 1892; "Process Burdeau gegen Drumont," NFP, 16 June 1892; "Scandale in Frankreich," NFP, 27 November 1892, and "Panama," NFP, 11 January 1893.

8. Byrnes, *Anti-semitism in Modern France*, pp. 329–31.

9. Byrnes, pp. 331–33.

10. "Französische Antisemiten," NFP, 3 September 1892; BuT 1: 512, 517.

11. Byrnes, pp. 335–39.

12. For Drumont's political failures, Byrnes, pp. 177–81, 235–37, 262; Michael Marrus, *The Politics of Assimilation*, p. 153; "Französische Antisemiten," NFP, 3 September 1892.

13. For this analysis of France in the 1890s, R. D. Anderson, *France, 1870–1914*, pp. 15, 30–32, 36–41, 63–64; in the elections of 1893 the majority moderate Republicans won 322 seats; the Radicals, as the second largest party, won 122 seats; the Socialists gained 49; the *Ralliés*, that part of the Catholic Right aligned with the Republic, won 35 seats; and the divided antirepublican Right won 58 seats, a sharp drop from its previous standing (Anderson, p. 168).

14. "Frankreich im Jahre 1891," NFP, 31 December 1891; "Frankreich im Jahre 1893, NFP, 30 December 1893.

15. Marrus, pp. 135–36, 202; "Frankreich im Jahre 1892," NFP, 31 December 1892; on French Socialists, "Frankreich im Jahre 1894," NFP, 30 December 1894. The Socialists achieved a major breakthrough in the parliamentary elections of 1893. From a handful of deputies, they now had a block of 40 seats. On the masses, "Frankreich im Jahre 1892."

16. On Socialist antisemitism, PB, p. 23; BuT 1: 509.

17. Schorske, pp. 156–57; "Frankreich im Jahre 1894."

18. Herzl, *L'Affaire Dreyfus*, trans. Léon Vogel, pp. 3–21.

19. Paléologue quoted in Stephen Wilson, *Ideology and Experience*, p. 10; Durkheim quoted in Steven Lukes, *Émile Durkheim* (New York: Penguin Books, 1973), p. 345; Bein, *Theodore Herzl*, p. 115; Elon has embellished Bein's conjecture: "In Vienna, that evening, his editors censored his story" (Elon, p. 129); Bein mentions elsewhere that the *Neue Freie Presse* regularly reported on Austrian and German antisemitism (Bein, p. 84).

20. For the reference to Jaurès, PB, pp. 127–28. The piece was written in February 1895; for references to Vienna, CD 1: 46, 125, 201, 243–44, 269. The sole reference to Dreyfus is on p. 273; JS, p. 43.

21. Bredin, p. 98.

22. For an authoritative and complete account of these political developments, Wilson, chapters 1 and 2.

23. ZW 2: 114.

24. ZW 2: 113; Herzl to Adolf Agai, 6 May 1898, in Tulo Nussenblatt, ed., *Theodor Herzl Jahrbuch*, p. 173; for Herzl's conversation with the military attaché, ZW 2: 112–13. Herzl says of the attaché that his "name has been frequently mentioned these days." Both Major Panizzardi and Colonel von Schwarzkoppen, the German military attaché, were in the news, suspected of espionage against France. That Herzl had the 1895 conversation about Dreyfus with Colonel von Schwarzkoppen rather than Pannizardi, is less credible, as most suspected that Dreyfus was spying for the Germans (Bredin, pp. 78–83, 272–73).

25. Herzl to Paul Goldmann, 22 November 1896, Bein, "Some Early Herzl Letters," in HYB, ed. Raphael Patai, 1: 312–13; for Lazare's brochure, Marrus, pp. 182–83; in 1894 Lazare was one of a handful of French Jews skeptical about the prospects of assimilation. Amazingly, one week after Herzl finished his play, Lazare published an article entitled, "Le nouveau ghetto." Marrus suggests Lazare and Herzl may have been in contact in 1894. Herzl's first mention of Lazare came only in July 1896 (Marrus, pp. 178–80, CD 1: 424).

26. CD 1: 9, 13; Herzl to Teweles, 19 May 1895, in Heinrich Teweles, *Theater und Publikum*, p. 122.

Selected Bibliography

Archival Materials

Central Zionist Archives, Jerusalem

H I A 2. Bar-Mizvah: Einladung zur "Konfirmation," 3.5, 1873.

H I K 4. Letter from Herzl's seconds, Heinrich Kana and Julius von Ludassy. Exchange of apologies with Ludwig Videcky.

H N IV B 9. *Das neue Ghetto.* Theaterkritiken. Press clippings of theater reviews of *The New Ghetto.* The name and date of the newspaper have been snipped off in some cases.

H IV B 14. *Das Ghetto.* Herzl's first handwritten draft of the play, includes revisions suggested by Arthur Schnitzler.

H IV B 79. "Lesehallias: Ein Kneipepos."

H IV C 1. "Die Resorption der Juden." These unpublished notes are dated April 17 in Herzl's hand. The Central Zionist Archives wrongly places them in 1894. They are identical in theme to Herzl's letters to Baron Leitenberger in January 1893. Herzl subtitled these notes "Letters on the Jewish question by Dr. S. Kohn," suggesting he was recording his ideas for eventual publication under a pseudonym. See also Bein, *Theodor Herzl,* pp. 149, 155.

H IV C 2. "Notizen zur Judenfrage," [1891?–1893?].

H VIII 34. Eduard Bacher's letters to Herzl.

H VIII 253a. Heinrich Friedjung's letter to Herzl.

H VIII 614/15. Max Nordau's letters to Herzl.

Pollak, Adolf. "Zionistische Chronologie." Typescript. 1949. An invaluable annotated index to articles in *Die Welt.*

Newspapers

Neue Freie Presse. Vienna.

Die Neuzeit: Wochenschrift für politische, religiöse und Cultur-Interessen. Vienna.

Oesterreichische Wochenschrift: Centralorgan für die gesammten Interessen des Judenthums. Vienna.

Herzl's Writings

L'Affaire Dreyfus: Reportages et Réflexions. Léon Vogel, trans. Paris: Imprimerie des 2 Artisans, 1958. This translation, done for the Fedération sioniste de France, includes all Herzl's dispatches and articles on the Dreyfus trial and Affair.

Briefe: Von der Jugendzeit bis zum Tode. Microfiche. Zug, Switzerland: Inter Documentation Company, 1977. All Herzl's letters, from the Central Zionist Archives collection.

Briefe und Tagebücher. Alex Bein et al., ed. Vol. 1, *Briefe und Autobiographische Notizen, 1866–1895.* Johannes Wachten, ed. Berlin: Verlag Ullstein, Propyläen, 1983.
Briefe und Tagebücher. Alex Bein et al., ed. Vol. 2, *Zionistisches Tagebuch, 1895–1899.* Johannes Wachten and Chayan Harel, eds. Berlin: Verlag Ullstein, Propyläen, 1984.
The Complete Diaries of Theodor Herzl. Raphael Patai, ed. Harry Zohn, trans. 5 vols. New York: Herzl Press and Thomas Yoseloff, 1960.
Feuilletons. 2 vols. 2d ed. Berlin: Verlag Benjamin Harz, 1911.
[H. Jungmann]. "Die Heimkehr." NFP, 23 March–15 April 1900.
The Jewish State. Harry Zohn, trans. New York: Herzl Press, 1970.
Das neue Ghetto. Vienna: Verlag der "Welt," 1897.
The New Ghetto. Heinz Norden, trans. New York: The Theodor Herzl Foundation, 1955.
Old-New Land. Lotta Levensohn, trans. Introduction by Jacques Kornberg. New York: Markus Wiener Publishing and Herzl Press, 1987.
Das Palais Bourbon: Bilder aus dem Französischen Parlamentsleben. Leipzig: Verlag von Duncker & Humblot, 1895.
Philosophische Erzählungen. Berlin: B. Harz Verlag 1919.
Theodor Herzl: A Portrait for This Age. Edited by Ludwig Lewisohn. New York: World, 1955. Selections from Herzl's writings.
Was wird man sagen? Vienna: Verlag von Gabor Steiner, 1890.
Zionist Writings: Essays and Addresses. Harry Zohn, trans. 2 vols. New York: Herzl Press.

Letters to Herzl

Schnitzler, Arthur. *Briefe, 1875–1912.* Therese Nickl and Heinrich Schnitzler, eds. Frankfurt am Main: S. Fischer, 1981.
Teweles, Heinrich. *Theater und Publikum: Erinnerungen und Erfahrungen.* Veröffentlichungen der Gesellschaft deutscher Bücherfreunde in Böhmen, no. 7. Prague: Gesellschaft deutscher Bücherfreunde in Böhmen, 1927.

Memoirs, Literary Works, Tracts, Essays

Achad Haam, *Am Scheidewege: Gesammelte Aufsätze.* Hugo Knöpfmacher and Ernst Müller, trans. Vol 2. Berlin: Jüdischer Verlag, 1923.
Achad Ha-Am. *Ten Essays on Zionism and Judaism.* Leon Simon, trans. 1922. Reprint. New York: Arno Press, 1973.
Bahr, Hermann. *Selbstbildnis.* Berlin: S. Fischer Verlag, 1923.
Bloch, Joseph S. *My Reminiscences.* Vienna: R. Löwit, 1923. Reprint. New York: Arno Press, 1973.
Dessauer, Adolf. *Grossstadtjuden.* Vienna: Wilhelm Braumüller, 1910.
Dohm, Christian Wilhelm. *Concerning the Amelioration of the Civil Status of the Jews.* Helen Lederer, trans. Readings in Modern Jewish History, edited by Ellis Rivkin. Mimeographed. Cincinnati: Hebrew Union College—Jewish Institute of Religion, 1957.
Gomperz, Theodor. *Ein Gelehrtenleben im Bürgertum der Franz-Josefs-Zeit: Auswahl seiner Briefe und Aufzeichnungen, 1869–1912, erläutert und zu einer Darstellung*

seines Lebens verknüpft Heinrich Gomperz. Robert A. Kann, ed. Österreichische Akademie der Wissenschaften. Philosophisch-Historische Klasse. Sitzungsberichte, vol. 295. Vienna: Verlag der Österreichischen Akademie der Wissenschaften, 1974.

Mayer, Sigmund. *Ein jüdischer Kaufmann, 1831 bis 1911: Lebenserinnerungen.* Leipzig: Verlag von Duncker & Humblot, 1911.

Plener, Ernst, *Erinnerungen.* Vol. 2, *Parlamentarische Tätigkeit 1873–1891.* Leipzig: Deutsche Verlags-Anstalt, 1921.

Ruppin, Arthur. *Memoirs, Diaries, Letters.* Alex Bein, ed. Karen Gershon, trans. New York: Herzl Press, 1971.

Schnitzler, Arthur. *My Youth in Vienna.* Catherine Hutter, trans. New York: Holt, Rinehart & Winston, 1970.

———. *The Road to the Open.* Horace Samuel, trans. New York: Alfred A. Knopf, 1923.

Schnitzler, Olga. *Spiegelbild der Freundschaft.* Salzburg: Residenz Verlag, 1962.

Treitschke, Heinrich von. *A Word about Our Jewry.* Helen Lederer, trans. Readings in Modern Jewish History, ed. Ellis Rivkin. Mimeographed. Cincinnati: Hebrew Union College—Jewish Institute of Religion, n.d.

Wassermann, Jacob. *My Life as German and Jew.* S. N. Brainin, trans. New York: Coward-McCann, 1933.

Zweig, Stefan. *The World of Yesterday: An Autobiography.* Lincoln: University of Nebraska Press, A Bison Book, 1964.

Herzl Biographies

Bein, Alex. *Theodor Herzl: Biographie.* Vienna: Fiba Verlag, 1934.

———. *Theodore Herzl: A Biography.* Maurice Samuel, trans. New York: Atheneum, A Temple Book, 1970. Note the different spellings of Theodor(e) which distinguish the above titles in the endnotes.

de Haas, Jacob. *Theodor Herzl: A Biographical Study.* 2 vols. Chicago: Leonard, 1927.

Elon, Amos. *Herzl.* New York: Holt, Rinehart & Winston, 1975.

Fränkel, Josef. *Theodor Herzl: Des Schöpfers erstes Wollen.* Vienna: Fiba Verlag, 1934.

Friedemann, Adolf. *Das Leben Theodor Herzls.* 2d ed., rev. Berlin: Jüdischer Verlag, 1919.

Handler, Andrew. *Dori: The Life and Times of Theodor Herzl in Budapest (1860—1878).* Tuscaloosa: University of Alabama Press, 1983.

Kellner, Leon. *Theodor Herzls Lehrjahre, 1860–1895.* Vienna: R. Löwit, 1920.

Pawel, Ernst. *The Labyrinth of Exile: A Life of Theodor Herzl.* New York: Farrar, Straus, Giroux, 1989.

Rosenberger, Erwin. *Herzl as I Remember Him.* Translated and abridged by Louis Jay Herman. New York: Herzl Press, 1959.

Stewart, Desmond. *Theodor Herzl: Artist and Politician.* Garden City, N.Y.: Doubleday, 1974.

Articles, Essays on Herzl

Bein, Alexander, "Herzl und der Dreyfus-Prozess," *Die Stimme* V (5 October 1934).

Cohn, Henry J. "Theodor Herzl's Conversion to Zionism." JSS 32 (1970): 101–10.

Diamant, Paul J. *Theodor Herzls väterliche und mütterliche Vorfahren: Eine familiengeschichtliche Studie mit einer Ahnentafel.* Jerusalem: Verlag Bamberger & Wahrmann, 1934.

Fränkel, Josef. "Theodor Herzl in der akademischen Burschenschaft 'Albia.'" *Die Neue Welt*, nos. 235, 236, 238 (1932).

———. "Wie 'Das neue Ghetto' entstand." *Selbstwehr*, 15 July 1938.

Herzog, Dietrich. "Theodor Herzl als Burschenschafter—und die Folgen." *Beiträge zur österreichischen Studentengeschichte.* 2 (1974): 73–88.

Kornberg, Jacques. "Ahad Ha-Am and Herzl." *At the Crossroads: Essays on Ahad Ha-Am.* Jacques Kornberg, ed. Albany: State University of New York Press, 1983. Pp. 106–29.

Nussenblatt, Tulo. "Aus Theodor Herzls Schul- und Universitätszeit." *Die Neue Welt*, nos. 229, 231, 232 (5, 19, 26 February 1932).

Rabinowicz, Oskar K. Review of Israel Cohen, "Theodor Herzl, Founder of Modern Zionism." JSS 22 (1960): 182–85.

———. "Herzl the Playwright." *Jewish Book Annual* 18 (1960–61): 100–115.

Salten, Felix. "Ein Judenstück," *Wiener Allgemeine Zeitung*, 8 January 1898.

Talmon, T. L. "Types of Jewish Self-Awareness: Herzl's 'Jewish State' after Seventy Years (1896–1966)," *Israel among the Nations.* London: Weidenfeld & Nicolson, 1970.

Memorial Volumes, Collected Articles, Documents on Herzl

Nussenblatt, Tulo. *Ein Volk unterwegs zum Frieden: (Theodor Herzl—Bertha von Suttner).* Vienna: Reinhold-Verlag. 1933.

———, ed. *Theodor Herzl Jahrbuch.* Vienna: Dr. Heinrich Glanz Verlag, 1937. Nussenblatt intended this as the first of a series of yearbooks devoted to documents and articles on Herzl. Born in Galicia in 1895, Nussenblatt was expelled to Poland after the *Anschluss*. He was deported and murdered in the Treblinka death camp in 1943.

———, ed. *Zeitgenossen über Herzl.* Brünn, Czechoslovakia: Jüdischer Buch- und Kunstverlag, 1929.

Ost und West: Illustrierte Monatsschrift für Modernes Judentum. "Herzl-Nummer." 4 (August-September 1904). An early memorial issue with a number of valuable assessments.

Patai, Raphael, ed. HYB. 7 vols. New York: Herzl Press, 1958–71.

Weisgal, Meyer W., ed. *Theodor Herzl: A Memorial.* New York: The New Palestine, 1929.

Die Welt, 3 July 1914. On the tenth anniversary of his death, *Die Welt* issued a special number devoted to remembrances of Herzl.

Austria

Documents and Reports

Jahresbericht der Akademischen Lesehalle in Wien über das zehnte Vereinsjahr 1879–80. Vienna: Selbstverlag der Akademischen Lesehalle [1880].

Kolmer, Gustav. *Parlament und Verfassung in Österreich.* 8 vols. 1905. Reprint. Graz: Akademische Druck- & Verlagsanstalt, 1972.
Die *Lesevereine der deutschen Hochschüler an der Wiener Universität.* Gedenkschrift, herausgegeben von Lese—u. Redevereine der deutschen Hochschüler in Wien "Germania." Vienna: Im Selbstverlage des Lese- und Redevereins der deutschen Hochschüler in Wien "Germania," 1912.

Books and Articles on Austria

Bahnwehr, Spulak von. *Geschichte der aus den Jahren 1859–1884 stammenden Wiener Couleurs.* Vienna: Im Selbstverlag des Verfassers, 1914.
Barea, Ilsa. *Vienna.* New York: Alfred A. Knopf, 1966.
Becke, Karl. *Wiener akademische Burschenschaft "Albia," 1870–1930.* Vienna: Im Selbstverlag der Wiener Akademische Burschenschaft "Albia" [1930].
Boyer, John W. *Political Radicalism in Late Imperial Vienna: Origins of the Christian Social Movement, 1848–1897.* Chicago: University of Chicago Press, 1981.
Bunzl, John, and Bernd Marin. *Antisemitismus in Österreich: Sozialhistorische und soziologische Studien.* Vergleichende Gesellschaftsgeschichte und politische Ideengeschichte der Neuzeit. Vol 3. Innsbruck: Inn-Verlag, 1983.
Charmatz, Richard. *Deutsch-österreichische Politik: Studien über den Liberalismus und über die auswärtige Politik Österreichs.* Leipzig: Verlag von Duncker & Humblot, 1907.
———. *Österreichs innere Geschichte von 1848 bis 1895.* 2 vols. 3d rev. ed. Leipzig: B. G. Taubner, 1918.
Geehr, Richard S., ed. and trans. *"I Decide Who Is A Jew!: The Papers of Dr. Karl Lueger.* Washington, D.C.: University Press of America, 1982.
Gross, N. T. "The Industrial Revolution in the Habsburg Monarchy." *The Fontana Economic History of Europe.* Vol 4, *The Emergence of Industrial Societies,* part 1, ed. Carlo M. Cipolla. London: Collins, Fontana Books, 1973.
Hein, Robert. *Studentischer Antisemitismus in Österreich.* Beiträge zur österreichischen Studentengeschichte. Vol. 10. Vienna: Österreichischer Verein für Studentengeschichte, 1984.
Jászi, Oscar. *The Dissolution of the Habsburg Monarchy.* Chicago: University of Chicago Press, Phoenix Books, 1961.
Jenks, William A. *Austria under the Iron Ring, 1879–1893.* Charlottesville: University Press of Virginia, 1965.
Knoll, Kurt. *Die Geschichte der schlesischen akademischen Landsmannschaft "Oppavia" in Wien, im Rahmen der allgemeinen studentischen Entwicklung an den Wiener Hochschulen.* 2 vols. Vienna: Im Selbstverlage der schlesischen akademischen Landsmannschaft "Oppavia" in Wien, 1923.
Matis, Herbert. *Österreichs Wirtschaft, 1848–1913: Konjunkturelle Dynamik und gesellschaftlicher Wandel im Zeitalter Franz Josephs I.* Berlin: Duncker & Humblot, 1972.
May, Arthur J. *The Hapsburg Monarchy, 1867–1914.* New York: W. W. Norton, The Norton Library, 1968.
McGrath, William T. "Student Radicalism in Vienna." *Journal of Contemporary History* 2 (1967): 183–201.
Molisch, Paul. *Geschichte der deutschnationalen Bewegung in Oesterreich: von ihren Anfängen bis zum Zerfall der Monarchie.* Jena: Verlag von Gustav Fischer, 1926.

————. *Politische Geschichte der deutschen Hochschulen in Österreich von 1848 bis 1918*. 2d rev. ed. Vienna: Wilhelm Braumüller, 1938.

[Oppenheimer, Ludwig John]. *Austriaca: Betrachtungen und Streiflichter*. Leipzig: Verlag von Duncker & Humblot, 1882.

Pichl, Eduard [Herwig]. *Georg Schönerer und die Entwicklung des Alldeutschtumes in der Ostmark*. 6 vols. 1912–1938. Vols. 1–4 were published in Vienna, vols. 5–6 in Berlin. Volumes carry the names of different publishers.

Pulzer, Peter G. J. *The Rise of Political Anti-Semitism in Germany and Austria*. New York: John Wiley & Sons, 1964.

Scheuer, Oskar F. *Burschenschaft und Judenfrage: Der Rassenantisemitismus in der deutschen Studentschaft*. Berlin: Verlag Berlin-Wien, 1927.

Schorske, Carl E. *Fin-de-Siècle Vienna: Politics and Culture*. New York: Alfred A. Knopf, 1980.

Seliger, Maren, and Karl Ucakar. *Wien: Politische Geschichte 1740–1934: Entwicklung und Bestimmungskräfte grossstädtischer Politik*. 2 vols. Vienna: Jugend und Volk, 1985.

Steed, Henry Wickham. *The Hapsburg Monarchy*. 4th ed. London: Constable, 1919.

Terzi, Alfred Otto Ritter von. "Aus der Geschichte der deutschnationalen Studentenbewegung in Österreich und ihre Bedeutung für das Deutsche Reich." *Akademische Rundschau: Zeitschrift für das gesamte Hochschulwesen und die Akademischen Berufe* [Leipzig]. 5 (1917–18): 365–94, 417–45.

Wagner-Rieger, Renate, ed. *Die Wiener Ringstrasse, Bild einer Epoche: Die Erweiterung der inneren Stadt Wien unter Kaiser Franz Joseph*. Vol. 5, Franz Baltzarek, Alfred Hoffmann, and Hannes Stekl. *Wirtschaft und Gesellschaft der Wiener Stadterweiterung*. Wiesbaden: Franz Stainer Verlag, 1975.

Wandruszka, Adam. "Österreichs politische Struktur." *Geschichte der Republik Österreich*. Heinrich Benedikt, ed. Munich: Verlag R. Oldenbourg, 1954.

————. "Die österreichische Presse in der franzisko-josephinischen Epoche." *Öffentliche Meinung in der Geschichte Österreichs*. Erich Zollner, ed. Schriften des Instituts für Österreichkunde, no. 34. Vienna: Österreichischer Bundesverlag, 1979.

Whiteside, Andrew G. "The Germans as an Integrative Force in Imperial Austria: The Dilemma of Dominance." *AHY*, vol. 3, pt. 1 (1967): 157–200.

————. *The Socialism of Fools: Georg Ritter von Schönerer and Austrian Pan-Germanism*. Berkeley: University of California Press, 1975.

Books and Articles on Austrian Jewry

Beller, Steven. *Vienna and the Jews, 1867–1938: A Cultural History*. Cambridge: Cambridge University Press, 1989.

Bernhard, Paul P. "Joseph II and the Jews: The Origins of the Toleration Patent of 1782." *AHY* 4–5 (1968–69): 101–19.

Cahnman, Werner J. "Adolf Fischhof and His Jewish Followers." *LBIYB* 4 (1959): 111–139.

Clare, George. *Last Waltz in Vienna: The Rise and Destruction of a Family, 1842–1942*. New York: Avon Books, 1983.

Drabek, Anna, Wolfgang Häusler, Kurt Schubert, Karl Stuhlpfarrer, and Nikolaus Vielmetti. *Das österreichische Judentum: Voraussetzungen und Geschichte*. Vienna: Jugend und Volk, 1974.

Fraenkel, Josef., ed. *The Jews of Austria: Essays on Their Life, History and Destruction.* London: Vallentine, Mitchell, 1967.

Grunwald, Max. *Vienna.* Jewish Communities Series. Philadelphia: The Jewish Publication Society of America, 1936.

Mayer, Sigmund. *Die Wiener Juden: Kommerz, Kultur, Politik, 1700–1900.* Vienna: R. Löwit Verlag, 1917.

Oxaal, Ivan, and Walter R. Weitzmann. "The Jews of Pre-1914 Vienna: An Exploration of Basic Sociological Dimensions." LBIYB 30 (1985): 395–432.

Pulzer, P. G. J. "Liberals and the Jewish Question, 1867–1914." *Journal of Central European Affairs* 23 (1963): 131–42.

Rabinbach, Anton G. "The Migration of Galician Jews to Vienna, 1857–1880," AHY II (1975): 44–54.

Rosensaft, Menachem Z. "Jews and Antisemites in Austria at the End of the Nineteenth Century." LBIYB 21 (1976): 57–86.

Rozenblit, Marsha L. *The Jews of Vienna, 1867–1914: Assimilation and Identity.* Albany: State University of New York Press, 1983.

Scheichl, Sigurd Paul. "The Contexts and Nuances of Anti-Jewish Language: Were All the 'Antisemites' Antisemites?" Ivan Oxaal, Michael Pollack, and Gerhard Botz. *Jews, Antisemitism and Culture in Vienna.* London: Routledge & Kegan Paul, 1987.

Schorsch, Ismar. "Moritz Güdemann: Rabbi, Historian and Apologist." LBIYB II (1966): 42–66.

Schubert, Kurt, ed. *Der Wiener Stadttempel, 1826–1976.* SJA, vol. 6. Eisenstadt: Edition Roetzer, 1978.

———, ed. *Zur Geschichte der Juden in den östlichen Ländern der Habsburgermonarchie.* SJA, vol. 8. Eisenstadt: Edition Roetzer, 1980.

Tietze, Hans. *Die Juden Wiens: Geschichte-Wirtschaft-Kultur.* Leipzig: E. P. Tal Verlag, 1935.

Wistrich, Robert S. *Socialism and the Jews: The Dilemmas of Assimilation in Germany and Austria-Hungary.* East Brunswick, N.J.: Associated University Presses, 1982.

Wolf, Gerson. *Die Juden.* Vienna: Verlag der k. k. Hofbuchhandlung Karl Prochaska, 1883.

Books and Articles on Jewish History, Antisemitism

Almog, Shmuel. *Zionism and History: The Rise of a New Jewish Consciousness.* Ina Friedman, trans. New York: St. Martin's Press, 1987.

Arendt, Hannah. *The Jew as Pariah: Jewish Identity and Politics in the Modern Age.* Ron H. Feldman, ed. New York: Grove Press, An Evergreen Book, 1978.

Aschheim, Steven E. *Brothers and Strangers: The East European Jew in German and German Jewish Consciousness, 1800–1923.* Madison: University of Wisconsin Press, 1982.

———. " 'The Jew Within': The Myth of 'Judaization' in Germany." *The Jewish Response to German Culture: From the Enlightenment to the Second World War.* Jehuda Reinharz and Walter Schatzberg, eds. Hanover, N. H.: University Press of New England, 1985.

Baron, Salo. "Ghetto and Emancipation: Shall We Revise the Traditional View." *The Menorah Journal* 14 (1928): 515–26.

Barzilay, Isaac Eisenstein. "The Jew in the Literature of the Enlightenment." JSS 4 (1956): 243–61.

Berlin, Isaiah. "Benjamin Disraeli, Karl Marx and the Search for Identity." *Against the Current: Essays in the History of Ideas*. Henry Hardy, ed. New York: Viking Press, Penguin Books, 1980.

Böhm, Adolf. *Die Zionistische Bewegung*. Vol. 2, *Die Zionistische Bewegung bis zum Ende des Weltkrieges*. Tel Aviv: Hozaah Ivrith, 1935.

Brandes, Georg. "Ludwig Jacobowski," *Gestalten und Gedanken*. Munich: Albert Langen, 1903.

Byrnes, Robert F. *Antisemitism in Modern France*. Vol. 1, *The Prologue to the Dreyfus Affair*. New Brunswick, N.J.: Rutgers University Press, 1950.

Endelman, Todd M. "Conversion as a Response to Antisemitism in Modern Jewish History." *Living with Antisemitism: Modern Jewish Responses*. Jehuda Reinharz, ed. Hanover, N. H.: University Press of New England, 1987.

Gelber, Mark H. "An Alternate Reading of the Role of the Jewish Scholar in Gustav Freytag's *Soll und Haben*." *The Germanic Review* 58 (1983): 83–88.

Gilman, Sander L. *Jewish Self-Hatred: Antisemitism and the Hidden Language of the Jews*. Baltimore: Johns Hopkins University Press, 1986.

Harkabi, Yehoshafat. *Israel's Fateful Hour*. Lenn Schramm, trans. New York: Harper & Row, 1988.

Hertzberg, Arthur, *The French Enlightenment and the Jews: The Origins of Modern Anti-Semitism*. New York: Schocken Books, 1970.

Katz, Jacob. *Out of the Ghetto: The Social Background of Jewish Emancipation, 1770–1870*. Cambridge: Harvard University Press, 1973.

———. *From Prejudice to Destruction: Anti-Semitism, 1700–1933*. Cambridge: Harvard University Press, 1980.

Klein, Dennis B. "Assimilation and the Demise of the Liberal Political Tradition in Vienna: 1860–1914." *Jews and Germans from 1860 to 1933*. David Bronsen, ed. Heidelberg: Carl Winter Universitätsverlag, 1979.

Kuznets, Simon. "Economic Structure and Life of the Jews." Finkelstein, Louis, ed. *The Jews: Their History, Culture, and Religion*, 3d ed. 2 vols. Philadelphia: The Jewish Publication Society of America, 1960.

Landes, David S. "The Jewish Merchant: Typology and Stereotypology in Germany." LBIYB 29 (1974): 11–30.

Lea, Charlene A. *Emancipation, Assimilation and Stereotype: The Image of the Jew in German and Austrian Drama (1800–1850)*. Modern German Studies. Peter Heller et al., ed. Vol. 2. Bonn: Bouvier Verlag Herbert Grundmann, 1978.

Loewenberg, Peter. "Antisemitismus und jüdischer Selbsthass." *Geschichte und Gesellschaft: Zeitschrift für historische Sozialwissenschaft* 5 (1979): 455–75.

Marrus, Michael. *The Politics of Assimilation: A Study of the French Jewish Community at the Time of the Dreyfus Affair*. Oxford: Oxford University Press, Clarendon Press, 1971.

Meyer, Michael A. *Response to Modernity: A History of the Reform Movement in Judaism*. New York: Oxford University Press, 1988.

Mosse, George L. *Germans & Jews: The Right, the Left, and the Search for a "Third Force" in Pre-Nazi Germany*. New York: Grosset & Dunlop, The Universal Library, 1971.

Poppel, Stephen M. *Zionism in Germany, 1897–1933: The Shaping of a Jewish Identity*. Philadelphia: The Jewish Publication Society of America, 1977.

Prawer, S. S. *Heine's Jewish Comedy: A Study of His Portraits of Jews and Judaism.* Oxford: Clarendon Press, 1983.

Ragins, Sanford. *Jewish Responses to Anti-Semitism in Germany, 1870–1914: A Study in the History of Ideas.* Cincinnati, Ohio: Hebrew Union College Press, 1980.

Ruppin, Arthur. *Die Juden der Gegenwart: Eine sozialwissenschaftliche Studie.* 3d ed. Berlin: Jüdischer Verlag, 1920.

Schorsch, Ismar. *Jewish Reactions to German Anti-Semitism, 1870–1914.* New York: Columbia University Press, 1972.

———. Introduction to *The Structure of Jewish History and Other Essays,* by Heinrich Graetz. Ismar Schorsch, trans. and ed. New York: The Jewish Theological Seminary of America, 1975.

Sorkin, David. *The Transformation of German Jewry, 1780–1840* New York: Oxford University Press, 1987.

Stern, Fred B. "Ludwig Jacobowski, der Autor von 'Werther, der Jude.' " *Bulletin des Leo Baeck Instituts* 7 (1964): 101–37.

Stoffers, Joannes. *Juden und Ghetto in der deutschen Literatur bis zum Ausgang des Weltkrieges.* Graz: Druckerei und Verlagsanstalt Heinrich Stiasnys Söhne, 1939.

Tal, Uriel. *Christians and Jews in Germany: Religion, Politics and Ideology in the Second Reich, 1870–1914.* Noah Jonathan Jacobs, trans. Ithaca: Cornell University Press, 1975.

Vital, David. *The Origins of Zionism.* Oxford: Oxford University Press, Clarendon Press, 1975.

Volkov, Shulamit. "Antisemitismus in Deutschland als Problem jüdischnationalen Denkens und jüdischer Geschichtsschreibung." *Geschichte und Gesellschaft: Zeitschrift für Historische Sozialwissenschaft* 5 (1979): 519–44.

Wilson, Stephen. *Ideology and Experience: Antisemitism in France at the Time of the Dreyfus Affair.* Rutherford, N.J.: Farleigh Dickinson University Press, 1982.

Books and Articles on European History

Anderson, R. D. *France, 1870–1914: Politics and Society.* London: Routledge & Kegan Paul, 1977.

Bramsted, Ernest K. *Aristocracy and the Middle Class in Germany: Social Types in German Literature, 1830–1900.* Rev. ed. Chicago: The University of Chicago Press, Phoenix Books, 1964.

Bredin, Jean-Denis. *The Affair: The Case of Alfred Dreyfus.* Jeffrey Mehlman, trans. New York: George Braziller, 1986.

Craig, Gordon A. *Germany, 1866–1945.* New York: Oxford University Press, 1978.

Hermand, Jost. "Der gründerzeitliche Parvenu." Akademie der Künste. *Aspekte der Gründerzeit.* Ausstellung in der Akademie der Künste vom 8. September bis zum 24. November 1974. Berlin: Akademie der Künste, 1974.

Hertz, Friedrich. "Des Duell als soziale Erscheinung." *Österreichische Rundschau* 22 (1910): 401–407.

Kiernan, V. G. *The Duel in European History.* New York: Oxford University Press, 1988.

Lorenzen, Ernest G. "The Negotiorum Gestio in Roman and Modern Civil Law." *Cornell Law Quarterly* 13 (1928): 190–210.

Rosenberg, Hans. "Political and Social Consequences of the Great Depression of 1873–1896 in Central Europe." *Economic History Review* 12 (1942): 58–73.

Index

Abeles, Heinrich, 78, 211*n*58

Academic Reading Hall (*Akademische Lesehalle*), 35, 38–41, 44, 51, 53, 67

Acculturation, 30

Adler, Viktor, 28, 44, 46, 47

Ahad Ha-Am, 110, 158, 170, 172, 186–87

Akademische Lesehalle (Academic Reading Hall), 35, 38–41, 44, 51, 53, 67

Albia (fraternity), 6, 35–37, 40–43, 120, 149, 205*n*13, 206*n*14, 206*n*18, 207*n*38, 211*n*70; antisemitism in, 49–51, 81, 106, 207*n*43; and dueling, 41–43, 67, 68, 70–71, 146, 209*n*28, 209*n*39; and German nationalism, 35–37, 40–43, 45, 46, 53, 54; Herzl's resignation from, 49, 50–51, 59, 77, 78, 81–82; and Jewish assimilation, 35, 48–49, 53, 59, 81–82, 211*n*68; and Zionism, 52, 53, 57

Ambivalence, 2, 80–85, 202*n*3

Amelungia (*Korps*), 42

Anarchism, 122–23, 194

Anticapitalism, 92–93, 96–99, 182

Antisemitism: in *Albia*, 49–51, 81, 106, 207*n*43; and assimilated Jews, 20–22, 90, 100, 103–105, 115, 203*n*19; in Austria, 2, 3, 6–7, 26, 31–34, 89–99, 99–109, 180, 190, 191, 194; as caused by Jews, 9, 85, 99, 116–17, 126–27, 138, 210*n*50; in the Christian Social Party, 6–7, 92–100, 101, 102, 104; in France, 1, 89–90, 99, 101, 191–200; and German nationalism, 105–107; in Germany, 20, 31, 120–21, 204*n*47, 217*n*16; and the Liberal Party, 107–109; in *The New Ghetto*, 154; racial, 20–22, 47–48, 51, 59, 82; and Zionism, 182–84

Arendt, Hannah, 62, 176

Aristocracy, 5, 59, 62–66

Aschheim, Steven, 80, 147, 164, 219*n*35

Aschner, Alfred, 39, 206*n*27

Assimilation, 16, 59, 84, 85, 110; and antisemitism, 3–8, 20–22, 90, 100, 103–105, 115, 203*n*19; compared to acculturation, 30; through conversion to Christianity, 9, 21, 24–26, 115–21, 160, 216*n*4, 216*n*12, 216*n*14, 217*n*15; and dueling, 9, 124–26, 217*n*28; through Germanization, 30, 46–51, 80;

Herzl's critique of, 137–45; through intermarriage, 24–25; in the Jewish state, 178; through Socialism, 9, 121–24; and Zionism, 159–64, 182. *See also* Emancipation

Auersperg, Carlos, 14

Austria, 205*n*4; antisemitism in, 2, 3, 6–7, 26, 31–34, 89–99, 99–109, 180, 190, 191, 194; aristocracy in, 5, 62–66; civil reform in, 14; and German nationalism, 5, 36–38, 43–46, 51, 54–57, 207*n*57; Jewish emancipation in, 26–31; its nouveau riche class, 72–76; the rise of mass parties in, 33–34, 90–94, 100–101, 212*n*6. *See also* Vienna

"Autobiography" (Herzl), 191

Bacher, Eduard, 102

Bachrach, Adolf, 39

Badeni, Count, 184

Bahr, Hermann, 41, 56, 70, 149–50, 211*n*68; and the Wagner memorial, 51, 54, 55

Bauer, Julius, 169–70

Becke, Karl, 41, 48, 50, 51, 205*n*13, 207*n*43

Beer, Samuel, 130, 132

Beer-Hofmann, Richard, 178

Bein, Alex, 1, 3, 35–36, 156, 191, 197, 224*n*19

Benedikt, Moriz, 28, 116, 117, 120, 126, 194

Bensen, Christian, 20

Berlin, Isaiah, 62–64, 85

Billroth, Theodor, 49

Bismarck, Otto von, 51, 55, 56, 167

Bloch, Joseph S., 95, 204*n*42, 219*n*28

Bodenheimer, Max, 176

Böhm, Adolf, 171, 184

Boxer, Oswald, 46, 83

Boyer, John W., 74, 75, 92, 159, 204*n*30, 205*n*57

Braun, Heinrich, 46

Bredin, Jean-Denis, 198

Buber, Martin, 177

Byrnes, Robert F., 194

Canon, Hans, 72–73

Capitalism: and antisemitism, 22, 32, 46, 121, 183, 196; and aristocracy, 5, 66. *See also* Anticapitalism

Paléologue, Maurice, 197
Palestine, 36, 57, 128, 170, 172, 176
Panama Canal scandal, 192–94, 195, 196
Panizzardi, Major, 199, 225*n*24
Pernersdorfer, Engelbert, 44–45, 47–48, 50, 109; on *The New Ghetto*, 153
Pius IX, 14
Plener, Ernst von, 95, 107, 108
Poachers (Wilddiebe) (Herzl), 71–72
Poppel, Stephen, 175, 176
Portheim, Paul von, 48
Prawer, S. S., 85, 177

Racism. *See* Antisemitism, racial
Rathenau, Walther, 119
Ravachol (anarchist), 122–24
Reading Society of German Students (*Leseverein der Deutschen Studenten*), 39
Rosenbacher, Arnold, 155
Rosenberg, Hans, 97
Rosenberger, Erwin, 148–49
Rothschild family, 127, 164, 192; and the proposed Jewish state, 162, 172, 173, 180, 183, 184
Rozenblit, Marsha, 27, 30, 204*n*38
Rumbold, Sir Horace, 73
Ruppin, Arthur, 173, 187
Russia, 22, 31; Zionist movement in, 170, 172–73, 188, 222*n*39

Salten, Felix, 148, 153, 157
Savonarola, Girolamo, 14, 15, 16, 22, 202*n*7(2)
Schmelkes, Heinrich, 78, 211*n*58
Schmerling, Anton von, 44
Schneider, Ernst, 94, 95
Schnitzler, Arthur, 28, 46, 49, 61, 149, 196, 209*n*27; and antisemitism, 31–32, 47; on Herzl's German nationalism, 40–41; *Lieutenant Gustl*, 68; and *The New Ghetto*, 132, 150–56, 158; *The Road to the Open*, 29, 218*n*18
Schnitzler, Olga, 178
Schönerer, Georg von: antisemitism of, 48, 82, 105, 211*n*70; and German nationalism, 32–33, 40, 42, 44, 46, 51, 54, 57, 91, 207*n*52; Herzl's fantasy duel with, 124–25
Schopenhauer, Arthur, 56
Schorske, Carl, 124, 191–92, 193, 196; on the *feuilleton*, 174; on Herzlean Zionism, 52–53; on Viennese culture, 60–61, 208*n*15
Schwarzkoppen, Colonel von, 199, 225*n*24
Siklósy, Josef, 212*n*1
Singer, Isador, 204*n*47

Social Democratic party, 44, 90–91, 121
Socialism, 121–24, 160, 217*n*18
Society of Jews, 167, 185
Sorkin, David, 203*n*26
Speidel, Ludwig, 131
Staerck, Franz, 41, 149
Staerk, Gustav, 82, 211*n*70
Steed, Henry Wickham, 56–57, 62, 72, 208*n*11, 208*n*13
Stewart, Desmond, 156, 191, 224*n*5
Stöcker, Adolf, 31
Stricker, Robert, 186
Suess, Eduard, 108
Suttner, Baron Arthur Gundaccar von, 96, 117, 179, 215*n*2

Tabarin (Herzl), 153
Talmon, Jacob, 162, 173, 186
Teweles, Heinrich, 132, 153, 155
Tietze, Hans, 74
Treitel, Emil, 72
Treitschke, Heinrich von, 31, 56, 76
Turnverein der Wiener Hochschulen (Gymnastic Club of the Viennese Universities), 49–50
Tur-Sinai, N. H., 78

United Christians (coalition), 91–92, 212*n*7. *See also* Christian Social party
University of Vienna, 13, 35, 38–44, 54–55; antisemitism of, 106; and the Catholic church, 93. See also *Akademische Lesehalle*; *Albia*; Fraternities

Videcky, Ludwig, 69
Vienna, 13; antisemitism in, 89, 92–94, 94–96, 100, 159, 198, 213*n*16; culture of, 60–62; Jews in, 27–31, 79–80, 82–83, 210*n*49, 214*n*44
Violence against Jews, 95–96, 213*nn*19–20, 214*n*31
Vital, David, 2, 173, 188, 189, 191
Vogelsang, Karl von, 32, 98
Volkov, Shulamit, 184

Wagner, Adolf, 56
Wagner, Richard, 50–51, 52, 54, 55, 56, 162
Waldeck-Rousseau, René, 193, 199
Wandruszka, Adam, 56, 92, 205*n*6
Wassermann, Jacob, 82, 85
"We Shall Not Go to Canossa" (Herzl), 15, 22
Welt, Die (newspaper), 179, 186
Wertheimstein, Josefine von, 73

JACQUES KORNBERG teaches in the Department of History at the University of Toronto. The author of numerous articles on German intellectual history and on Zionism, he is editor of *At the Crossroads: Essays on Ahad Ha-Am.*

www.ingramcontent.com/pod-product-compliance
Ingram Content Group UK Ltd.
Pitfield, Milton Keynes, MK11 3LW, UK
UKHW022304260525
458860UK00005B/48